CAIRO

Beyond the Pyramids

A comprehensive travel guide to exploring the Magic of Egypt's Ancient Capital

Wren A. Rove

© 2025 Wren A. Rove All rights reserved.

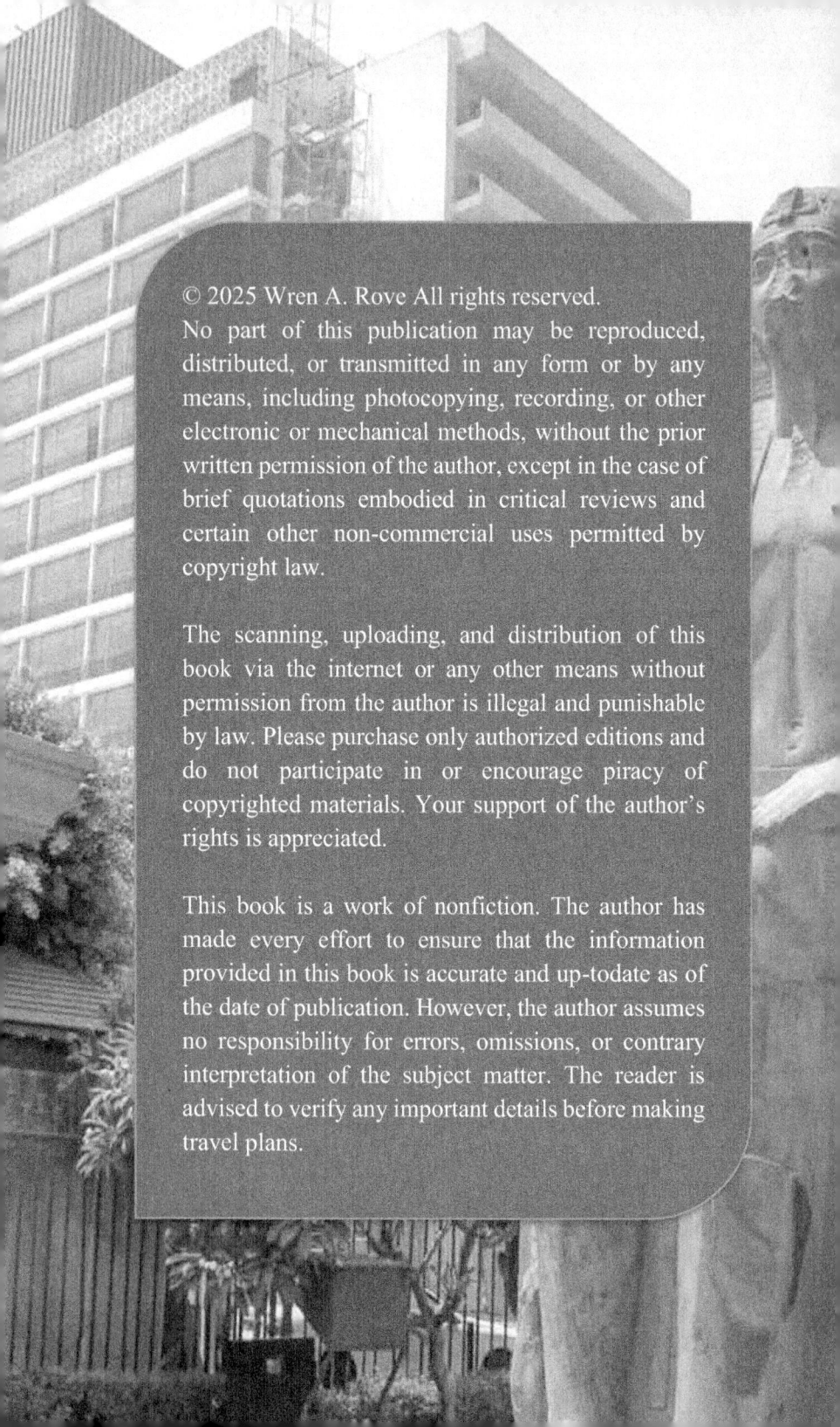

No part of this publication may be reproduced, distributed, or transmitted in any form or by any means, including photocopying, recording, or other electronic or mechanical methods, without the prior written permission of the author, except in the case of brief quotations embodied in critical reviews and certain other non-commercial uses permitted by copyright law.

The scanning, uploading, and distribution of this book via the internet or any other means without permission from the author is illegal and punishable by law. Please purchase only authorized editions and do not participate in or encourage piracy of copyrighted materials. Your support of the author's rights is appreciated.

This book is a work of nonfiction. The author has made every effort to ensure that the information provided in this book is accurate and up-todate as of the date of publication. However, the author assumes no responsibility for errors, omissions, or contrary interpretation of the subject matter. The reader is advised to verify any important details before making travel plans.

Gratitude

Thank you so much for choosing this guide to accompany you on your journey to Cairo! We truly appreciate you investing in this book, and we're excited to be part of your adventure. It's our goal to ensure that your time on this beautiful island is filled with unforgettable moments, and we hope this guide helps you make the most of every step along the way. Whether you're seeking adventure, relaxation, or cultural discovery, we trust this guide will be a valuable resource as you explore all that Cairo has to offer.

Wishing you incredible experiences, great memories, and safe travels throughout your trip. Thank you once again for your trust in us. Here's to making your time in Cairo absolutely unforgettable!

This Guide Belongs To:

_____

_____

_____

TABLE OF CONTENTS

TABLE OF CONTENTS 3
INTRODUCTION 9
WHY YOU SHOULD VISIT CAIRO 13
CHAPTER 1 19
PRACTICAL INFORMATION FOR TRAVELERS 19
    Visa and Entry Requirements 19
    Currency, Costs, and Budgeting 22
    Language and Common Phrases 26
    Transportation: Getting to Cairo 29
    Transportation: Getting Around Cairo 34
    The Best Time to Visit 37
    Safety and Health Information for Travelers 41
CHAPTER 2 47
EXPLORING CAIRO BY DISTRICT 47
    Giza 47
    Must-See Attractions 47
        The Great Pyramids of Giza: A Journey into Ancient History 47
        The Great Sphinx of Giza: A Timeless Symbol of Mystery and Power 51
        The Solar Boat Museum 55

Things to Do in Giza: Camel Rides, Light and Sound Show, and Exploring the Pyramid Complex 60

Accommodation Options in Giza 63

Luxury Stays: Resorts with Pyramid Views in Giza, Cairo, Egypt 63

Mid-Range Options: Comfortable hotels near the Giza Plateau 67

Budget Choices: Hostels and Guesthouses with Easy Access to Attractions in Giza, Cairo, Egypt 70

Islamic Cairo 74

Must-See Attractions 74

Al-Azhar Mosque: A Timeless Center of Learning and Spirituality 74

Khan El Khalili Bazaar 79

The Citadel of Cairo 83

Things to Do: Walking Tours, Shopping for Local Handicrafts, and Visiting Traditional Coffeehouses 89

Accommodation Options 93

Luxury Stays: Boutique Hotels with Historic Charm in Islamic Cairo, Cairo, Egypt 93

Mid-Range Options: Stylish Lodgings in Bustling Neighborhoods in Islamic Cairo, Cairo, Egypt 97

Downtown Cairo 105

Must-See Attractions 105

Tahrir Square 105

The Egyptian Museum 110

Abdeen Palace: A Glimpse into Egypt's Royal Past . 115

Things to Do: Exploring Modern Cairo's Art Galleries and Cafes 120

Accommodation Options 124

    Luxury Stays: High-End Hotels with Nile Views in Downtown Cairo, Egypt 124

    Mid-Range Options: Contemporary City Hotels in Downtown Cairo, Egypt 128

    Budget Choices: Budget-Friendly Lodgings Close to Public Transport in Downtown Cairo, Egypt 132

Aisha Fahmy Palace: A Hidden Gem of Art and Elegance in Zamalek 141

The Gezira Art Center... 146

Things to Do: Strolling Along the Nile, Visiting Boutiques, and Enjoying Rooftop Restaurants 151

Accommodation Options 155

    Luxury Stays: Boutique Hotels on Gezira Island in Zamalek, Cairo, Egypt 155

    Mid-Range Options: Riverside Hotels with Modern Amenities in Zamalek, Cairo, Egypt......................... 159

    Budget Choices: Co-Living Spaces and Budget Lodgings in Zamalek, Cairo, Egypt 163

Old Cairo (Coptic Cairo) 167

Must-See Attractions 167

The Hanging Church: A Jewel of Coptic Cairo's Heritage 167

Ben Ezra Synagogue 173

Amr Ibn Al-As Mosque 179

Things to Do: Visiting Religious Landmarks and Coptic Museum 184

Accommodation Options 188

Mid-Range Options: Cozy Hotels with Easy Access to Historic Sites in Old Cairo (Coptic Cairo), Cairo, Egypt 193

Budget Choices: Affordable Stays for Culture Enthusiasts in Old Cairo (Coptic Cairo), Cairo, Egypt 197

CHAPTER 3 201

ITINERARIES FOR EVERY TRAVELER 201

How To Craft Your Desired Itinerary 201

Bonus: 14-Day Itinerary Planner 204

3-Day Itinerary for Cairo, Egypt: A Solo Traveler's Guide 206

7-Day Itinerary 210

14-Day Itinerary: Cairo and Beyond (Luxor, Alexandria, and Aswan) 215

CHAPTER 4 221

SHOPPING AND SOUVENIRS 221

Khan El Khalili Bazaar: The Heart of Cairo's Souks 221

- Local Markets for Spices, Perfumes, and Textiles 225
- Unique Souvenirs: Papyrus, Jewelry, and Egyptian Art 229

CHAPTER 5 235

CUISINE AND DINING IN CAIRO 235

- Traditional Egyptian Dishes You Must Try 235
- Street Food Hotspots and Market Snacks 239
- Top Restaurants and Nile-Side Dining Experiences 243

CHAPTER 6 249

DAY TRIPS FROM CAIRO 249

- Saqqara 249
- Dahshur 253
- Fayoum Oasis: Waterfalls, Lakes, and Wildlife 256

CHAPTER 7 261

OUTDOOR ACTIVITIES AND NATURE SPOTS 261

- Exploring Al-Azhar Park 261
- Nile Cruises and Evening Felucca Rides 264
- Desert Safari Adventures 268

CHAPTER 8 273

CAIRO'S HIDDEN GEMS 273

- Al-Moez Street 273
- The Cave Church of St. Simon 277
- Zabbaleen Garbage City 281

CHAPTER 9 287

CULTURAL EXPERIENCES AND HISTORY 287
   Attending a Sufi Dance Performance 287
   Exploring Egypt's Coptic Heritage 291
   Festivals and Religious Events in Cairo 295
CHAPTER 10 301
PRACTICAL TIPS AND RESOURCES 301
   Essential Packing List for Cairo 301
   Useful Travel Phrases in Arabic 305
   Staying Connected: Internet and Mobile Data Options . 309
CONCLUSION 313

INTRODUCTION

Cairo is home to some of the most iconic historical treasures in the world. It is where the Great Pyramids of Giza stand proudly, monuments that have stood the test of time and continue to amaze visitors from all over the globe. But Cairo is not just about pyramids; it's a vibrant city alive with sounds, colors, and flavors that reflect its rich culture and traditions. Walking through the streets of Cairo feels like stepping into a living museum, where every corner tells a story. Yet, this is also a city that moves forward, blending its ancient roots with the pulse of modern life.

The heart of Cairo beats in its neighborhoods. From the maze-like streets of Islamic Cairo, where mosques, madrasas, and historic houses stand side by side, to the bustling markets of Khan el-Khalili, where traders have been selling their goods for centuries, the city is a kaleidoscope of experiences. You'll find locals going about their day, shopkeepers calling out to customers, and a lively atmosphere that's as much a part of Cairo's charm as its historic landmarks. These streets aren't just places; they're experiences that invite you to be a part of them.

Food lovers will find themselves in paradise here. Cairo's food scene is as diverse as its history, offering everything from street food like koshari and taameya to hearty dishes such as molokhia and grilled meats. The city's coffeehouses, where locals gather to sip tea or puff on shisha pipes, are also a cultural experience not to be missed. Dining in Cairo isn't just about eating; it's about immersing yourself in a way of life.

Cairo also offers a unique window into Egypt's artistic and cultural heritage. You'll discover museums brimming with ancient artifacts, including the famed Egyptian Museum, where you can get up close with treasures from King Tutankhamun's tomb. You'll also find a city that loves its art, from traditional music and dance to contemporary galleries showcasing modern Egyptian artists. The richness of culture is palpable in every corner, whether it's through the ornate architecture of historic buildings or the stories passed down through generations.

One of the things that makes Cairo truly special is its people. Cairenes are known for their warmth and hospitality. They'll welcome you into their world with open arms, happy to share stories, offer directions, or even invite you to experience local traditions. Their friendliness turns every interaction into a memorable part of your journey. Whether you're navigating a busy souk or simply enjoying a stroll along the Nile, you'll find that the people of Cairo are what make this city feel alive. While Cairo is undeniably ancient, it is also modern and evolving. Skyscrapers rise alongside historic mosques, and bustling highways crisscross ancient streets. The city's energy is infectious, a blend of old and new that creates an atmosphere unlike anywhere else. It's a city where you can step out of a centuries-old mosque and into a modern café, or take a ride on the metro after marveling at the oldest stone structures in the world. This blend of eras makes Cairo endlessly exciting to explore.

As you read through this guide, you'll find detailed insights to help you make your trip unforgettable. From practical tips on getting around the city to recommendations for must-visit attractions, hidden gems, and the best spots to experience local life, this book is your companion for navigating Cairo with ease. We've gathered all the information you need so that you can spend less time planning and more time enjoying everything this city has to offer.

Cairo is a place that stays with you long after you leave. It's a city of contrasts and surprises, where the past and present coexist in the most beautiful way. With every page of this guide, you'll gain a deeper appreciation for its wonders and the memories it offers to those who explore it. Whether you're here to marvel at its history, savor its flavors, or simply soak in its lively atmosphere, Cairo promises an experience like no other. Let this introduction be the beginning of your journey into a city that has captivated travelers for centuries. The adventure starts here.

WHY YOU SHOULD VISIT CAIRO

Cairo is a city unlike any other, a destination that offers something extraordinary for every traveler. Whether you are drawn to history, culture, food, or simply the chance to experience a place that feels alive with energy, Cairo is a city that will capture your imagination and leave a lasting impression. There are countless reasons why you should visit Cairo, but let's take a closer look at what makes it truly special and worth exploring.

Cairo's most famous claim to fame is its rich history, which stretches back thousands of years. It is one of the oldest cities in the world and has been a center of civilization for millennia. The pyramids at Giza, located just outside the city, are a testament to ancient engineering and human achievement. These towering monuments, built as tombs for the pharaohs, remain one of the Seven Wonders of the Ancient World and continue to awe visitors with their sheer size and complexity. Seeing the Great Pyramid, standing in front of the Sphinx, and walking among the ancient stones is an experience that feels almost otherworldly.

But Cairo's history goes far beyond the pyramids. The city is a living museum of Egyptian culture and heritage. The Egyptian Museum is home to one of the most impressive collections of artifacts in the world, including treasures from the tomb of King Tutankhamun and mummies of ancient rulers. Visiting this museum allows you to connect with the past in a way that is both educational and deeply moving.

Other historic landmarks, like the Citadel of Saladin and the Hanging Church, showcase Cairo's diverse and layered history, from its Islamic golden age to its Christian heritage.

Cairo's culture is another reason why this city is a must-visit destination. It is a place where tradition and modernity coexist in a way that feels vibrant and authentic. Walking through the streets of Cairo, you'll see locals going about their daily lives, whether they're shopping for fresh produce in the markets, sipping tea at a street-side café, or attending Friday prayers at one of the city's many mosques. The people of Cairo are known for their warmth and hospitality, and they take pride in sharing their culture with visitors. Whether it's through a conversation, a shared meal, or an invitation to learn more about local customs, you'll find that the people are a big part of what makes Cairo so unforgettable.

The food in Cairo is another highlight that makes the city worth visiting. Egyptian cuisine is flavorful, hearty, and satisfying, and there's no better place to enjoy it than in the capital. From street food stalls to fine dining restaurants, Cairo offers a wide range of culinary experiences. You can try koshari, a beloved dish made with rice, lentils, and pasta topped with a tangy tomato sauce, or sink your teeth into freshly made falafel, known locally as taameya. The city is also famous for its sweets, like basbousa and konafa, which are perfect for anyone with a sweet tooth. Eating in Cairo is not just about the food itself but about the experience of sharing a meal, whether it's with friends, family, or even strangers who quickly become acquaintances.

Cairo's bustling markets are another draw for visitors. Perhaps the most famous is Khan el-Khalili, a sprawling bazaar that has been a hub of trade for centuries. Here, you can shop for everything from handmade jewelry and textiles to spices and perfumes. Bargaining is part of the experience, and the lively atmosphere of the market is something that stays with you long after you leave. The markets are not just places to shop but places to observe local life, soak in the sights and sounds, and enjoy the unique energy that makes Cairo so special.

Beyond its history, culture, and food, Cairo is a city of incredible contrasts. On one hand, it is a place where you can step into the ancient past, visiting sites that are thousands of years old. On the other hand, it is a modern city with all the conveniences and energy of urban life. This blend of old and new is one of the things that makes Cairo so unique. You might find yourself standing in a centuries-old mosque in the morning and then enjoying a meal at a trendy rooftop restaurant overlooking the Nile River in the evening. This mix of experiences is what makes exploring Cairo so exciting and rewarding.

The Nile itself is another reason to visit Cairo. This iconic river has been the lifeblood of Egypt for thousands of years, and spending time by the Nile is a must when you're in the city. Whether you take a felucca ride at sunset, enjoy a dinner cruise with traditional music and dance, or simply stroll along the riverbanks, the Nile adds a sense of tranquility and beauty to your time in Cairo. It's a reminder of the city's deep connection to the natural world and its importance in shaping Egypt's history and culture.

Cairo is also a gateway to exploring more of Egypt. From here, you can easily visit other parts of the country, such as Luxor, Aswan, and Alexandria. Whether you're planning a longer trip or just looking for a base from which to see the sights, Cairo is the perfect starting point. The city is well-connected, making it easy to travel to other destinations while still enjoying everything Cairo has to offer.

Cairo is a city that offers endless reasons to visit. Its history, culture, food, and people create an experience that is rich, rewarding, and unforgettable. Whether you're an adventurer, a history enthusiast, or someone simply looking for a new perspective, Cairo has something to offer you. It is a city that stays with you long after you leave, and once you've experienced its magic, you'll understand why so many people around the world dream of visiting Cairo.

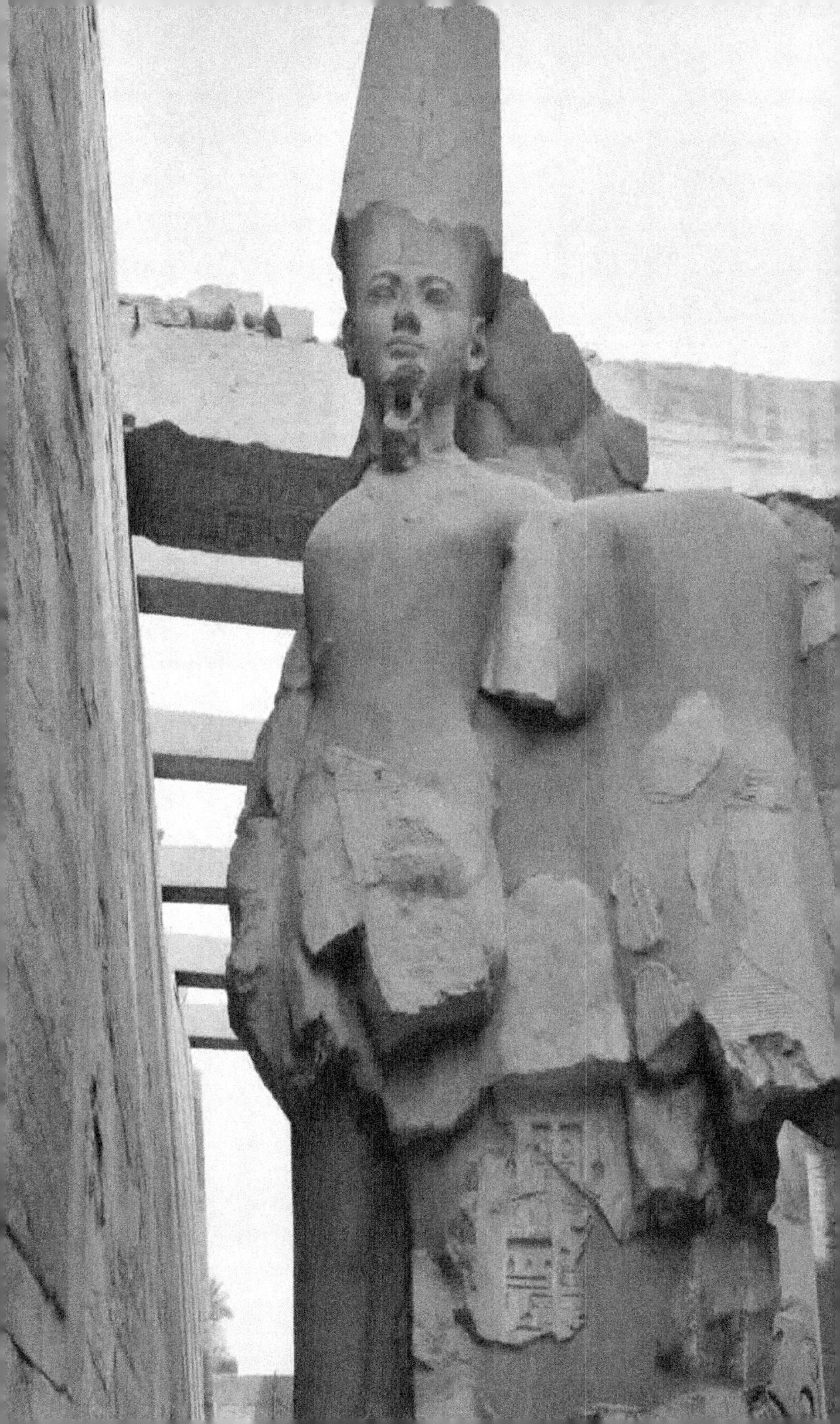

CHAPTER 1

PRACTICAL INFORMATION FOR TRAVELERS

Visa and Entry Requirements

Traveling to Cairo, Egypt, as a tourist is an exciting opportunity to explore one of the world's most fascinating destinations, but before packing your bags, it's essential to understand the visa and entry requirements. Egypt has specific rules and procedures for tourists entering the country, and being well-informed about these can save you time, money, and potential complications during your trip.

Most travelers visiting Cairo as tourists will need a visa to enter Egypt. The good news is that Egypt offers several types of tourist visas, making it relatively easy for visitors to gain access. For many nationalities, there is an option to obtain a visa upon arrival at major airports in Egypt, including Cairo International Airport. This type of visa is convenient and allows you to skip the process of applying in advance. However, to ensure a smooth entry, it's important to understand how the process works and whether your nationality is eligible for this option. A visa on arrival is usually valid for 30 days and costs approximately 25 USD, though it's always a good idea to confirm the latest fees before your trip.

For those who prefer to have everything prepared before arrival, Egypt also offers an e-Visa system. This allows travelers to apply online for their tourist visa in advance. The e-Visa process is straightforward and can be completed from the comfort of your home. You'll need to visit the official website, fill out the application form, and upload the required documents, such as a copy of your passport. Payment is made online using a credit or debit card, and once approved, the e-Visa will be sent to your email. This option is ideal for travelers who want to avoid potential delays at the airport and prefer to have their visa ready before they depart.

It's also important to check whether your country has a specific agreement with Egypt that might exempt you from needing a visa. For instance, citizens of some countries are granted visa-free entry for a limited period, while others may require special permissions. Always verify the specific requirements for your nationality to avoid surprises when you arrive in Cairo.

Another critical aspect of preparing for your trip is ensuring your passport is valid. Egypt requires that your passport be valid for at least six months beyond your planned departure date from the country. If your passport is close to expiring, make sure to renew it before you apply for a visa or travel to Egypt. Border officials are strict about this rule, and failure to meet it could result in being denied entry.

Travelers visiting Cairo should also be prepared to provide certain documents upon arrival. In addition to your passport and visa, you may be asked to show proof of your travel plans, such as a return ticket or an onward ticket to another destination. Some visitors may also be asked to provide proof of accommodation, such as a hotel booking or an invitation letter from a host if you are staying with friends or family.

These documents help demonstrate that you have a clear plan for your stay and that you intend to leave Egypt after your visit. Health-related entry requirements are another important consideration. While Egypt does not typically require tourists to have vaccinations to enter, it is always a good idea to check for any updated health advisories before you travel. Travelers coming from countries where yellow fever is common may need to provide proof of vaccination upon arrival. It's also wise to ensure that your routine vaccinations, such as measles and tetanus, are up to date for your safety during your stay.

For visitors planning extended stays or those who wish to explore beyond Cairo, it's worth noting that Egypt also offers multi-entry visas. These allow travelers to leave and re-enter the country multiple times within a specified period, usually six months. If you plan to travel to neighboring countries and then return to Egypt, this type of visa can save you the hassle of reapplying for a new visa each time.

Finally, it's essential to stay informed about any changes to entry requirements, as rules can evolve based on government policies or global events. For example, during periods of heightened health concerns or security measures, additional documentation or screenings might be required at the border. Checking the official website of the Egyptian Ministry of Foreign Affairs or contacting the nearest Egyptian embassy or consulate in your country can provide the most accurate and up-to-date information for your trip.

Currency, Costs, and Budgeting

When planning a trip to Cairo, Egypt, understanding the local currency, costs, and how to budget effectively is crucial for ensuring a smooth and enjoyable experience. Cairo offers a wide range of experiences and services that cater to different budgets, but having a clear understanding of the financial aspects will help you make the most of your visit without unnecessary stress or overspending.

The official currency in Egypt is the Egyptian Pound, often abbreviated as EGP or LE (from the French term "livre égyptienne"). The pound is divided into 100 piastres, and both coins and banknotes are used. Banknotes are available in denominations ranging from 1 pound to 200 pounds, while coins are commonly used for smaller amounts such as 1, 5, 10, 25, and 50 piastres. It's essential to familiarize yourself with the appearance of the currency to avoid confusion, as some denominations look similar at first glance.

When you arrive in Cairo, it's a good idea to have some local currency on hand for immediate expenses such as transportation, tips, or small purchases. Currency exchange services are available at airports, banks, and authorized exchange offices throughout the city. While exchanging money at the airport is convenient, the exchange rates may not always be the most favorable. For better rates, consider using reputable exchange offices or withdrawing cash from ATMs, which are widely available in Cairo. However, be aware of potential international transaction fees and ensure your bank card is compatible with local ATMs.

Costs in Cairo are generally affordable compared to many other major cities worldwide, making it a popular destination for budget-conscious travelers. Accommodation options range from budget-friendly hostels and guesthouses to mid-range hotels and luxury resorts. Depending on your preferences and budget, you can find a comfortable place to stay without spending a fortune. A bed in a hostel dormitory might cost around 150-250 EGP per night, while a mid-range hotel room could range from 500-1,500 EGP per night. Luxury hotels in prime locations near the Nile or historic sites can cost significantly more, but they often provide exceptional service and amenities.

Transportation in Cairo is also inexpensive and offers various options to suit different budgets. The city's metro system is one of the cheapest and most efficient ways to get around, with tickets costing as little as 5-10 EGP depending on the number of stops. Taxis are widely available, but it's important to agree on a fare beforehand or ensure the driver uses the meter. Ride-hailing apps like Uber and Careem are also popular and provide a reliable alternative to traditional taxis, often with transparent pricing. For longer distances, private drivers or organized tours can be arranged, though these tend to be more expensive.

Food is another area where Cairo offers excellent value for money. Egyptian cuisine is flavorful and satisfying, and you'll find options to suit every budget. Street food is incredibly affordable, with dishes like koshari, falafel (taameya), and shawarma costing as little as 20-50 EGP per meal. Local restaurants and cafés provide more variety, with meals typically costing between 50-150 EGP. For a more upscale dining experience, you can expect to pay 200-400 EGP per person at a high-end restaurant. Tipping is customary in Cairo, with 10-15% of the bill being standard in restaurants and cafés. Keep small denominations of cash handy for tips, as it's also common to tip hotel staff, taxi drivers, and tour guides.

Sightseeing and activities in Cairo can be enjoyed on almost any budget. Entry fees to major attractions like the Pyramids of Giza, the Egyptian Museum, and the Citadel of Saladin are generally affordable, ranging from 100-300 EGP per ticket. Some sites may offer discounted rates for students, so carrying a valid student ID can be beneficial. Guided tours and private excursions are more expensive but often provide added convenience and insight into the city's history and culture. For those looking to save money, self-guided visits and free attractions like local markets and neighborhoods can be equally rewarding.

Shopping in Cairo is a unique experience, especially in traditional markets like Khan el-Khalili. Bargaining is an integral part of the shopping culture, and negotiating prices can help you secure a good deal on souvenirs, handicrafts, and other items. It's important to have cash on hand when shopping in markets, as many vendors do not accept credit cards. For more modern shopping experiences, Cairo has malls and stores that accept cards, but carrying cash is still advisable for smaller purchases and tips.

When budgeting for your trip, consider additional expenses such as travel insurance, mobile data plans, and any personal preferences for comfort or luxury. Travel insurance is highly recommended to cover unforeseen circumstances, including medical emergencies or trip cancellations. Many travelers also opt to purchase a local SIM card or data plan upon arrival, which can be a cost-effective way to stay connected during your trip.

Language and Common Phrases

When planning a visit to Cairo, Egypt, understanding the local language and learning some common phrases can greatly enhance your experience. Arabic is the official language of Egypt, and while many people in Cairo speak English, especially in tourist areas, knowing a few basic words and phrases in Arabic can help you navigate the city more smoothly and connect with the local people. It shows respect for the culture and can often lead to warmer interactions and helpful responses.

Arabic is a rich and expressive language, but don't worry if you're not fluent. Egyptian Arabic, the dialect spoken in Cairo and across the country, is widely understood in the Arabic-speaking world due to Egypt's influence in media and entertainment. It's a good idea to familiarize yourself with some key phrases and words that you can use in everyday situations. Even a small effort to speak Arabic can make a big difference, as locals appreciate visitors who try to communicate in their language.

To start, it's helpful to know how to greet people. Greetings are an essential part of Egyptian culture and are often exchanged before any conversation or interaction. The most common greeting is "As-salamu alaykum," which means "Peace be upon you." The typical response to this is "Wa alaykum as-salam," which means "And upon you, peace." If you prefer something simpler, you can say "Sabah al-khayr" in the morning, which means "Good morning," and the response would be "Sabah al-noor," meaning "Morning of light." In the evening, you can say "Masa' al-khayr" for "Good evening," with the response being "Masa' al-noor," meaning "Evening of light."

Politeness is highly valued in Egyptian culture, so knowing how to say "Thank you" and "Please" is important. "Shukran" means "Thank you," and if you want to say "Thank you very much," you can say "Shukran gazilan." To say "Please," you can use "Min fadlak" when speaking to a man or "Min fadlik" when speaking to a woman. If someone does something kind for you, a good response is "Alhamdulillah," which means "Praise be to God," often used to express gratitude or contentment.

When you're out and about in Cairo, you'll likely need to ask for help or directions. Some useful phrases include "Fein?" which means "Where?" and "Ana 'awez arooh…" meaning "I want to go to…" You can add the name of the place you're looking for. For example, "Ana 'awez arooh al-Ahramat" means "I want to go to the Pyramids." If you need to ask how much something costs, you can say "Bekam da?" which means "How much is this?" Knowing numbers in Arabic can also be helpful when dealing with prices, especially in markets where bargaining is common.

When traveling, it's also important to know phrases for basic interactions, such as introducing yourself or explaining your needs. If you want to say your name, you can use "Ismi…" followed by your name, which means "My name is…" To ask someone's name, you can say "Ismak eh?" when speaking to a man or "Ismik eh?" when speaking to a woman. If you don't understand something, you can say "Ana mish fahem" (for men) or "Ana mish fahma" (for women), which means "I don't understand." Similarly, if you need someone to speak more slowly, you can say "Momken tetkallem bshwaya?" which means "Can you speak slowly?"

For dining and shopping, there are a few key phrases that can be especially useful. If you're ordering food, you can say "Ana 'awez…" for men or "Ana 'awza…" for women, followed by the name of the dish. For example, "Ana 'awez koshari" means "I want koshari." When shopping, if you want to ask for a discount, you can say "Momken tkhafed shwaya?" which means "Can you lower the price a little?" Bargaining is a common practice in Cairo's markets, so don't be afraid to negotiate politely.

Getting around Cairo often involves using taxis or public transportation. If you're in a taxi, you might need to say "Ruh al-shamal" for "Go left" or "Ruh al-yemeen" for "Go right." To ask the driver to stop, you can say "Law samaht, wa'af hina," which means "Please, stop here." If you're lost, you can approach someone and say "Momken tsa'edni?" which means "Can you help me?"

Beyond practical phrases, learning a few cultural expressions can also enrich your interactions. Egyptians often use the phrase "Insha'Allah," meaning "God willing," to express hope or intention for something in the future. Another common phrase is "Maalesh," which means "It's okay" or "Never mind" and is used to reassure someone or ease a situation.

While you don't need to master Arabic to enjoy your trip to Cairo, knowing these basic phrases can make a significant difference in your experience. It can help you feel more confident navigating the city, build connections with locals, and show respect for the culture. Cairo is a welcoming city, and the effort you put into learning even a little of the language will go a long way in making your visit more enjoyable and memorable.

Transportation: Getting to Cairo

Getting into Cairo, Egypt, as a tourist involves understanding the various transportation options available, each with its own set of advantages depending on your preferences, budget, and travel plans. Cairo, being the capital and a major hub of the Middle East, is accessible through several means, making it convenient for travelers from around the globe to reach this historic city. Knowing your options and planning ahead can make your journey smoother and more enjoyable.

The most common way to get into Cairo is by air. Cairo International Airport (CAI) is the primary gateway for international travelers and one of the busiest airports in Africa. Located approximately 15 kilometers northeast of the city center, the airport serves as a hub for numerous airlines, including EgyptAir, the national carrier. Flights to Cairo are available from major cities worldwide, and depending on your location, you can find direct or connecting flights. Booking your tickets in advance is advisable, as it can save you money and secure your preferred travel dates. Upon arrival at the airport, travelers will find a range of services, including currency exchange counters, ATMs, car rental agencies, and airport shuttles.

Once you arrive at Cairo International Airport, getting to the city center or your accommodation is straightforward. Many tourists opt for taxis, which are readily available outside the terminals. While taxis are a convenient choice, it's important to agree on a fare beforehand or ensure the driver uses the meter to avoid overpaying. Alternatively, ride-hailing apps like Uber and Careem are widely used in Cairo and offer a more transparent pricing system, which can provide peace of mind, especially for first-time visitors. Airport shuttles and private car services are also available for those who prefer a more organized and comfortable transfer.

For travelers coming from neighboring countries, Cairo can also be reached by land. Buses are a popular option, with several international routes connecting Cairo to cities in Jordan, Sudan, and Libya. These long-distance buses are often operated by private companies and offer varying levels of comfort, from basic seating to more luxurious options with reclining seats and air conditioning. While buses are generally affordable, the journey can be long and tiring, so it's important to weigh the cost savings against the time and effort involved. Tickets can usually be purchased online or at the bus company's office, and it's advisable to book in advance during peak travel seasons.

Another way to travel to Cairo by land is through private or shared cars, which are commonly used for cross-border travel from nearby countries. This option provides more flexibility in terms of scheduling and stops along the way, but it may require additional paperwork, such as border permits or insurance, depending on the country of origin. If you're planning to drive your own vehicle into Egypt, be aware that you'll need an international driving permit and the appropriate documentation for your car. Border crossings can involve lengthy inspections, so patience and preparation are key.

For those traveling from Europe or other Mediterranean countries, arriving in Cairo by sea is an option, though it is less common. Egypt has several ports along the Mediterranean and Red Sea coasts, with Alexandria and Port Said being the most prominent for passenger travel. From these ports, travelers can continue their journey to Cairo by road or train. While cruises occasionally stop in Egypt as part of larger itineraries, ferry services between certain countries and Egypt also operate, providing a unique and scenic way to enter the country.

Once you're in Egypt, getting to Cairo from other cities is relatively easy due to the country's well-connected transportation network. Domestic flights are a quick and efficient way to travel, with several airlines offering daily services to Cairo from cities like Luxor, Aswan, and Sharm El-Sheikh. These flights are ideal for those with limited time who want to maximize their exploration of Egypt's diverse regions.

Another popular option for domestic travel is the train. Egypt's railway system connects Cairo with major cities across the country, providing a scenic and comfortable way to travel. The trains offer different classes of service, ranging from basic seating to air-conditioned sleeper cars, making it a suitable option for all types of travelers. Tickets can be purchased at train stations or online, and it's recommended to book in advance, especially for sleeper trains and during holiday periods.

Buses are another reliable way to travel within Egypt, with multiple companies operating routes to Cairo from other cities. These buses are often equipped with air conditioning and comfortable seating, making them a budget-friendly choice for travelers. Some companies also offer luxury buses with additional amenities, such as onboard entertainment and refreshments. Bus terminals in Cairo are well-organized, and schedules are typically frequent, allowing for flexibility in planning your trip.

In addition to these options, private transfers and tours are available for those who prefer a more personalized travel experience. Many tour operators offer packages that include transportation to Cairo, along with guided tours of the city's landmarks and attractions. This can be a convenient option for travelers who want to combine transportation with sightseeing.

Transportation: Getting Around Cairo

Getting around Cairo, Egypt, as a tourist can be an exciting and unique experience, but it's essential to understand the transportation options available to ensure your journey is smooth and enjoyable. Cairo is a large and busy city with a population of over 20 million people, which means traffic can be overwhelming at times, but the variety of transport options caters to different needs, budgets, and levels of convenience.

One of the most affordable and efficient ways to travel within Cairo is the Cairo Metro. The metro system is one of the oldest in Africa and the Middle East and serves as a vital part of the city's public transport network. It has three main lines, with plans for expansion in the future. The metro connects many major neighborhoods and landmarks, making it a convenient choice for tourists. Tickets are inexpensive, with fares depending on the number of stops your travel, typically ranging between 5 and 10 Egyptian pounds. The metro is clean, relatively punctual, and much faster than traveling by road during rush hours. Additionally, the first two cars of each train are reserved for women, offering a safe and comfortable space for female travelers.

Taxis are another common mode of transportation in Cairo and are widely available throughout the city. There are three main types of taxis: the older black-and-white cabs, newer white taxis, and yellow taxis, which are equipped with meters. While the older taxis often require you to negotiate the fare before starting your journey, the newer white and yellow taxis generally use meters, which can make the pricing more transparent. However, it's important to ensure the meter is running or agree on a price beforehand to avoid disputes. While taxis are affordable, be prepared for the possibility of traffic delays, especially during peak hours. For a smoother experience, it helps to know some basic Arabic phrases or have your destination written in Arabic to show the driver.

Ride-hailing apps like Uber and Careem have become increasingly popular in Cairo due to their convenience and reliability. These apps allow you to book a ride using your smartphone, providing upfront pricing and an estimated time of arrival. Uber and Careem are often more comfortable and safer than traditional taxis, and their drivers are generally professional and polite. They are also particularly useful for tourists who are unfamiliar with the city, as the app's GPS navigation ensures you won't get lost. Payment can be made via credit card through the app or in cash, depending on your preference.

Microbuses are a common form of shared transportation used by locals, but they can be challenging for tourists who are unfamiliar with the city. These small vans operate on fixed routes and are a very cheap way to get around Cairo, but they don't follow strict schedules or designated stops, making them difficult to navigate for newcomers. Additionally, they tend to be crowded and lack air conditioning, which may not be the most comfortable option, especially during the summer months. Unless you are accompanied by a local or have a good understanding of the city's layout, it's generally better to opt for more tourist-friendly transportation.

Buses are another option for getting around Cairo, and the city has a mix of public and private bus services. Public buses are very affordable, but like microbuses, they can be confusing for tourists due to the lack of clear signage and schedules. Private buses, on the other hand, are slightly more expensive but offer a more comfortable and organized experience. Some companies operate air-conditioned buses with modern amenities, making them a viable option for longer trips within the city. Tickets can usually be purchased on board or at bus terminals.

For tourists who prefer more control over their itinerary, renting a car is an option, but it comes with significant challenges. Driving in Cairo can be daunting, as traffic is often chaotic, and local driving habits may be unfamiliar to visitors. Parking can also be difficult to find in busy areas, and navigation can be tricky without a good GPS system. If you decide to rent a car, it's important to familiarize yourself with local traffic laws and driving customs. Alternatively, hiring a private driver is a more comfortable and stress-free way to explore the city, allowing you to focus on enjoying the sights without worrying about the logistics of driving.

Walking is another way to explore certain parts of Cairo, especially historic areas like Islamic Cairo or the streets around the Khan el-Khalili bazaar. While the city is not known for being particularly pedestrian-friendly, with its busy roads and lack of sidewalks in some areas, walking can be a rewarding experience in specific neighborhoods. It's a great way to soak in the local atmosphere, discover hidden gems, and take photos of the city's vibrant street life. However, it's important to stay aware of your surroundings, especially when crossing streets, as traffic can be unpredictable.

For tourists looking to enjoy the Nile River, ferries and feluccas (traditional wooden sailboats) offer a unique and scenic way to travel. Ferries operate on fixed routes and provide an affordable way to cross the river or travel along its banks. Feluccas, on the other hand, are more of a leisure activity, offering short rides that allow you to relax and enjoy the view of the city from the water. Renting a felucca is a peaceful and picturesque experience, especially at sunset.

The Best Time to Visit

Choosing the best time to visit Cairo, Egypt, is an important step in planning your trip, as the weather, events, and overall atmosphere of the city can vary greatly depending on the time of year. Cairo is a year-round destination, but certain seasons offer more comfortable weather, better opportunities for sightseeing, and unique cultural experiences that can enhance your visit. Understanding the city's climate and its seasonal characteristics will help you make an informed decision about when to go.

Cairo has a desert climate, which means hot summers, mild winters, and very little rainfall throughout the year. The city's weather is heavily influenced by its location in the northeastern part of Egypt, close to the Nile River and surrounded by arid landscapes. While the weather is generally predictable, it's important to consider how temperatures and conditions during different months may affect your plans, especially if you intend to spend a lot of time outdoors exploring landmarks like the Pyramids of Giza or walking through bustling markets.

The period between October and April is widely regarded as the best time to visit Cairo for several reasons. During these months, the weather is cooler and more pleasant compared to the scorching summer heat. Daytime temperatures typically range from 18 to 26 degrees Celsius (64 to 79 degrees Fahrenheit), making it much easier to enjoy outdoor activities and sightseeing. The evenings can be cooler, with temperatures sometimes dropping to around 10 degrees Celsius (50 degrees Fahrenheit), so it's a good idea to bring a light jacket or sweater. This time of year is especially popular with tourists, as the milder weather allows for comfortable exploration of Cairo's historical sites, such as the Citadel, Islamic Cairo, and the Pyramids.

December and January are the coolest months in Cairo, and they are also part of the peak tourist season. Many visitors choose to come during this time to escape colder weather in their home countries and enjoy the relatively mild Egyptian winter. While the cooler temperatures make sightseeing more comfortable, this is also when attractions are busiest, and accommodation prices may be higher. If you plan to visit during this period, it's advisable to book your hotel and tours well in advance to secure your preferred options.

Spring, from March to April, is another excellent time to visit Cairo. The weather during these months remains comfortable, with slightly warmer temperatures than winter. This is a great time to enjoy the city's outdoor spaces, such as Al-Azhar Park or the banks of the Nile. However, it's worth noting that spring can occasionally bring strong winds and dust storms known as "khamsin." These storms, which occur when hot winds blow in from the desert, can reduce visibility and make outdoor activities less enjoyable for a day or two. Checking the weather forecast and staying flexible with your plans can help you manage this possibility.

The summer months, from May to September, are the hottest time of year in Cairo, with temperatures often exceeding 35 degrees Celsius (95 degrees Fahrenheit) during the day. In July and August, the heat can become intense, especially for those not accustomed to desert climates. While the city is less crowded with tourists during this time, the high temperatures can make outdoor sightseeing challenging, particularly at midday. If you choose to visit Cairo in the summer, it's best to plan your activities for early morning or late afternoon when the heat is less intense. Wearing light, breathable clothing, staying hydrated, and taking breaks in shaded or air-conditioned areas are essential for staying comfortable.

Despite the heat, summer can still be an appealing time to visit for budget-conscious travelers. Accommodation and flight prices are generally lower during the summer months, and popular attractions may be less crowded. Additionally, some cultural events and festivals take place during this period, providing unique opportunities to experience local traditions and celebrations.

Religious and cultural holidays also play a role in determining the best time to visit Cairo. The Islamic calendar, which is based on lunar cycles, includes significant holidays such as Ramadan and Eid. During Ramadan, a holy month of fasting and prayer for Muslims, the daily rhythm of the city changes. Many restaurants and businesses operate on reduced hours, and some tourist sites may have shorter opening times. However, evenings during Ramadan are vibrant, with streets and markets coming alive after sunset as locals break their fast and gather to celebrate. If you visit during Ramadan, it's an opportunity to experience a unique cultural aspect of Cairo, but it's important to be respectful of local customs, such as refraining from eating or drinking in public during daylight hours.

Eid al-Fitr, the festival that marks the end of Ramadan, and Eid al-Adha, the festival of sacrifice, are also significant holidays in Cairo. These celebrations are marked by feasts, family gatherings, and public events. While some businesses may close during the holidays, the festive atmosphere and special activities can add a memorable dimension to your visit.

In addition to seasonal and cultural considerations, personal preferences and travel goals should influence your decision about when to visit Cairo. If you prefer cooler weather and don't mind larger crowds, the winter and early spring months are ideal. For those looking for budget-friendly options and fewer tourists, the summer months can still provide an enjoyable experience with careful planning. If you're interested in experiencing local traditions, timing your visit around Ramadan or one of the major festivals can offer a unique perspective on Cairo's culture.

Safety and Health Information for Travelers

Traveling to Cairo, Egypt, as a tourist can be an exciting and rewarding experience, but like any destination, it is essential to stay informed about safety and health considerations to ensure your trip is enjoyable and trouble-free.

Cairo is generally safe for tourists, and millions of visitors travel there each year without incident. However, as with any major city, it is important to be aware of your surroundings and take basic precautions to protect yourself and your belongings. Pickpocketing and petty theft can occur, especially in crowded areas like markets, public transportation, and tourist sites. To reduce the risk, keep your valuables secure and out of sight. Use a money belt or a secure bag to carry cash, passports, and other important items. Avoid displaying expensive jewelry, electronics, or large amounts of money, as this can attract unwanted attention.

When exploring Cairo, staying vigilant in busy areas is key. Markets such as Khan el-Khalili are lively and vibrant but can be overwhelming for first-time visitors. Be mindful of your belongings and avoid becoming distracted. If someone offers unsolicited help or a service, exercise caution, as they may expect a tip or attempt to sell you something. While most interactions with locals are friendly and genuine, it is always good to maintain a polite but cautious demeanor.

Taxis and ride-hailing services like Uber and Careem are popular modes of transportation in Cairo, but safety measures are still important. If using traditional taxis, agree on the fare before starting the journey, as meters are not always used. For added safety and convenience, ride-hailing apps are often a better choice, as they provide a clear fare estimate and a record of your trip. Avoid accepting rides from unlicensed drivers or those who approach you directly at airports or train stations.

Crossing the street in Cairo can be challenging due to the chaotic traffic. Pedestrian crossings are often ignored, and drivers rarely yield to pedestrians. Exercise caution and use footbridges or traffic lights where available. If you must cross a busy street, wait for a gap in traffic and cross with confidence, but always remain alert. Following the lead of locals can also be helpful, as they are familiar with the flow of traffic.

Health considerations are another important aspect of planning your trip to Cairo. The tap water in Cairo is not recommended for drinking, as it can cause stomach upset for visitors who are not accustomed to it. Stick to bottled or filtered water, which is widely available and affordable. When eating out, choose reputable restaurants and avoid street food that appears unhygienic. While Egyptian cuisine is delicious and safe in most establishments, it is wise to ensure that food is freshly prepared and served hot.

Travelers should also be aware of the risk of sun exposure, especially during the hotter months. Cairo's climate can be harsh, with intense sunlight and high temperatures. Protect yourself by wearing lightweight, breathable clothing that covers your skin, a wide-brimmed hat, and sunglasses. Apply sunscreen with a high SPF regularly, even on cloudy days. Stay hydrated by drinking plenty of water throughout the day, particularly if you are engaging in outdoor activities or visiting sites like the Pyramids of Giza.

Medical care in Cairo is generally accessible, with both public and private healthcare facilities available. However, the quality of care can vary, and private hospitals are often a better option for tourists. It is highly recommended to purchase travel insurance that covers medical emergencies and evacuation if necessary. Before traveling, make sure you are up to date on routine vaccinations and consult your doctor about any additional vaccines or medications you may need for Egypt. While there is no requirement for specific vaccinations for entry into Egypt, travelers from certain countries may need proof of yellow fever vaccination.

Air pollution in Cairo can be a concern, particularly for individuals with respiratory issues or allergies. The city's dense population and heavy traffic contribute to poor air quality, especially during the cooler months when temperature inversions can trap pollution. If you are sensitive to air pollution, consider bringing a face mask or avoiding outdoor activities on days with high pollution levels. Checking air quality forecasts can help you plan your activities accordingly. Another aspect of safety to consider is cultural sensitivity. Egypt is a predominantly Muslim country, and respecting local customs and traditions is important for a positive experience.

Dress modestly, particularly when visiting religious sites, by covering your shoulders and knees. Women may also consider carrying a scarf to cover their heads when entering mosques. Public displays of affection should be avoided, as they may be considered inappropriate. Being respectful of local customs not only helps you avoid potential misunderstandings but also allows you to connect more authentically with the local culture.

Tourists should also be aware of potential scams or overly aggressive sales tactics, especially in tourist-heavy areas. Vendors and touts may approach you offering goods, services, or tours, sometimes at inflated prices. It is perfectly acceptable to decline politely and walk away if you are not interested. If you choose to engage, bargaining is expected in markets and for certain services, so don't hesitate to negotiate a fair price.

Emergency services are available in Cairo, but response times can vary. The general emergency number for police, fire, and ambulance services is 122. It is a good idea to keep a list of important contacts, including your embassy or consulate, as well as the address and phone number of your accommodation. In case of minor issues, many hotels and tour operators have staff who can assist you with translations or advice.

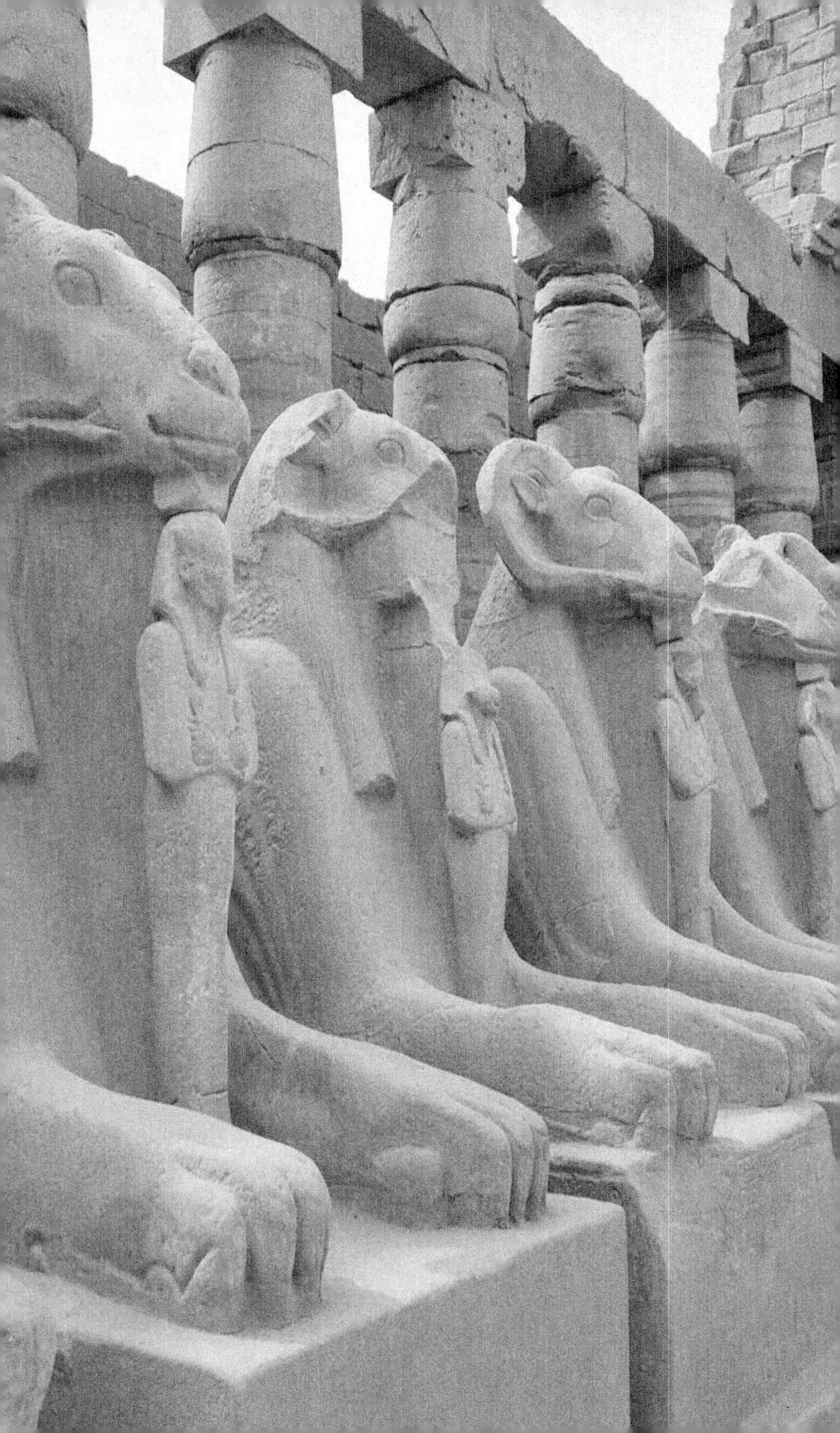

CHAPTER 2

EXPLORING CAIRO BY DISTRICT

Giza

Must-See Attractions

The Great Pyramids of Giza: A Journey into Ancient History

The Great Pyramids of Giza, standing proudly on the Giza Plateau just outside Cairo, are among the most iconic landmarks in the world. These ancient structures have drawn travelers for thousands of years, and visiting them is a bucket-list experience for anyone with an interest in history, architecture, or human achievement. Each pyramid carries its own story, and exploring the site is both awe-inspiring and educational.

The Location and How to Get There
The pyramids are located about 13 kilometers (8 miles) southwest of central Cairo, making them easily accessible from the city. If you're staying in Cairo, the most convenient way to reach the site is by taxi or ride-hailing apps like Uber or Careem. These services provide direct transport to the Giza Plateau, and the fares are generally reasonable. If you prefer public transportation, you can take the metro to Giza Station

and then catch a microbus or taxi to the entrance. Organized tours are another popular option, offering hassle-free transport along with guided visits.

What You Will See and Do
The Giza Plateau is home to three main pyramids: the Great Pyramid of Khufu (Cheops), the Pyramid of Khafre (Chephren), and the Pyramid of Menkaure. Each pyramid is unique and worth exploring.

The Great Pyramid of Khufu
This is the largest and most famous pyramid, built over 4,500 years ago during the reign of Pharaoh Khufu. It originally stood at 146 meters (481 feet) and was the tallest man-made structure in the world for nearly 4,000 years. You can walk around its massive base and marvel at the precision of the limestone blocks. For an additional fee, you can enter the pyramid and navigate narrow corridors to reach the King's Chamber, where you'll feel the weight of history in the still, solemn atmosphere.

The Pyramid of Khafre
This pyramid appears slightly taller than Khufu's due to its elevated location but is slightly smaller in size. Khafre's Pyramid is known for retaining some of its original limestone casing at the top, giving visitors a glimpse of how these structures originally appeared. It also features a satellite pyramid nearby, which is smaller but equally intriguing.

The Pyramid of Menkaure
The smallest of the three main pyramids, Menkaure's Pyramid is no less impressive. Its base is made of granite, a material that adds to its distinct appearance. The pyramid is surrounded by several smaller "Queen's Pyramids," which were likely built for the wives and family members of the pharaoh.

You can also visit the surrounding necropolis, which contains tombs, temples, and smaller pyramids that give insight into the burial practices and beliefs of ancient Egypt.

The Best Times to Visit
The Giza Plateau is open year-round, but the best time to visit is between October and April, when the weather is cooler and more comfortable for outdoor exploration. During this period, temperatures range from 18°C to 26°C (64°F to 79°F), making it ideal for walking around the site. To avoid crowds, it's best to arrive early in the morning when the site opens at 8:00 AM. Late afternoons are also less busy and provide excellent lighting for photography.

Ticket Information and Booking
Tickets can be purchased at the entrance or online through authorized platforms. A general entry ticket grants access to the Giza Plateau, while additional tickets are required to enter the Great Pyramid or the other pyramids. Prices vary depending on whether you are an adult, student, or child, with discounts available for students who present a valid ID. Guided tours often include tickets, transportation, and expert commentary, offering a convenient way to visit.

Facilities and Accessibility
The site is equipped with restrooms, cafes, and gift shops where you can purchase water, snacks, and souvenirs. Accessibility has been improved in recent years, with ramps and pathways for wheelchair users, although some areas, like the interiors of the pyramids, may still be challenging to navigate. Visitors with mobility needs can arrange for assistance, and it's advisable to check in advance for specific accessibility services.

Photography Tips and Rules
Photography is allowed on the Giza Plateau, but tripods and drones are generally not permitted without special permission. The best time for photos is during sunrise or sunset when the soft lighting enhances the beauty of the pyramids. For creative shots, consider framing the pyramids with the desert in the foreground or capturing reflections in nearby water features.

Cultural and Historical Context
The Great Pyramids are the last surviving wonder of the ancient world and a testament to the skill and ambition of ancient Egyptian builders. Constructed as tombs for pharaohs, they were designed to ensure safe passage to the afterlife. Each pyramid was part of a larger complex that included temples, causeways, and burial chambers, reflecting the intricate rituals and beliefs of the time.

Rules, Etiquette, and Safety Tips
While visiting the pyramids, it's important to respect the site by not climbing on the structures or touching artifacts. Dress modestly, as Egypt is a conservative country, and wear

comfortable shoes for walking on uneven terrain. Bring sunscreen, a hat, and plenty of water, especially if you're visiting during warmer months. Be cautious of vendors and camel ride operators who may charge inflated prices; always agree on a price upfront.

Why You Should Visit
The Great Pyramids of Giza are more than just architectural marvels; they are a window into an ancient civilization that continues to fascinate the world. Visiting these monuments allows you to connect with the past, experience the ingenuity of human achievement, and create memories that will last a lifetime.

The Great Sphinx of Giza: A Timeless Symbol of Mystery and Power

The Great Sphinx of Giza is one of the most iconic landmarks in Egypt and the world. Located on the Giza Plateau, near the Great Pyramids, the Sphinx stands as a silent sentinel, embodying the mystery, power, and ingenuity of ancient Egyptian civilization. Visiting the Sphinx is an unforgettable experience, offering you a chance to marvel at its sheer size, intricate craftsmanship, and deep historical significance.

Location and How to Get There
The Sphinx is situated on the eastern edge of the Giza Plateau, just in front of the Pyramid of Khafre. It is approximately 13 kilometers (8 miles) southwest of central Cairo, making it accessible by various means of transport. The most convenient way to get there is by taxi or ride-hailing apps like Uber or

Careem, which provide direct service to the site. If you're feeling adventurous, you can take the metro to Giza Station and then hop on a microbus or taxi to the plateau entrance. Many organized tours also include the Sphinx as part of a broader visit to the Giza Pyramids, offering transportation and a guided experience.

What You Will See and Do
As you approach the Great Sphinx, the first thing you'll notice is its immense size. Carved from a single block of limestone, the Sphinx measures 73 meters (240 feet) in length and 20 meters (66 feet) in height. Its body resembles a reclining lion, symbolizing strength and protection, while its human head, thought to represent Pharaoh Khafre, symbolizes wisdom. The combination of these two forms reflects the ancient Egyptians' belief in the divine power of their rulers.

The Sphinx faces east, greeting the rising sun, and is surrounded by a carefully designed temple complex that adds to its grandeur. While exploring the site, you can walk along pathways that offer close views of the statue's intricate details, such as the headdress known as the "nemes" and the faint remnants of paint that hint at how it might have looked in its original state. Although time and erosion have worn down parts of the Sphinx, including its nose and beard, the statue retains an aura of majesty that leaves a lasting impression.

One of the most intriguing features near the Sphinx is the Valley Temple, believed to have been part of the funerary complex of Pharaoh Khafre. The temple, made from massive limestone and granite blocks, was used for mummification rituals and other ceremonies. Walking through the temple ruins gives you a sense of the architectural skill and spiritual practices of the ancient Egyptians.

The Best Times to Visit
The Sphinx is best visited during the cooler months, from October to April, when the weather is mild and comfortable for outdoor activities. Arriving early in the morning, as soon as the site opens at 8:00 AM, allows you to enjoy the attraction with fewer crowds and better lighting for photography. Late afternoons are also a good time to visit, as the soft golden light creates a stunning backdrop for the Sphinx and the surrounding desert.

Ticket Information and Booking
Access to the Sphinx is included in the general entry ticket for the Giza Plateau, which can be purchased at the entrance or online through authorized platforms. If you're booking a guided tour, the Sphinx is usually part of the itinerary, so you won't need to worry about separate tickets. It's always a good idea to check current prices and availability before your visit. Discounts are often available for students who present a valid ID.

Facilities and Accessibility
The area around the Sphinx is well-maintained and offers basic facilities, including restrooms and a visitor center with information about the site. Nearby cafes and shops provide water, snacks, and souvenirs. While pathways around the Sphinx have been improved to accommodate visitors, some

areas may still be challenging for those with mobility issues due to uneven terrain. If you have specific needs, it's advisable to contact the site in advance to inquire about accessibility options.

Photography Tips and Rules
The Great Sphinx is a dream destination for photographers, and there are many angles and perspectives to capture its beauty. For the best photos, aim to visit during sunrise or sunset when the light is softer and highlights the details of the statue. A popular spot for photos is the platform that offers a side view of the Sphinx with the Pyramid of Khafre in the background. While photography is generally allowed, tripods and drones require special permits, so it's best to plan accordingly.

Cultural and Historical Context
The Great Sphinx was built during the Fourth Dynasty of ancient Egypt, around 2500 BCE, as part of Pharaoh Khafre's mortuary complex. Its purpose was likely symbolic, serving as a guardian of the pyramids and a representation of the king's divine power. The Sphinx has inspired countless myths and legends over the centuries, from ancient tales of its protective role to modern theories about its construction and symbolism. Its enigmatic expression and missing nose have fueled debates among historians, archaeologists, and adventurers, adding to its allure.

Rules, Etiquette, and Safety Tips
When visiting the Sphinx, it's important to respect the site and follow the rules. Climbing on the statue is strictly prohibited,

as it can cause further damage to the already fragile structure. Dress modestly, as Egypt is a conservative country, and wear comfortable shoes for walking on uneven paths. Bring sunscreen, a hat, and plenty of water to stay hydrated, especially during warmer months. Be cautious of vendors around the site and agree on prices upfront if you decide to purchase souvenirs or hire a camel for photos.

Why You Should Visit
The Great Sphinx of Giza is more than just an ancient statue—it's a symbol of the enduring legacy of Egypt's civilization. Standing in its presence connects you to a time when humans achieved extraordinary feats of creativity, ambition, and spiritual devotion. Visiting the Sphinx allows you to immerse yourself in this rich history, marvel at its artistry, and reflect on the mysteries it still holds.

The Solar Boat Museum

Located near the Great Pyramid on the Giza Plateau, the Solar Boat Museum offers an extraordinary glimpse into the advanced craftsmanship and spiritual beliefs of ancient Egypt. This museum houses one of the most well-preserved artifacts from the time of the pharaohs: the Solar Boat of Pharaoh Khufu. Visiting this museum not only complements your exploration of the pyramids but also deepens your understanding of ancient Egyptian rituals and their exceptional engineering skills.

What Is the Solar Boat?
The Solar Boat, also known as the Khufu Ship, is an ancient wooden vessel that was discovered buried in a pit near the Great Pyramid in 1954. This extraordinary find dates back over 4,500 years to the reign of Pharaoh Khufu. The boat was likely built for ceremonial purposes, symbolizing the journey of the pharaoh's soul to the afterlife. Some scholars also believe it may have been used to transport Khufu's body during his funeral. The ship is made entirely of wood, including cedar imported from Lebanon, and its design reflects the advanced shipbuilding techniques of the time.

The Museum's Location and How to Get There
The Solar Boat Museum is situated on the southern side of the Great Pyramid, within the Giza Plateau. If you're visiting the pyramids, it's easy to include the museum in your itinerary since it's only a short walk from the main structures. To reach the plateau, you can take a taxi or use ride-hailing services like Uber and Careem from central Cairo. Alternatively, public transportation such as the metro to Giza Station and a connecting taxi or microbus will get you there. Many guided tours also include the museum as part of a package that covers the major attractions on the plateau.

What You Will See and Do
When you enter the Solar Boat Museum, you'll immediately notice the modern, climate-controlled design that protects this ancient artifact. The boat itself is displayed in a specially built glass enclosure, elevated off the ground to allow visitors to view it from all angles. As you walk around the exhibit, you'll see the intricate details of the ship, from its carefully fitted

wooden planks to the ropes and oars that were used for navigation.

The museum also includes informative displays and diagrams that explain the boat's construction, purpose, and the process of its excavation and restoration. You'll learn about how the boat was buried in a pit, disassembled into over 1,200 pieces, and carefully reassembled by experts over several years. These exhibits provide context and help you appreciate the skill and effort that went into preserving this remarkable artifact.

The highlight of the visit is seeing the Solar Boat up close. Its size is impressive, measuring approximately 43.6 meters (143 feet) in length, and the craftsmanship is astonishing considering the tools and techniques available at the time. As you walk around, you'll gain a deeper appreciation for the ancient Egyptians' engineering expertise and their belief in the afterlife.

The Best Times to Visit
The museum is open year-round, and the best time to visit is during the cooler months from October to April. The site opens at 8:00 AM, and arriving early allows you to avoid larger crowds and enjoy a quieter experience. If you're visiting during the summer months, the museum's air-conditioned interior provides a welcome escape from the heat, making it a good stop during the hottest part of the day.

Ticket Information and Booking
Entry to the Solar Boat Museum requires a separate ticket in addition to your Giza Plateau ticket. You can purchase tickets at the entrance to the museum, and prices are generally affordable. Discounts are available for students with valid ID. If you're booking a guided tour, check whether the museum is included in the package, as some tours bundle the cost of all main attractions for convenience.

Facilities and Accessibility
The Solar Boat Museum is equipped with modern facilities, including clean restrooms, a small gift shop, and an information desk where you can ask questions or learn more about the exhibits. The museum is wheelchair-accessible, with ramps and elevators available for visitors with mobility challenges. The climate-controlled environment ensures that the museum is comfortable to visit regardless of the weather outside.

Photography Tips and Rules
Photography is allowed inside the museum, but flash photography is prohibited to protect the ancient wood from damage. The lighting in the museum is carefully designed to highlight the details of the Solar Boat, so you can capture excellent photos without additional equipment. Consider taking shots from different angles to showcase the ship's size and craftsmanship. If you're using a smartphone, adjust your settings to capture the intricate details of the wood and ropes.

Cultural and Historical Context
The Solar Boat is not just a fascinating artifact; it is a powerful symbol of ancient Egyptian beliefs about the afterlife. The ancient Egyptians believed that the pharaoh's soul needed a vessel to navigate the heavens and join the sun god Ra on his eternal journey. This concept of a solar journey was central to their religious practices, and the construction of the Solar Boat reflects the importance of this belief.

The discovery of the Solar Boat also sheds light on the advanced construction techniques of the Old Kingdom. The use of imported cedar wood, the precise fitting of planks without nails, and the overall design demonstrate the ingenuity and ambition of ancient Egyptian shipbuilders.

Rules, Etiquette, and Safety Tips
When visiting the museum, it's important to respect the rules, such as refraining from touching the displays and maintaining a quiet atmosphere to allow others to enjoy the experience. Dress modestly and wear comfortable shoes, as you may be walking around the plateau before or after your visit. Bring water to stay hydrated, especially if you're visiting in warmer months, but note that food and drinks are not allowed inside the museum.

Why You Should Visit
The Solar Boat Museum is a must-see attraction for anyone interested in ancient history, engineering, or spirituality. It offers a unique opportunity to see one of the world's oldest and best-preserved boats, providing a tangible connection to the beliefs and practices of ancient Egypt. A visit to the Solar

Boat Museum will not only deepen your appreciation for ancient Egyptian culture but also leave you with a sense of wonder at their incredible achievements.

Things to Do in Giza: Camel Rides, Light and Sound Show, and Exploring the Pyramid Complex

Exploring the Pyramid Complex near Giza is an extraordinary experience that offers visitors the chance to connect with some of the most iconic landmarks in the world. The Great Pyramids of Giza, including the Pyramid of Khufu, the Pyramid of Khafre, and the Pyramid of Menkaure, are monuments that stand as a testament to ancient Egypt's architectural brilliance and cultural achievements. When you visit, there are several activities you can enjoy to make your trip even more memorable and immersive. Among these, camel rides, the evening light and sound show, and exploring the pyramid complex on foot or by vehicle are some of the most engaging ways to appreciate this UNESCO World Heritage Site fully.

One of the most popular activities around the Pyramids of Giza is taking a camel ride. Riding a camel is not only a unique and fun way to navigate the desert terrain, but it also provides a chance to experience a mode of transport that has been used for centuries in Egypt. As you sit high on the camel's back, you'll get an elevated view of the vast pyramid complex, the golden sands of the surrounding desert, and the dramatic skyline of Cairo in the distance. Camel rides are particularly popular at sunrise or sunset when the soft light enhances the beauty of the pyramids and the surrounding landscape. The warm hues of the sun create a magical atmosphere, making it the perfect time to take photographs. Many local guides offer camel rides near the main entrance of the complex, and it's a good idea to agree on a price before starting your ride to ensure a fair deal. Some guides also provide traditional scarves to protect you from the desert sun and sand, adding an authentic touch to your experience.

The light and sound show at the Giza pyramid complex is another highlight that visitors should not miss. This evening event combines history, storytelling, and spectacular visuals to bring the ancient world to life. As darkness falls, the pyramids and the Sphinx are illuminated with vibrant lights that highlight their grandeur and details. A narrator recounts the history of the pharaohs, the construction of the pyramids, and the significance of these structures to ancient Egyptian civilization. The story is accompanied by dramatic music and sound effects, creating a truly immersive experience. The show is available in multiple languages, so you can choose a performance that suits you. Many visitors find that the light and sound show is an excellent way to deepen their understanding of the pyramids after seeing them during the day. The show runs for about an hour, and tickets can be purchased at the site or online in advance. Be sure to dress warmly if you're visiting during cooler months, as the temperature can drop in the evening.

Exploring the pyramid complex itself is an essential part of any visit. Walking among these massive stone structures allows you to appreciate their scale and craftsmanship up close. Each of the three main pyramids has its own unique features and history. The Pyramid of Khufu, also known as the Great Pyramid, is the largest and most famous. Its precise construction and enormous size continue to amaze engineers and archaeologists to this day. You can even enter the Great Pyramid, though the passageways are narrow and may not be suitable for everyone. Inside, you'll find chambers that once housed the king's sarcophagus and other treasures. The Pyramid of Khafre, slightly smaller but equally impressive, retains some of its original smooth limestone casing at the top, offering a glimpse of how all the pyramids once looked. The Pyramid of Menkaure, the smallest of the three, is notable for its elegant proportions and its historical significance.

As you explore, you'll also come across smaller satellite pyramids, tombs, and temples that form part of the larger necropolis. The Great Sphinx of Giza, located near the pyramids, is another must-see. This massive limestone statue with the body of a lion and the head of a pharaoh has stood guard over the complex for thousands of years. The Sphinx is shrouded in mystery, and its enigmatic expression has inspired countless legends and theories. Walking around the Sphinx and viewing it from different angles will give you a deeper appreciation of its size and artistry.

To enhance your visit, consider hiring a knowledgeable guide who can explain the history, construction techniques, and cultural significance of the pyramids and the surrounding structures. Guides are available on-site, and many are fluent in multiple languages. They can share fascinating stories and details that you might not discover on your own. If you prefer to explore independently, informational signs and maps are available to help you navigate the site.

For those who prefer not to walk long distances, horse-drawn carriages and small tour vehicles are available to take you around the complex. These options are especially helpful for families with young children or visitors with mobility challenges. No matter how you choose to explore, be sure to bring water, wear comfortable shoes, and protect yourself from the sun with a hat and sunscreen.

Accommodation Options in Giza

Luxury Stays: Resorts with Pyramid Views in Giza, Cairo, Egypt

For an unforgettable trip to Giza, there's nothing quite like staying in a luxury resort with direct views of the iconic pyramids. These accommodations combine world-class amenities with the unbeatable experience of waking up to one of the most awe-inspiring sights on earth. Below, we've detailed the best luxury stays, complete with practical information to help you choose the perfect resort for your visit.

1. Marriott Mena House, Cairo
Price Range: Approx. $300–$600 per night, depending on the season and room type.

Amenities: At Marriott Mena House, you'll find an unparalleled blend of history and luxury. This historic property boasts elegantly furnished rooms and suites, many with private balconies or terraces that directly face the pyramids. Enjoy free Wi-Fi, a spacious outdoor pool, a fully equipped fitness center, and a spa offering a range of treatments. The hotel's dining options are equally impressive, including an outdoor terrace restaurant where you can dine with the pyramids as your backdrop.

Best Area to Stay: The resort is ideally located at the base of the Giza Plateau, just a short walk from the entrance to the pyramids. This makes it a top choice for convenience, offering easy access to the ancient wonders while maintaining a tranquil atmosphere.

Contact Details:
Website: Marriott Mena House
Phone: +20 2 33773222
Email: reservations@marriott.com

2. **Four Seasons Hotel Cairo at The First Residence**
Price Range: Approx. $250–$500 per night.
Amenities: This luxurious five-star hotel offers rooms and suites with refined interiors, some providing panoramic views of the pyramids and the Nile River. Indulge in a relaxing spa experience, swim in the heated outdoor pool, and enjoy gourmet dining at the hotel's multiple restaurants and lounges. The rooftop lounge is particularly popular for its stunning views and exceptional service. A dedicated concierge is available to help you plan your stay, from arranging tours to recommending local attractions.

Best Area to Stay: Located in Giza's upscale district, this hotel is slightly farther from the pyramids but provides easy access to both the ancient sites and downtown Cairo. Its location near upscale shops and dining makes it a great choice for those seeking a mix of exploration and leisure.
Contact Details:
Website: Four Seasons Cairo First Residence
Phone: +20 2 35672000
Email: reservations.cairo@fourseasons.com

3. Le Meridien Pyramids Hotel & Spa
Price Range: Approx. $150–$400 per night.
Amenities: Le Meridien Pyramids is known for its stunning pyramid views and excellent hospitality. The hotel features spacious rooms and suites, many with pyramid-facing balconies. You can relax in the large outdoor pool, complete with a swim-up bar, or unwind at the on-site spa, which offers a variety of rejuvenating treatments. Multiple dining options, including an international buffet and a specialty restaurant, cater to a range of tastes.

Best Area to Stay: Situated just minutes from the pyramids, the hotel offers incredible convenience for sightseeing. It is also close to local restaurants and shops, making it easy to explore the area.
Contact Details:
Website: Le Meridien Pyramids
Phone: +20 2 33773222

4. Steigenberger Pyramids Cairo
Price Range: Approx. $200–$450 per night.
Amenities: This elegant hotel offers a modern take on luxury, with stylish rooms and suites that provide unobstructed views of the pyramids. Guests can enjoy a relaxing swim in the outdoor pool, dine at the gourmet on-site restaurant, or sip cocktails at the rooftop bar while soaking in the panoramic scenery. The hotel also features free Wi-Fi, a fitness center, and a friendly concierge team to assist with travel plans.
Best Area to Stay: Conveniently located near the pyramids and the Giza Plateau, this hotel provides easy access to the main attractions while offering a peaceful retreat from the city's hustle and bustle.
Contact Details:
Website: [Steigenberger Pyramids Cairo](#)
Phone: +20 2 33870070

5. Pyramids Valley Boutique Hotel
Price Range: Approx. $100–$250 per night.
Amenities: A boutique experience with personalized service, this hotel offers cozy rooms with direct pyramid views, ensuring a more intimate and unique stay. Enjoy complimentary breakfast on the terrace, free Wi-Fi, and friendly staff ready to assist with sightseeing plans. The hotel also arranges private pyramid tours and camel rides for an authentic Egyptian experience.

Best Area to Stay: Located just steps from the pyramid complex, this hotel is perfect for travelers who want to maximize their time exploring the Giza Plateau. Its proximity

to the attractions and peaceful ambiance make it an excellent choice for a quiet and convenient stay.
Contact Details:
Website: Pyramids Valley Boutique Hotel
Phone: +20 2 35877033

Mid-Range Options: Comfortable hotels near the Giza Plateau

If you're looking for a balance of comfort, convenience, and affordability, the mid-range hotels near the Giza Plateau offer excellent choices for your stay in Cairo. These accommodations provide modern amenities, friendly service, and easy access to the iconic pyramids, ensuring a memorable and comfortable experience without stretching your budget. Here are some highly recommended mid-range options to consider:

1. Panorama Pyramids Inn
Price Range: Approx. $50–$100 per night.
Amenities: This cozy and welcoming inn offers clean and comfortable rooms, many of which come with private balconies or terraces boasting direct pyramid views. Guests enjoy free Wi-Fi, complimentary breakfast served on the rooftop terrace, and the option to arrange guided tours and airport transfers through the hotel. The rooftop is a highlight, providing an incredible vantage point to watch the sunset over the pyramids while sipping a refreshing drink.

Best Area to Stay: Located just a short walk from the Giza Plateau entrance, Panorama Pyramids Inn is ideal for travelers looking to maximize their time exploring the ancient wonders. Its proximity to local restaurants and shops adds to the convenience.
Contact Details:
Website: Panorama Pyramids Inn
Phone: +20 2 35698745

2. Pyramids View Inn
Price Range: Approx. $60–$120 per night.
Amenities: Pyramids View Inn lives up to its name, offering breathtaking views of the pyramids from its rooftop terrace. The hotel features air-conditioned rooms with en-suite bathrooms, free Wi-Fi, and a complimentary breakfast buffet. The staff is known for their warm hospitality and can assist with organizing camel rides, guided tours, and airport pickups. The cozy rooftop seating area is perfect for unwinding after a day of sightseeing.

Best Area to Stay: Situated right next to the Giza Plateau, the hotel's location ensures you're within walking distance of the pyramid complex and the Sphinx. It's an excellent choice for travelers who value convenience and a personal touch.
Contact Details:
Website: Pyramids View Inn
Phone: +20 2 33849711

3. Hayat Pyramids View Hotel
Price Range: Approx. $70–$130 per night.

Amenities: This hotel offers modern and spacious rooms, many featuring pyramid views from private balconies. Guests can enjoy free Wi-Fi, daily housekeeping, and a complimentary breakfast buffet. The on-site restaurant serves a variety of local and international dishes, and the rooftop terrace is a standout feature, offering panoramic views of the pyramids. The hotel also provides transportation services and tour assistance.

Best Area to Stay: Conveniently located just steps from the pyramid complex, Hayat Pyramids View Hotel makes it easy to explore Giza's most famous attractions. Its central location also ensures access to nearby dining and shopping options.

Contact Details:
Website: Hayat Pyramids View Hotel
Phone: +20 2 33871030

4. Best View Pyramids Hotel
Price Range: Approx. $65–$120 per night.
Amenities: This family-friendly hotel features comfortable rooms with air conditioning, flat-screen TVs, and private bathrooms. Complimentary breakfast is served on the rooftop terrace, which offers stunning views of the pyramids and the Sphinx. The hotel staff is attentive and can assist with organizing tours, airport transfers, and local excursions. Free Wi-Fi is available throughout the property.

Best Area to Stay: Located within walking distance of the Giza Plateau, this hotel is perfect for travelers who want to

wake up to pyramid views and spend their days exploring the area's rich history.
Contact Details:
Website: Best View Pyramids Hotel
Phone: +20 2 33991234

5. Giza Pyramids Inn
Price Range: Approx. $55–$100 per night.
Amenities: This charming inn offers a welcoming atmosphere and excellent value for money. Rooms are clean and well-equipped with modern amenities, including air conditioning, free Wi-Fi, and flat-screen TVs. Guests enjoy a hearty complimentary breakfast, served on a terrace overlooking the pyramids. The hotel also provides guided tour packages, airport transfers, and 24-hour front desk service.

Best Area to Stay: The inn is located just across the street from the Sphinx entrance to the Giza Plateau, making it one of the most convenient options for travelers who want to maximize their time at the pyramids.
Contact Details:
Website: Giza Pyramids Inn
Phone: +20 2 35880077

Budget Choices: Hostels and Guesthouses with Easy Access to Attractions in Giza, Cairo, Egypt

For travelers on a budget, Giza offers a variety of affordable accommodations that provide comfortable stays and easy access to the iconic pyramids and other local attractions.

Staying at a budget-friendly hostel or guesthouse doesn't mean sacrificing convenience or quality—many of these options come with helpful amenities and warm hospitality, ensuring you'll feel right at home while exploring one of the world's most historic destinations. Here's a guide to some of the best budget accommodations in Giza.

1. Guardian Guest House
Price Range: Approx. $40–$70 per night.
Amenities: Guardian Guest House is a highly-rated budget option with a homely atmosphere. The property offers free Wi-Fi, complimentary breakfast, and clean, comfortable rooms with en-suite bathrooms. The rooftop terrace is a standout feature, providing stunning, uninterrupted views of the Great Pyramids and the Sphinx. The friendly staff is available to help organize tours and transportation.

Best Area to Stay: Located directly across from the Sphinx entrance to the Giza Plateau, this guesthouse is as close to the pyramids as you can get without staying inside the complex itself. The central location makes it easy to explore the surrounding area.
Contact Details:
Website: Guardian Guest House
Phone: +20 2 35697823
Email: info@guardianguesthouse.com

2. Pyramids Loft Homestay
Price Range: Approx. $30–$60 per night.

Amenities: Pyramids Loft Homestay is a charming, family-run property that offers a relaxed and welcoming environment. Rooms are simple but comfortable, with air conditioning and free Wi-Fi. Guests have access to a shared kitchen, and breakfast is included. The rooftop terrace provides breathtaking pyramid views, making it a great spot for morning coffee or evening relaxation. The staff is known for their exceptional hospitality and personalized service.

Best Area to Stay: This homestay is a short walk from the Giza Plateau entrance, making it an excellent choice for travelers who want to focus on exploring the pyramids and the Sphinx.

Contact Details:
Website: Pyramids Loft Homestay
Phone: +20 2 35798712

3. Egypt Pyramids Inn
Price Range: Approx. $25–$50 per night.
Amenities: Egypt Pyramids Inn offers clean and cozy rooms with free Wi-Fi, air conditioning, and private bathrooms. A complimentary breakfast is served each morning, and the rooftop terrace provides excellent views of the pyramids and the Sphinx. The staff is helpful and can assist with booking tours, arranging transportation, and offering local tips.

Best Area to Stay: Positioned just steps away from the Giza Plateau entrance, this guesthouse is perfect for travelers looking for convenience on a budget. Its location also puts you close to local shops and casual dining options.

Contact Details:

Website: Egypt Pyramids Inn
Phone: +20 2 33840981

4. Great Pyramid Inn
Price Range: Approx. $35–$70 per night.
Amenities: This guesthouse combines affordability with fantastic views of the pyramids. Rooms are well-maintained and include free Wi-Fi, air conditioning, and flat-screen TVs. Guests can enjoy a complimentary breakfast on the rooftop terrace, which offers some of the best views in the area. The on-site restaurant serves Egyptian and international cuisine, making dining convenient. The staff is known for their friendly and accommodating service.

Best Area to Stay: Located directly opposite the Sphinx, Great Pyramid Inn is ideally situated for sightseeing and offers unbeatable pyramid views at an affordable price.
Contact Details:
Website: Great Pyramid Inn
Phone: +20 2 35678456

5. Happy Days Pyramids Inn
Price Range: Approx. $20–$40 per night.
Amenities: Happy Days Pyramids Inn provides basic but comfortable accommodations, including free Wi-Fi, air-conditioned rooms, and complimentary breakfast. The guesthouse has a laid-back atmosphere, with a rooftop terrace that offers clear views of the pyramids. The staff is eager to help with travel arrangements and can recommend local restaurants and attractions.

Best Area to Stay: Located within walking distance of the Giza Plateau and several public transport options, this inn is a great base for budget travelers exploring Giza and beyond.

Contact Details:
Website: Happy Days Pyramids Inn
Phone: +20 2 35870643

These budget accommodations in Giza provide excellent value for travelers who want a comfortable stay with easy access to the pyramids and other attractions.

Islamic Cairo

Must-See Attractions

Al-Azhar Mosque: A Timeless Center of Learning and Spirituality

Al-Azhar Mosque is one of the most iconic landmarks in Islamic Cairo, standing as a symbol of religious devotion, education, and architectural brilliance. Located in the heart of Cairo's historic Islamic district, this mosque is not only a place of worship but also one of the oldest universities in the world. Visiting Al-Azhar Mosque offers you a chance to connect with over a thousand years of history while experiencing the serenity and beauty of one of Egypt's most revered spiritual sites.

Location and How to Get There
Al-Azhar Mosque is situated in Islamic Cairo, a short distance from other famous landmarks such as the Khan el-Khalili Bazaar and Al-Hussein Mosque. The mosque's exact location is near Al-Azhar Street, making it easy to reach from most parts of the city. If you're staying in central Cairo or Downtown, you can take a taxi or use ride-hailing services like Uber or Careem for a direct and convenient journey. For those using public transport, the nearest metro station is Ataba, from where you can take a short taxi ride or walk to the mosque. Many guided tours of Islamic Cairo also include a visit to Al-Azhar Mosque, making transportation and navigation effortless.

What You Will See and Do
As you approach Al-Azhar Mosque, you'll immediately notice its striking architecture, which reflects centuries of Islamic art and design. Built in 970 CE during the Fatimid dynasty, the mosque has been expanded and renovated over the years, resulting in a blend of architectural styles that tell the story of its long history.

The mosque's five minarets, each with its own unique design, are among its most distinctive features. These towering structures are intricately decorated and serve as a visual reminder of the mosque's spiritual and cultural significance. The mosque's main entrance leads you into a spacious courtyard, surrounded by elegant arcades supported by columns. The courtyard is a peaceful space where you can take a moment to absorb the beauty of the mosque's design.

Inside the mosque, you'll find the prayer hall, which is adorned with beautifully carved wooden panels, intricate calligraphy, and traditional Islamic motifs. The prayer hall is vast and serene, with natural light streaming in through stained-glass windows. Even if you're not a practicing Muslim, you can appreciate the sense of tranquility and the craftsmanship that went into creating this sacred space.

One of the most fascinating aspects of Al-Azhar Mosque is its role as a center of learning. Al-Azhar University, which grew out of the mosque, is one of the oldest and most respected Islamic universities in the world. Established in 972 CE, it has been a hub for Islamic scholarship for over a millennium, attracting students from across the globe. While exploring the mosque, you can imagine the generations of scholars who have studied and debated within its walls.

The Best Times to Visit
Al-Azhar Mosque is open to visitors throughout the year, but the best times to visit are during the cooler months from October to April. The weather during this period is pleasant, making it easier to explore the mosque and the surrounding Islamic Cairo district. Visiting in the morning or early afternoon is ideal, as the mosque is generally quieter, allowing you to fully appreciate its peaceful atmosphere. Fridays, which are holy days in Islam, tend to be busier due to prayers, so plan your visit accordingly if you prefer a less crowded experience.

Entry Requirements and Etiquette

Visiting Al-Azhar Mosque is free, though donations are appreciated to help with its upkeep. As it is an active place of worship, it's important to dress modestly and respect Islamic customs. Women are advised to cover their heads with a scarf and wear clothing that covers their arms and legs. Men should also dress modestly, avoiding shorts and sleeveless shirts. Shoes must be removed before entering the mosque, and plastic bags are often provided to carry them.

Photography is generally allowed, but it's best to ask for permission before taking pictures inside the mosque. Flash photography is discouraged to maintain the serene atmosphere.

Facilities and Accessibility
The mosque is equipped with basic facilities, including clean restrooms and designated areas for ablution. While the historic structure has limitations in terms of accessibility, efforts have been made to accommodate visitors with mobility challenges. Ramps and pathways are available in certain areas, but it's a good idea to contact the mosque in advance if you have specific needs. There are also shops and cafes nearby where you can enjoy refreshments after your visit.

Cultural and Historical Context
Al-Azhar Mosque was built by Jawhar al-Siqilli, a general of the Fatimid Caliphate, as part of the establishment of Cairo as the new capital of the Fatimid dynasty. Over the centuries, the mosque evolved into a global center for Islamic learning, where scholars studied the Quran, jurisprudence, philosophy,

and the sciences. The name "Al-Azhar" is thought to be a reference to Fatima al-Zahra, the daughter of the Prophet Muhammad, highlighting the mosque's spiritual connection to Islamic heritage.

The mosque's history is intertwined with the development of Cairo as a cultural and intellectual hub. Its influence extends far beyond Egypt, shaping Islamic thought and education worldwide. Today, Al-Azhar University continues to play a significant role in the academic and spiritual life of the Muslim world.

Nearby Attractions
A visit to Al-Azhar Mosque can easily be combined with exploring other landmarks in Islamic Cairo. The Khan el-Khalili Bazaar, just a short walk away, offers a lively shopping experience with its vibrant stalls and traditional crafts. The Al-Hussein Mosque, another important religious site, is also nearby and worth visiting. For a deeper dive into the history of the area, consider exploring Al-Muizz Street, which is lined with historic mosques, madrasas, and palaces.

Why You Should Visit
Al-Azhar Mosque is more than just a religious building—it's a testament to the enduring legacy of Islamic culture and education. Visiting this mosque allows you to step into a world of architectural beauty, spiritual devotion, and intellectual achievement.

Khan El Khalili Bazaar

Khan El Khalili Bazaar is one of the most famous and lively attractions in Cairo. Located in the heart of Islamic Cairo, this bustling marketplace has been a hub of trade, culture, and craftsmanship for centuries. Visiting Khan El Khalili is like stepping back in time, as you wander through its maze-like streets lined with shops, stalls, and cafes that reflect Egypt's rich heritage. It's not just a place to shop—it's an experience that immerses you in the sights, sounds, and smells of traditional Cairo.

Location and How to Get There
Khan El Khalili is situated in the Islamic Cairo district, near Al-Azhar Mosque and Al-Hussein Mosque. Its central location makes it easily accessible from most parts of Cairo. If you're coming from downtown or nearby neighborhoods, you can take a taxi or use ride-hailing apps like Uber or Careem for a convenient and direct route. For a more adventurous approach, you can use the metro and stop at Ataba Station, followed by a short taxi ride or walk to the bazaar. Many guided tours of Islamic Cairo include Khan El Khalili in their itinerary, allowing you to visit the market alongside other historic landmarks.

What You Will See and Do
As you enter Khan El Khalili, you'll be greeted by a lively and colorful scene that feels like a living postcard of Cairo's past. The market's narrow alleys are lined with small shops and stalls selling a dazzling array of goods. You'll find everything from handmade jewelry, intricate brass lamps, and finely

crafted textiles to perfumes, spices, and traditional souvenirs. The bazaar is famous for its artisans, and many shops feature craftsmen working on their wares, offering you a chance to see their skill and dedication up close.

The market is divided into sections, each specializing in a particular type of product. If you're a fan of Egyptian culture, you'll find statues, papyrus scrolls, and hieroglyphic-themed items that make excellent souvenirs. For food lovers, there are stalls selling dried fruits, nuts, and fragrant spices that capture the essence of Egyptian cuisine.

Beyond shopping, Khan El Khalili is a cultural experience. The streets are alive with the sound of vendors calling out their wares, the scent of spices and incense wafting through the air, and the sight of locals and tourists mingling in the vibrant atmosphere. Take your time to explore, and don't hesitate to engage with the shopkeepers, who are often friendly and eager to share stories about their products.

The Best Times to Visit
Khan El Khalili is open every day, typically from mid-morning until late evening. To fully enjoy the bazaar, it's best to visit during the cooler months from October to April, when the weather is more comfortable for walking around. Arriving in the late morning or early afternoon allows you to explore at a leisurely pace before the evening crowds arrive. The market becomes especially lively after sunset, with its shops brightly lit and the surrounding cafes bustling with activity. Fridays,

being a holy day in Islam, may see some shops open later in the day.

Tips for Shopping and Bargaining
Shopping at Khan El Khalili is an art in itself, as bargaining is a common practice. Prices are often negotiable, and haggling is expected, so don't be shy about offering a lower price and negotiating with the shopkeepers. Approach the process with a friendly attitude, as bargaining is seen as a social interaction as much as a transaction. Start by asking for the price and countering with an offer that feels fair. If you're not satisfied, feel free to walk away—often, this will lead the seller to lower the price further. While most vendors accept cash, it's a good idea to carry smaller denominations of Egyptian pounds to make transactions smoother. Some shops may also accept credit cards, but this is less common in smaller stalls.

Nearby Attractions
Khan El Khalili's location in Islamic Cairo makes it easy to combine your visit with nearby historic sites. Al-Azhar Mosque, just a short walk away, is a masterpiece of Islamic architecture and a center of learning. The Al-Hussein Mosque, another significant religious site, is located right next to the bazaar and is worth visiting for its serene atmosphere and stunning interior. If you're interested in history, you can also explore Al-Muizz Street, lined with historic mosques, madrasas, and old buildings that tell the story of Cairo's past.

Dining and Resting Spots
After a day of exploring and shopping, you'll likely want to relax and soak in the atmosphere. Khan El Khalili is home to

several traditional cafes and restaurants where you can enjoy a meal or a refreshing drink. The most famous is El Fishawy, a historic cafe that has been serving visitors for over 200 years. Here, you can sit on wooden chairs, sip a cup of mint tea, and enjoy the lively ambiance of the market. Many cafes also offer shisha (water pipes), allowing you to experience a quintessential Egyptian tradition. If you're hungry, nearby restaurants serve a variety of Egyptian dishes, such as koshari, grilled meats, and stuffed pigeon. These meals are often hearty and flavorful, providing a perfect end to your visit.

Cultural and Historical Context
Khan El Khalili dates back to the 14th century, when it was established during the reign of the Mamluk Sultan Al-Zahir Barquq. Originally built as a caravanserai—a resting place for merchants and their goods—it quickly grew into a bustling marketplace that became central to Cairo's commercial and cultural life. Over the centuries, the bazaar has been shaped by various influences, from Ottoman architecture to modern tourism, while maintaining its traditional charm.
Today, Khan El Khalili is not just a market but a living piece of history. Walking through its alleys, you're surrounded by centuries of trade, craftsmanship, and cultural exchange that reflect Cairo's unique character.

Rules, Etiquette, and Safety Tips
When visiting Khan El Khalili, it's important to respect local customs and traditions. Dress modestly, especially if you plan to visit nearby mosques, and be polite when interacting with shopkeepers and vendors. Keep an eye on your belongings, as

the crowded streets can be a target for pickpockets. It's also a good idea to stay hydrated and wear comfortable shoes, as you'll likely be walking for an extended period.

If you're unsure about a particular area or shop, don't hesitate to ask locals or tour guides for advice—they're usually happy to help. Avoid rushing through the market; instead, take your time to absorb the atmosphere and enjoy the unique experience.

Why You Should Visit
Khan El Khalili Bazaar is more than just a shopping destination—it's a vibrant slice of Cairo's culture and history. Its rich history, colorful displays, and warm interactions with locals make it a must-see attraction for anyone visiting Cairo. As you wander through its alleys, you'll discover not just treasures to take home but also a deeper connection to the soul of the city.

The Citadel of Cairo

The Citadel of Cairo, also known as the Saladin Citadel, is one of the most iconic landmarks in Islamic Cairo. Perched on a hill in the Mokattam area, it offers stunning views of the city and serves as a window into Egypt's fascinating history. Built as a military fortress and later expanded into a royal residence and government center, the Citadel is a must-see attraction that blends architectural beauty with deep historical significance.

Location and How to Get There
The Citadel is located in the Mokattam district of Cairo, approximately 3 kilometers southeast of Downtown Cairo. It

is situated on a prominent hill, making it visible from many parts of the city. To reach the Citadel, you can take a taxi or use ride-hailing services like Uber or Careem, which are convenient and affordable options. Public buses and microbuses also pass near the Citadel, though these can be more challenging to navigate if you're unfamiliar with the routes. Many guided tours of Islamic Cairo include the Citadel as part of their itinerary, providing transport and expert commentary to enhance your visit.

What You Will See and Do
When you arrive at the Citadel, you'll immediately notice its imposing walls and towers, which were originally built for defense against potential invaders. The Citadel complex is vast, housing several important structures, including mosques, museums, and palaces, each offering unique insights into Cairo's rich history and culture.

The Mosque of Muhammad Ali (The Alabaster Mosque)
The most prominent feature of the Citadel is the Mosque of Muhammad Ali, easily recognizable by its large domes and towering minarets. Built in the Ottoman style between 1830 and 1848, this mosque is a masterpiece of architecture and one of the most photographed landmarks in Cairo. Its interior is equally impressive, with intricate designs, large chandeliers, and colorful k,stained-glass windows. From the courtyard of the mosque, you can enjoy panoramic views of Cairo, and on a clear day, you might even spot the Pyramids of Giza in the distance.

The Mosque of Sultan al-Nasir Muhammad:
Another significant structure within the Citadel is the Mosque of Sultan al-Nasir Muhammad, built in the 14th century during the Mamluk period. This mosque is known for its unique green-tiled domes and columns that were repurposed from earlier structures, showcasing the resourcefulness of Mamluk architects. The mosque has a quieter and more intimate atmosphere compared to the grandiose Muhammad Ali Mosque.

The National Military Museum: Located within the Citadel, the National Military Museum showcases Egypt's military history from ancient times to the modern era. The museum features a wide range of artifacts, including weapons, uniforms, and vehicles, as well as detailed exhibits about significant battles and leaders. If you're interested in history, this museum provides a fascinating look at the evolution of Egypt's military power.

The Gawhara Palace (Jewel Palace)
Built by Muhammad Ali in the early 19th century, the Gawhara Palace was designed as a royal residence. Its elegant architecture and intricate decorations reflect the luxury of the time. Though parts of the palace have been damaged over the years, it still offers a glimpse into the opulence of Muhammad Ali's reign.

The Best Times to Visit
The Citadel is open to visitors year-round, but the best time to visit is during the cooler months from October to April. During this period, the weather is mild, making it comfortable to explore the outdoor areas and enjoy the views. Arriving early in the morning is ideal, as the site is less crowded, and the lighting is perfect for photography. Late afternoons are also a good time to visit, allowing you to witness the sunset over the city from the mosque's courtyard.

Ticket Information and Booking
Tickets to the Citadel can be purchased at the entrance or through authorized tour operators if you're booking a guided visit. The ticket price includes access to the main attractions within the complex, such as the mosques, museums, and palaces. Discounts are available for students with valid ID, so be sure to bring it along if applicable. Guided tours often include transportation, tickets, and detailed explanations of the site's history, which can enhance your experience.

Facilities and Accessibility
The Citadel is equipped with basic facilities, including restrooms and small kiosks selling water and snacks. While the

site has made efforts to improve accessibility, some areas, such as the older mosques and sections with uneven pathways, may be challenging for visitors with mobility issues. Comfortable walking shoes are highly recommended, as you'll be exploring a large and varied terrain.

Photography Tips and Rules
Photography is allowed throughout the Citadel, and there are countless opportunities to capture stunning shots. The courtyard of the Muhammad Ali Mosque is a popular spot for panoramic photos of Cairo, while the intricate details of the mosque interiors offer excellent close-up shots. If you're visiting during sunrise or sunset, the lighting enhances the beauty of the structures and creates dramatic effects. Tripods and professional photography equipment may require special permission, so check in advance if you plan to bring them.

Cultural and Historical Context
The Citadel was constructed in 1176 by Salah al-Din (Saladin) to protect Cairo from Crusader attacks. Its strategic location on a hill provided a vantage point for monitoring potential threats and served as a stronghold for Egypt's rulers. Over the centuries, the Citadel evolved from a military fortress into a political and administrative center, housing royal palaces, mosques, and government offices.

The Ottoman influence on the Citadel is evident in its architecture, particularly in the Muhammad Ali Mosque, which was built to rival the great mosques of Istanbul. The complex also reflects the Mamluk period, during which Cairo was a major cultural and political hub in the Islamic world. Visiting the Citadel allows you to trace the layers of history that shaped Egypt's identity.

Rules, Etiquette, and Safety Tips
As the Citadel is a historical and religious site, it's important to dress modestly, especially when visiting the mosques. Women should cover their shoulders and knees, and men should avoid wearing shorts. Shoes must be removed before entering the mosques, and plastic bags are often provided to carry them.

Bring water to stay hydrated, especially if you're visiting during warmer months, and wear sunscreen and a hat to protect yourself from the sun. Be cautious of uneven pathways and steps, and take your time exploring the site to avoid accidents. Vendors may approach you to sell souvenirs or guide services, so be polite but firm if you're not interested.

Why You Should Visit
The Citadel of Cairo is more than just a historic site—it's a journey through Egypt's rich past, offering a glimpse into the lives of sultans, kings, and rulers who shaped the nation's destiny. From the stunning architecture of the mosques to the sweeping views of Cairo's skyline, every corner of the Citadel tells a story.

Things to Do: Walking Tours, Shopping for Local Handicrafts, and Visiting Traditional Coffeehouses

Islamic Cairo is one of the most fascinating parts of the city, offering a unique blend of history, culture, and daily life that draws visitors from around the world. Walking through this historic district is like stepping into the past while still being surrounded by the vibrant energy of modern Cairo. There are many things to do in this area, but some of the most rewarding activities include taking walking tours, shopping for local handicrafts, and visiting traditional coffeehouses. These experiences allow you to immerse yourself in the rich heritage of Islamic Cairo while also engaging with the people and traditions that keep it alive today.

Walking tours are an excellent way to explore Islamic Cairo and learn about its history and architecture. The area is home to some of the most iconic landmarks in the city, including mosques, madrasas, and ancient streets that date back hundreds of years. As you walk, you can admire the intricate designs of buildings like the Al-Azhar Mosque, which is one of the oldest universities in the world and a center of Islamic scholarship. Nearby, you'll find the Sultan Hassan Mosque, a masterpiece of Mamluk architecture known for its towering height and beautifully carved stonework. Many walking tours also take you through Al-Muizz Street, a historic thoroughfare lined with stunning examples of Islamic architecture, such as the Qalawun Complex and the Mosque of Al-Aqmar. This street is a living museum, where each building tells a story of Egypt's past rulers, artisans, and communities.

As you explore, you'll notice that Islamic Cairo is not just about its buildings but also about the life that takes place in its streets. The area is filled with bustling markets, small workshops, and street vendors selling everything from fresh bread to handmade goods. Joining a guided tour is a great way to uncover the hidden gems of the district, as experienced guides can point out details you might otherwise miss and share fascinating stories about the area's history and significance. Walking tours can vary in length and focus, so you can choose one that suits your interests, whether you're passionate about architecture, history, or local culture.

Shopping for local handicrafts in Islamic Cairo is another highlight of visiting this historic area. The district is home to some of Cairo's most famous markets, including Khan El Khalili, a sprawling bazaar that has been a center of trade and commerce for centuries. This market is a treasure trove of traditional goods, from intricately woven rugs and hand-carved wooden items to brass lamps, jewelry, and colorful fabrics. As you wander through the narrow alleys of Khan El Khalili, you'll find stalls overflowing with goods that reflect the craftsmanship and creativity of local artisans. Many of the items are made using techniques that have been passed down through generations, giving them a sense of authenticity and connection to Egypt's cultural heritage.

Shopping in Islamic Cairo is not just about buying souvenirs—it's also an opportunity to interact with the people who make and sell these items. Vendors are often happy to explain the stories behind their products, such as the symbolism of certain designs or the traditional methods used to create them. Bargaining is a common practice in the markets, so don't hesitate to negotiate prices in a friendly and respectful way. This can be a fun and engaging part of the shopping experience, and it allows you to connect with the culture on a deeper level.

In addition to the markets, you'll also find small workshops and artisan studios tucked away in the streets of Islamic Cairo. These spaces offer a chance to see craftspeople at work, whether they're weaving textiles, shaping pottery, or engraving metal. Visiting these workshops can be a rewarding experience, as it gives you a behind-the-scenes look at the effort and skill that go into making traditional goods. Some workshops even offer hands-on activities, where you can try your hand at making something yourself, such as a piece of jewelry or a painted tile.

No visit to Islamic Cairo would be complete without spending time in one of its traditional coffeehouses. These establishments are an integral part of Egyptian culture, serving as places where people gather to relax, socialize, and enjoy a cup of strong, aromatic coffee or tea. Coffeehouses in Islamic Cairo are often located in historic buildings, adding to their charm and atmosphere. Many of them feature intricate woodwork, colorful tile patterns, and cozy seating areas where you can unwind and watch the world go by.

At these coffeehouses, you can enjoy a variety of traditional drinks, such as Turkish coffee, which is served in small cups and prepared with a layer of thick coffee grounds at the bottom. For something lighter, you might try mint tea, a refreshing and fragrant beverage that is a favorite among locals. Some coffeehouses also offer snacks like fresh bread, pastries, or small plates of mezze, which are perfect for sharing. While you sip your drink, you may hear the sound of oud music or the rhythmic tapping of backgammon players enjoying a game. The coffeehouses are also a great place to meet locals and strike up a conversation, as they are welcoming spaces where people from all walks of life come together.

In the evenings, some coffeehouses host cultural performances, such as traditional music or storytelling, which add to the experience. These events provide insight into

Egypt's rich artistic traditions and create a lively atmosphere that is both entertaining and educational. Visiting a coffeehouse in Islamic Cairo is not just about having a drink—it's about immersing yourself in the rhythms of local life and experiencing the hospitality and warmth of the Egyptian people.

Accommodation Options

Luxury Stays: Boutique Hotels with Historic Charm in Islamic Cairo, Cairo, Egypt

Islamic Cairo is a treasure trove of history, culture, and architectural beauty, making it an incredible place to stay if you're seeking accommodations that offer both luxury and character. The boutique hotels in this district combine modern comforts with a strong connection to the area's historic roots, providing you with an unforgettable experience. Here are some of the top boutique hotels in Islamic Cairo that perfectly blend historic charm with five-star service.

1. Al Moudira Hotel
Price Range: Approx. $200–$400 per night.
Amenities: Al Moudira Hotel offers a perfect mix of elegance and tradition. This boutique hotel features spacious rooms with vintage furnishings, hand-painted ceilings, and antique decor. You'll enjoy complimentary Wi-Fi, an on-site restaurant serving authentic Egyptian cuisine, and beautifully landscaped courtyards where you can relax after a day of exploring. The

staff provides personalized service, ensuring that your stay is both luxurious and intimate.

Best Area to Stay: Located near the bustling Al-Muizz Street, the hotel places you in the heart of Islamic Cairo, surrounded by mosques, madrasas, and historic markets. This central location allows you to immerse yourself in the area's rich culture while enjoying a tranquil retreat.
Contact Details:
Website: [Al Moudira Hotel](#)
Phone: +20 2 35678910
Email: reservations@almoudirahotel.com

2. Le Riad Hotel de Charme
Price Range: Approx. $250–$500 per night.
Amenities: This boutique gem boasts luxurious suites, each uniquely designed to reflect Cairo's rich heritage. Expect spacious accommodations with traditional Egyptian decor, private balconies, and all modern conveniences like air conditioning and Wi-Fi. The rooftop restaurant offers breathtaking views of the surrounding mosques and minarets, and the concierge team is available to arrange personalized tours of the area. A complimentary breakfast is served daily, with both local and international options.

Best Area to Stay: Le Riad Hotel de Charme is nestled in the heart of Al-Muizz Street, one of the most historic and vibrant streets in Islamic Cairo. Staying here means you'll be within walking distance of landmarks like the Sultan Hassan Mosque and the Khan El Khalili Bazaar.

Contact Details:
Website: Le Riad Hotel de Charme
Phone: +20 2 35672345
Email: info@leriadhotel.com

3. Bayt Al-Suhaymi Boutique Hotel
Price Range: Approx. $180–$350 per night.
Amenities: This hotel offers an authentic cultural experience in a restored 17th-century mansion. Rooms are elegantly furnished with traditional Egyptian motifs and modern amenities like flat-screen TVs, free Wi-Fi, and air conditioning. The inner courtyard is a serene space where you can relax with a cup of tea. The on-site restaurant serves a variety of Middle Eastern dishes, and guided tours of the surrounding area can be arranged directly through the hotel.

Best Area to Stay: Located near the historic Bayt Al-Suhaymi house, the hotel is perfectly situated for exploring Islamic Cairo's architectural wonders. You'll be steps away from cultural landmarks and vibrant bazaars, making it an ideal choice for history enthusiasts.

Contact Details:
Website: Bayt Al-Suhaymi Hotel
Phone: +20 2 35789123

4. Wekalet El Ghouri Boutique Stay
Price Range: Approx. $150–$300 per night.
Amenities: This charming boutique hotel is housed in a beautifully restored caravanserai, blending history with

luxury. The rooms feature traditional Egyptian design with modern touches, such as plush bedding, air conditioning, and free Wi-Fi. Guests can enjoy a complimentary breakfast, relax in the hotel's serene courtyards, or attend a nearby Tanoura dance performance.

Best Area to Stay: Wekalet El Ghouri is located in the heart of Islamic Cairo, close to the iconic Al-Azhar Mosque and the vibrant Khan El Khalili Bazaar. Its central location makes it easy to explore the area on foot while offering a peaceful escape from the bustling streets.

Contact Details:
Website: Wekalet El Ghouri Stay
Phone: +20 2 35679098

5. Al-Tanoura Boutique Hotel
Price Range: Approx. $120–$250 per night.
Amenities: Al-Tanoura Boutique Hotel offers cozy yet elegant accommodations with a focus on cultural immersion. Each room is decorated with handcrafted furnishings and traditional textiles. The hotel provides free Wi-Fi, a rooftop terrace with panoramic views of Islamic Cairo, and a small library with books on Egyptian history and culture. Guests are welcomed with a complimentary drink and a detailed guide to local attractions.

Best Area to Stay: Situated near Bab Zuweila, this hotel places you in the heart of Islamic Cairo's historic district, surrounded by ancient gates, mosques, and traditional markets.

Its location is perfect for exploring both iconic landmarks and hidden gems.

Contact Details:
Website: Al-Tanoura Hotel
Phone: +20 2 35981234

Each of these boutique hotels in Islamic Cairo offers a unique experience that combines luxurious comfort with a deep connection to the area's history and culture. Staying in Islamic Cairo allows you to immerse yourself in the heart of the city's cultural and architectural heritage, making your visit both enriching and unforgettable.

Mid-Range Options: Stylish Lodgings in Bustling Neighborhoods in Islamic Cairo, Cairo, Egypt

Islamic Cairo offers an exciting mix of history, culture, and local life, and staying in this area gives you the chance to be at the heart of it all. If you're looking for accommodations that are comfortable, stylish, and reasonably priced, there are several excellent mid-range options to choose from. These lodgings combine modern amenities with easy access to the vibrant neighborhoods, making them ideal for travelers who want convenience and charm without overspending. Below are some great options to consider.

1. Arabian Nights Hotel
Price Range: Approx. $60–$90 per night.
Amenities: This cozy hotel provides comfortable rooms with traditional Egyptian decor and modern conveniences like air

conditioning, free Wi-Fi, and private bathrooms. Guests enjoy a complimentary breakfast served on the rooftop terrace, which offers panoramic views of Islamic Cairo's minarets. The hotel also offers 24-hour front desk service, laundry facilities, and assistance with booking local tours.

Best Area to Stay: Located in the lively Al-Darb Al-Ahmar district, Arabian Nights Hotel is just a short walk from landmarks like the Al-Azhar Mosque and the historic Bab Zuweila gate. The neighborhood's vibrant atmosphere, filled with local shops and cafes, makes it a perfect base for exploring Islamic Cairo.

Contact Details:
Website: Arabian Nights Hotel
Phone: +20 2 35679820
Email: info@arabiannightshotel.com

2. Hotel Royal Cairo
Price Range: Approx. $50–$80 per night.
Amenities: Hotel Royal Cairo offers spacious rooms with comfortable beds, flat-screen TVs, and en-suite bathrooms. Free Wi-Fi is available throughout the property, and guests are treated to a complimentary breakfast. The hotel also features a small lounge area and provides concierge services to help you plan your stay.

Best Area to Stay: This hotel is conveniently located near Al-Muizz Street, a historic thoroughfare known for its incredible Islamic architecture. Staying here puts you within walking distance of key attractions like the Sultan Hassan Mosque and the Khan El Khalili Bazaar, as well as local restaurants and street food vendors.

Contact Details:
Website: Hotel Royal Cairo
Phone: +20 2 35781234
Email: reservations@hotelroyalcairo.com

3. Al-Fustat Guesthouse
Price Range: Approx. $70–$100 per night.
Amenities: This charming guesthouse offers a boutique experience with stylishly decorated rooms featuring Egyptian-inspired furnishings. Guests enjoy free Wi-Fi, complimentary breakfast, and access to a communal lounge area. The rooftop terrace is a standout feature, offering stunning views of the historic district. The friendly staff provides personalized service, including tour recommendations and transportation arrangements.

Best Area to Stay: Al-Fustat Guesthouse is situated near the historic Coptic Cairo area, making it an ideal choice for visitors interested in exploring both Islamic and Coptic landmarks. The neighborhood is known for its peaceful streets and proximity to key sites like the Hanging Church and Amr Ibn Al-As Mosque.

Contact Details:
Website: Al-Fustat Guesthouse
Phone: +20 2 35698045

4. Cairo Heritage Inn
Price Range: Approx. $65–$95 per night.
Amenities: This mid-range hotel offers modern comfort with a touch of traditional charm. Rooms are well-equipped with air conditioning, flat-screen TVs, and free Wi-Fi. Guests can enjoy a hearty breakfast each morning, and the hotel's central courtyard provides a quiet space to relax. Concierge services and guided tours are available upon request.

Best Area to Stay: The inn is located near the Khan El Khalili Bazaar, making it a great choice for travelers who want to explore the bustling markets and historic streets of Islamic Cairo. It's also close to public transportation, making it easy to access other parts of the city.

Contact Details:
Website: Cairo Heritage Inn
Phone: +20 2 35870123

5. Minaret View Hotel
Price Range: Approx. $55–$85 per night.
Amenities: As the name suggests, this hotel offers stunning views of the nearby minarets from its rooftop terrace. Rooms are clean and comfortable, featuring air conditioning, private bathrooms, and free Wi-Fi. The hotel serves a complimentary breakfast and offers 24-hour reception and tour planning services.

Best Area to Stay: Minaret View Hotel is located in a lively part of Islamic Cairo, close to Al-Muizz Street and the Sultan

Hassan Mosque. The area is rich with local markets, historic landmarks, and authentic eateries, making it an excellent choice for travelers who want to be in the heart of the action.

Contact Details:
Website: Minaret View Hotel
Phone: +20 2 35987654

These mid-range accommodations in Islamic Cairo combine comfort, style, and affordability, making them ideal for travelers who want a convenient and enjoyable stay. With their central locations, thoughtful amenities, and friendly service, these lodgings will ensure your visit to Islamic Cairo is both memorable and stress-free.

Budget Choices: Affordable Hotels Near Cultural Landmarks in Islamic Cairo, Cairo, Egypt

Islamic Cairo is one of the most vibrant and historically rich districts in Cairo, making it a prime destination for travelers interested in culture, history, and authentic local experiences. If you're traveling on a budget, there are plenty of affordable hotels that offer comfortable accommodations close to some of the most famous cultural landmarks in the area. These options provide excellent value, convenient locations, and warm hospitality, ensuring you can enjoy the best of Islamic Cairo without overspending. Below are some of the best budget-friendly accommodations to consider.

1. Arabian Nights Hostel
Price Range: Approx. $20–$40 per night.

Amenities: Arabian Nights Hostel is a charming and budget-friendly choice for travelers seeking a simple and clean place to stay. Rooms are air-conditioned and equipped with free Wi-Fi. Guests can enjoy a complimentary breakfast each morning and access a rooftop terrace with views of the surrounding area. The hostel also provides 24-hour reception, luggage storage, and the option to book local tours directly through the staff.

Best Area to Stay: Located in the heart of the Al-Darb Al-Ahmar district, this hostel places you within walking distance of landmarks like Bab Zuweila, the Al-Azhar Mosque, and the Khan El Khalili Bazaar. The area is lively and full of traditional shops and cafes, giving you an authentic taste of local life.

Contact Details:
Website: Arabian Nights Hostel
Phone: +20 2 35781234
Email: info@arabiannightshostel.com

2. Cairo Moon Hotel
Price Range: Approx. $25–$50 per night.
Amenities: Cairo Moon Hotel offers basic yet comfortable accommodations with free Wi-Fi, air-conditioned rooms, and complimentary breakfast. The hotel has a rooftop terrace where you can relax and enjoy views of the bustling streets of Islamic Cairo. Friendly staff members are available to help arrange airport pickups, tours, and transportation.

Best Area to Stay: This hotel is situated near the famous Al-Muizz Street, a historic area known for its stunning Islamic architecture and vibrant markets. The location is ideal for travelers who want to explore cultural landmarks like the Sultan Hassan Mosque and the Al-Rifa'i Mosque.

Contact Details:
Website: Cairo Moon Hotel
Phone: +20 2 35870345

3. Traveler's House Hostel
Price Range: Approx. $15–$30 per night.
Amenities: This hostel is a great option for solo travelers or backpackers looking for affordable and sociable accommodations. The rooms are clean and simple, with free Wi-Fi and shared bathrooms. Guests can enjoy a complimentary breakfast, access to a communal kitchen, and a shared lounge area to meet other travelers. The hostel also offers guided walking tours of Islamic Cairo at an additional cost.

Best Area to Stay: Located near the Khan El Khalili Bazaar, Traveler's House Hostel puts you at the center of Islamic Cairo's bustling market scene. The hostel is also close to public transport options, making it convenient for exploring other parts of Cairo.

Contact Details:
Website: Traveler's House Hostel
Phone: +20 2 35791111

4. Pension Roma Cairo
Price Range: Approx. $30–$60 per night.
Amenities: Pension Roma Cairo offers a blend of historic charm and budget-friendly comfort. Rooms are furnished with vintage-style decor and include basic amenities like free Wi-Fi, air conditioning, and en-suite or shared bathrooms. A simple breakfast is included, and the friendly staff is happy to help with local recommendations and transportation arrangements.

Best Area to Stay: This guesthouse is located in a quieter section of Islamic Cairo, offering easy access to landmarks like the Mosque of Ibn Tulun and the Gayer-Anderson Museum. Its peaceful location makes it a great choice for travelers who prefer a quieter environment while staying close to cultural sites.

Contact Details:
Website: Pension Roma Cairo
Phone: +20 2 35870987

5. Nour Hostel
Price Range: Approx. $20–$40 per night.
Amenities: Nour Hostel provides affordable accommodations with a focus on comfort and community. The rooms are simple but clean, with free Wi-Fi and air conditioning. Guests can start their day with a complimentary breakfast and enjoy the hostel's rooftop terrace, which offers a great view of Islamic

Cairo's skyline. The hostel also organizes local excursions, including guided visits to cultural landmarks.

Best Area to Stay: Situated close to the Al-Azhar Mosque and the vibrant Al-Muizz Street, Nour Hostel is perfectly located for exploring Islamic Cairo's architectural wonders and historic bazaars. The neighborhood is full of energy, giving you a front-row seat to local life.
Contact Details:
Website: Nour Hostel
Phone: +20 2 35988012

These budget-friendly accommodations in Islamic Cairo offer excellent value for travelers who want to immerse themselves in the district's rich culture and history. With their welcoming atmospheres, helpful staff, and prime locations near cultural landmarks, these affordable options ensure that you'll have a memorable stay without breaking the bank.

Downtown Cairo

Must-See Attractions

Tahrir Square

Tahrir Square is one of the most famous and historically significant landmarks in Cairo. Located in the heart of Downtown Cairo, this bustling public square is not only a central hub for transportation and activity but also a site deeply tied to Egypt's modern history. Visiting Tahrir Square allows you to experience a dynamic part of the city that blends contemporary culture with important political and historical events.

Location and How to Get There
Tahrir Square is situated in the center of Downtown Cairo, making it easily accessible from virtually any part of the city. If you're staying in Downtown or nearby, you can reach the square on foot or by taking a short taxi or Uber ride. For those using public transportation, the Sadat Metro Station, located directly beneath the square, is a convenient option. The square is well-connected by major roads and serves as a transportation hub, making it a starting point for exploring other parts of Cairo.

What You Will See and Do
When you arrive at Tahrir Square, you'll immediately notice its vast open layout surrounded by important landmarks and modern infrastructure. The square is often bustling with activity, from locals commuting to work to tourists exploring the area. While the square itself is a large circular space, its true significance lies in the landmarks and institutions surrounding it.

The Egyptian Museum:
One of the most prominent buildings on the square is the Egyptian Museum, a treasure trove of ancient artifacts and historical wonders. The museum is home to the world's largest collection of ancient Egyptian antiquities, including the iconic

treasures of Tutankhamun. Visiting the museum is a must if you're in Tahrir Square, as it provides a fascinating journey through thousands of years of history.

The Mogamma Building:
Another notable structure is the Mogamma, a massive government building known for its imposing architecture. While the Mogamma itself is not a tourist attraction, its historical and administrative significance makes it an integral part of the square's identity.

The Central Monument and Fountain:
In the center of Tahrir Square, you'll find a large monument surrounded by a fountain. This space has been redesigned over the years, with modern touches added to reflect its historical significance. The area around the monument often serves as a gathering place for visitors and locals alike.

Street Art and Murals:
Tahrir Square has also become a canvas for political and cultural expression. Walking around the square, you may spot murals and graffiti commemorating important moments in Egypt's history, particularly from the 2011 Egyptian Revolution. These works of art provide a glimpse into the emotions and aspirations of the Egyptian people during pivotal times.

The Best Times to Visit
Tahrir Square is lively throughout the day, but the best time to visit depends on what you want to experience. If you're

interested in seeing the area at its busiest, late mornings and early afternoons are ideal. However, if you prefer a quieter atmosphere to take photos or enjoy the surroundings, visiting early in the morning or later in the evening is a better choice. During the cooler months from October to April, the weather is more comfortable for walking and exploring the area.

Cultural and Historical Context
Tahrir Square has a long and complex history that reflects Egypt's journey through modern times. Originally called Ismailia Square after Khedive Ismail, it was renamed Tahrir Square, meaning "Liberation Square," after the 1952 revolution that led to Egypt's independence. The square became a symbol of national pride and political change.

In 2011, Tahrir Square gained international attention as the epicenter of the Egyptian Revolution during the Arab Spring. The square was filled with millions of protesters calling for political reform, and it became a symbol of resilience, unity, and the power of the people. Walking through Tahrir Square today, you can still feel its significance as a place where history was made.

Facilities and Accessibility
Tahrir Square is a well-maintained public area with access to basic facilities. Nearby cafes and restaurants offer plenty of options for food and refreshments, ranging from quick snacks to full meals. The Egyptian Museum has restrooms, a gift shop, and other amenities for visitors. The square is easily accessible for people with mobility challenges, with smooth

walkways and public transportation connections like the metro providing convenience.

Photography Tips and Rules

Tahrir Square offers excellent photo opportunities, especially if you're interested in capturing the energy of the city or the striking architecture of the surrounding buildings. The best time for photography is during the golden hours of sunrise or sunset when the light is softer. If you're taking photos of murals or street art, be mindful of people around you and avoid obstructing foot traffic.

While photography is allowed in public areas, some nearby buildings may have restrictions due to security reasons. Always check for signs or ask for permission if you're unsure.

Nearby Attractions

Tahrir Square serves as a gateway to many of Cairo's top attractions. After exploring the square, you can walk to the Egyptian Museum to admire its incredible collection of artifacts. Al-Muizz Street, a historic thoroughfare filled with Islamic architecture, is also within easy reach. If you're interested in shopping or dining, Downtown Cairo is home to numerous cafes, shops, and restaurants where you can relax and enjoy the local atmosphere.

Rules, Etiquette, and Safety Tips

While Tahrir Square is a public space, it's important to be respectful of its cultural and historical significance. Dress modestly, as Egypt is a conservative country, and be mindful of local customs. Stay aware of your belongings, especially in crowded areas, as pickpocketing can occur. If you're visiting during a busy time, such as public events or holidays, follow any instructions from local authorities or security personnel to ensure your safety.

Why You Should Visit
Tahrir Square is more than just a public space—it's a symbol of Egypt's modern identity and a reflection of its historical journey. Whether you're exploring the surrounding landmarks, learning about its role in pivotal events, or simply soaking in the energy of Downtown Cairo, a visit to Tahrir Square offers a deeper connection to the city and its people. It's a place where the past and present come together, inviting you to be part of Cairo's ongoing story.

The Egyptian Museum

The Egyptian Museum in Cairo is one of the most important museums in the world, housing an unparalleled collection of artifacts that tell the story of ancient Egypt's fascinating history. Located in the heart of Downtown Cairo, this iconic museum is a must-see for anyone visiting the city. With thousands of artifacts on display, from statues and jewelry to mummies and the treasures of Tutankhamun, the museum offers an unforgettable journey into the world of the pharaohs.

Location and How to Get There
The Egyptian Museum is situated in Tahrir Square, a central location in Downtown Cairo that is easy to reach from most parts of the city. If you're staying nearby, you can walk to the

museum or take a short taxi ride. Ride-hailing services like Uber and Careem are also convenient options. For those using public transportation, the Sadat Metro Station, located directly beneath Tahrir Square, provides quick and easy access to the museum. Many guided tours of Cairo include a visit to the Egyptian Museum, offering transportation and expert commentary to enhance your experience.

What You Will See and Do
As you step into the Egyptian Museum, you'll be greeted by an awe-inspiring collection of artifacts that span over 5,000 years of history. The museum is home to more than 120,000 items, with many more stored in its archives. Each piece offers a glimpse into the life, culture, and beliefs of ancient Egypt. Here are some of the highlights you can expect to see:

The Treasures of Tutankhamun
One of the most famous exhibits in the museum is the collection of treasures from the tomb of King Tutankhamun, discovered by Howard Carter in 1922. The golden mask of the young pharaoh, intricately crafted and adorned with precious stones, is a masterpiece that draws visitors from all over the world. Alongside the mask, you'll find golden coffins, jewelry, furniture, and other items that were buried with the king to accompany him in the afterlife.

The Royal Mummies
The museum's Royal Mummies Room is a fascinating and slightly eerie exhibit where you can see the preserved remains of some of ancient Egypt's most famous pharaohs, including Ramses II and Hatshepsut. These mummies provide a direct

connection to the past, showcasing the advanced embalming techniques used by the ancient Egyptians.

Statues and Sculptures
The museum is filled with statues of gods, pharaohs, and other figures, many of which are remarkably well-preserved. Highlights include the statue of Khafre, the builder of the second pyramid at Giza, and the strikingly lifelike statues of Rahotep and Nofret.

Jewelry and Daily Life Artifacts:
In addition to monumental sculptures and royal treasures, the museum displays jewelry, pottery, tools, and household items that give insight into the daily lives of ancient Egyptians. These smaller artifacts reveal how people lived, worked, and worshiped thousands of years ago.

The Rosetta Stone Replica:
While the original Rosetta Stone is housed in the British Museum, the Egyptian Museum has a detailed replica and information about this vital artifact that helped scholars decode ancient Egyptian hieroglyphs.

The Best Times to Visit
The Egyptian Museum is open year-round, and the best time to visit is during the cooler months from October to April. Arriving early in the morning, when the museum opens at 9:00 AM, allows you to explore the exhibits with fewer crowds. If you're unable to visit in the morning, late afternoons can also be a good time, but keep in mind that the museum closes at

5:00 PM. Fridays and weekends tend to be busier, so plan your visit accordingly if you prefer a quieter experience.

Ticket Information and Booking
Tickets to the Egyptian Museum can be purchased at the entrance, and prices are generally affordable. There are separate fees for general admission and access to special exhibits, such as the Royal Mummies Room. Discounts are available for students who present a valid ID. Guided tours, which can be booked in advance through tour operators or online platforms, often include admission fees and provide in-depth explanations of the exhibits.

Facilities and Accessibility
The museum is equipped with essential facilities to make your visit comfortable. Restrooms, a gift shop, and a small cafe are available on-site. While the building is historic and not originally designed for modern accessibility, efforts have been made to accommodate visitors with mobility challenges, such as ramps and elevators in certain areas. If you have specific needs, it's a good idea to contact the museum in advance to ensure a smooth visit.

Photography Tips and Rules
Photography is permitted in most parts of the museum, but flash photography is prohibited to protect the artifacts. If you're capturing images of the exhibits, try to use natural lighting and steady your hand for clear shots. Certain areas, such as the Royal Mummies Room, may have additional

restrictions on photography, so always check for signs or ask museum staff if you're unsure.

Cultural and Historical Context
The Egyptian Museum was established in 1902 and is one of the oldest museums dedicated to ancient Egyptian history. It was designed to showcase Egypt's incredible archaeological discoveries and preserve its cultural heritage. Over the decades, the museum has become a symbol of national pride and an essential destination for scholars and tourists alike.

Although some of the museum's collections are being transferred to the new Grand Egyptian Museum near the Giza Plateau, the Egyptian Museum remains a vital cultural institution with a rich and varied collection that continues to inspire visitors.

Rules, Etiquette, and Safety Tips
When visiting the museum, it's important to respect the rules and the cultural significance of the artifacts. Avoid touching the exhibits, and keep your voice low to maintain a peaceful environment. Dress modestly, as Egypt is a conservative country, and wear comfortable shoes, as you'll be walking through large galleries. Carry a water bottle to stay hydrated, but note that food and drinks are not allowed inside the exhibition halls.

Nearby Attractions
After exploring the Egyptian Museum, you can visit other landmarks in Tahrir Square, such as the Mogamma Building and the central monument. Downtown Cairo is also home to

numerous cafes and restaurants where you can relax and enjoy local or international cuisine. If you're interested in shopping, the area around Talaat Harb Square offers a mix of traditional and modern stores.

Why You Should Visit
The Egyptian Museum is a treasure trove of history and culture, offering a rare opportunity to connect with the ancient world through its incredible collection of artifacts. From the golden treasures of Tutankhamun to the hauntingly preserved mummies of Egypt's great rulers, every corner of the museum tells a story that captivates the imagination.

Abdeen Palace: A Glimpse into Egypt's Royal Past

Abdeen Palace is one of Cairo's most remarkable landmarks, offering a fascinating look at Egypt's royal history, architectural beauty, and political evolution. Located in Downtown Cairo, this majestic palace was once the seat of power for Egypt's monarchy and now serves as a museum and cultural treasure. Visiting Abdeen Palace is an opportunity to explore opulent interiors, learn about Egypt's royal family, and see collections of artifacts that span centuries.

Location and How to Get There
Abdeen Palace is conveniently located in the heart of Downtown Cairo, just a short distance from iconic landmarks like Tahrir Square and the Egyptian Museum. The exact address is on Qasr al-Nil Street, and it's easy to reach from most parts of the city. If you're staying in Downtown Cairo,

you can walk to the palace or take a short taxi ride. Ride-hailing services like Uber and Careem are widely available and offer a comfortable and direct way to get there. For those using public transportation, buses and microbuses frequently pass through Downtown, and the nearest metro station, Ataba, is within walking distance.

What You Will See and Do
When you arrive at Abdeen Palace, the first thing you'll notice is its grand architecture. Built in the 19th century by Khedive Ismail, the palace was designed to reflect the luxury and prestige of Egypt's ruling class. Its exterior features a blend of European and Islamic architectural styles, with intricate details that set the tone for the elegance you'll find inside.

The Palace Interior
Stepping into the palace, you'll be greeted by opulent halls, grand staircases, and beautifully decorated rooms. Each space is adorned with ornate chandeliers, gilded furniture, and exquisite artwork. The Throne Room is particularly impressive, with its luxurious furnishings and ceremonial atmosphere, providing a glimpse into the royal court's grandeur.

The Museum Collections
Abdeen Palace is home to several museums that showcase a wide range of artifacts, including gifts received by Egypt's monarchs, historical documents, and weapons. The **Museum of Arms** features an extensive collection of swords, firearms, and military equipment from various periods and countries.

The **Silver Museum** displays intricate silverware and decorative items, while the **Royal Family Museum** offers personal items that belonged to Egypt's former rulers, including clothing, jewelry, and photographs. These exhibits provide a deeper understanding of Egypt's royal history and connections with other nations.

The Gardens
Surrounding the palace are beautifully landscaped gardens that offer a peaceful retreat from the busy streets of Cairo. You can take a leisurely stroll and admire the greenery, fountains, and sculptures that enhance the palace's charm.

The Best Times to Visit
Abdeen Palace is open to visitors year-round, and the best time to visit is during the cooler months from October to April. The weather is more comfortable during this period, making it easier to explore both the palace and its gardens. The palace typically opens in the morning and remains accessible through the afternoon, so arriving early ensures you have ample time to enjoy the exhibits and avoid crowds. Weekdays are generally quieter than weekends, offering a more relaxed experience.

Ticket Information and Booking
Tickets to Abdeen Palace can be purchased at the entrance, and the prices are reasonable. Admission fees typically vary depending on which museums and exhibits you wish to visit, so it's a good idea to check in advance. Students with valid ID cards may receive discounts. Guided tours are available and

highly recommended, as they provide detailed explanations of the palace's history and significance. These tours can be arranged through local tour operators or directly at the site.

Facilities and Accessibility

Abdeen Palace is equipped with facilities to make your visit comfortable. Restrooms and a small gift shop are available on-site, and there are cafes and restaurants nearby where you can enjoy refreshments. While the palace's historic nature limits some accessibility features, ramps and elevators are provided in certain areas to accommodate visitors with mobility challenges. If you have specific needs, contacting the palace in advance is a good idea to ensure a smooth visit.

Photography Tips and Rules

Photography is generally allowed in most parts of the palace, but flash photography is prohibited to protect the artifacts and interiors. The grand halls, intricate details of the furniture, and beautiful gardens offer excellent opportunities for photos. If you're taking pictures indoors, use natural light and steady your hand to capture clear images. Some areas, such as the museums, may have additional restrictions, so always check with the staff before taking photos.

Cultural and Historical Context

Abdeen Palace was constructed between 1863 and 1874 under the orders of Khedive Ismail, who wanted to create a residence that rivaled the grandeur of European palaces. It became the official residence of Egypt's monarchs and a symbol of the country's modernization during the 19th century. Over the years, the palace witnessed significant events, including royal ceremonies, political meetings, and the transition of Egypt from a monarchy to a republic.

Today, Abdeen Palace serves as a museum and a reminder of Egypt's royal past. Its collections reflect the cultural exchanges and diplomatic relationships that shaped the country's history. Visiting the palace allows you to explore this legacy and gain a deeper appreciation for Egypt's role on the global stage.

Rules, Etiquette, and Safety Tips
When visiting Abdeen Palace, it's important to respect the rules and the cultural significance of the site. Dress modestly, as Egypt is a conservative country, and avoid touching artifacts or furnishings. Speak quietly in the museum areas to maintain a peaceful atmosphere for other visitors. Wear comfortable shoes, as you'll be walking through large halls and gardens, and carry a water bottle to stay hydrated. If you're visiting during peak hours or weekends, be mindful of the crowds and plan your visit accordingly.

Nearby Attractions
Abdeen Palace is centrally located in Downtown Cairo, making it easy to combine your visit with other nearby attractions. Tahrir Square, the Egyptian Museum, and the iconic Qasr El-Nil Bridge are all within a short distance. The bustling streets of Downtown also offer plenty of cafes, shops, and restaurants where you can relax and enjoy the local atmosphere after your visit.

Why You Should Visit

Abdeen Palace is more than just a historic building—it's a living testament to Egypt's royal heritage and architectural splendor. It's an opportunity to step back in time and connect with a pivotal era in Egypt's history, making it a must-see destination for anyone exploring Cairo.

Things to Do: Exploring Modern Cairo's Art Galleries and Cafes

Downtown Cairo is a vibrant area that blends the charm of its historic roots with the dynamic energy of modern life. One of the most engaging ways to experience this part of the city is by exploring its art galleries and cafes. These two aspects of Downtown Cairo offer a window into the city's evolving cultural scene, providing opportunities to appreciate contemporary art, enjoy unique culinary experiences, and interact with the creative community that drives Cairo's modern spirit.

The art galleries in Downtown Cairo are a reflection of the city's growing role as a hub for artistic expression. Scattered throughout the area, these spaces showcase works by local and international artists, spanning a wide range of styles and mediums. Many of these galleries are tucked away in historic buildings, adding an extra layer of character to the experience. As you step into these spaces, you'll notice a shift in atmosphere—a quiet, thoughtful environment where the focus is on creativity and interpretation. Exhibitions often feature paintings, sculptures, photography, and installations that address both global and local themes, from identity and social change to heritage and modernity.

One of the notable galleries in Downtown Cairo is Townhouse Gallery, a cornerstone of the contemporary art scene in Egypt. Located in an industrial-style building, the gallery hosts rotating exhibitions that feature cutting-edge works from established and emerging artists. The space itself is as much a part of the experience as the art it houses, with its minimalist design providing a stark contrast to the vibrant colors and textures of the artworks on display. Townhouse Gallery is known for its focus on experimental and thought-provoking pieces, making it a must-visit for anyone interested in contemporary art.

Another significant venue is Darb 1718, a cultural center that supports a wide range of artistic disciplines. Though technically located on the edge of Old Cairo, its proximity to Downtown makes it easily accessible and worth the visit. Darb 1718 features open-air exhibitions, workshops, and live performances, offering a more interactive and community-focused approach to art. The center is also home to a rooftop space that provides stunning views of the city, making it a great spot to reflect on the art you've seen.

As you move between galleries, you'll likely notice the role of street art in Downtown Cairo's cultural landscape. Murals and graffiti can be found on walls, bridges, and alleyways, adding a layer of urban vibrancy to the area. This public art often reflects the voices of Cairo's youth, expressing social and political themes in bold and creative ways. Walking through Downtown Cairo with an eye for street art can feel like exploring an open-air gallery, where every turn reveals a new piece of visual storytelling.

While art galleries provide a formal setting for artistic expression, the cafes of Downtown Cairo offer a more casual and equally enriching experience. These establishments are not just places to enjoy food and drinks—they are spaces where people gather to share ideas, create, and connect. Many of the cafes in this area have a bohemian vibe, with eclectic decor, vintage furniture, and walls adorned with artwork or photographs. Some cafes even double as galleries, hosting small exhibitions or live performances that add to their creative atmosphere.

A standout example is Eish + Malh, a cozy café that combines contemporary design with a warm, welcoming ambiance. Known for its delicious food and artistic touches, this café is a popular spot for locals and visitors alike. Eish + Malh frequently hosts cultural events, such as poetry readings and live music, making it a dynamic part of Downtown Cairo's cultural scene.

Another favorite is Kafein, a trendy café that takes coffee culture seriously. Located in a quieter corner of Downtown, Kafein is known for its expertly crafted drinks and minimalist design. The café attracts a diverse crowd, from students and artists to professionals taking a break from their busy schedules. Kafein's focus on quality and presentation makes it a great place to relax and recharge while appreciating the finer details of modern café culture.

Downtown Cairo's cafés also include historic establishments that have been part of the city's social fabric for decades. Places like Café Riche and Groppi are iconic landmarks that offer a glimpse into Cairo's past while remaining relevant today. Café Riche, for example, has long been a gathering place for intellectuals, writers, and revolutionaries, earning its place as a symbol of Egypt's cultural and political history. Visiting such a café allows you to sit where great thinkers once discussed ideas that shaped the country, adding depth to your experience of the area.

As you explore Downtown Cairo's art galleries and cafes, you'll also find opportunities to interact with the people who make this cultural scene so vibrant. Artists, baristas, curators, and visitors all contribute to the lively and welcoming atmosphere that defines this part of the city. Engaging in conversations, whether about art, coffee, or life in Cairo, adds a personal dimension to your visit and helps you connect with the city on a deeper level.

The combination of art and café culture in Downtown Cairo offers a unique way to experience the city's modern identity while staying connected to its rich history. The galleries provide a platform for creative voices to be heard, showcasing the talent and perspectives of those shaping Egypt's cultural narrative. Meanwhile, the cafes serve as gathering spaces where ideas are exchanged, and community bonds are strengthened. Together, these elements create a dynamic environment that invites exploration, reflection, and enjoyment.

Accommodation Options

Luxury Stays: High-End Hotels with Nile Views in Downtown Cairo, Egypt

Downtown Cairo is the perfect place to immerse yourself in the energy and charm of Egypt's capital while enjoying stunning views of the Nile River. If you're looking for luxurious accommodations that combine modern amenities with breathtaking scenery, the area offers a selection of high-end hotels that cater to your every need. These properties provide an exceptional level of service, elegant rooms, and prime locations, ensuring a memorable stay in Cairo. Below are some top recommendations for luxury hotels with views of the Nile.

1. The Nile Ritz-Carlton, Cairo
Price Range: Approx. $400–$700 per night.
Amenities: The Nile Ritz-Carlton delivers five-star luxury with spacious, beautifully designed rooms and suites, many featuring private balconies overlooking the Nile. Guests can enjoy a range of dining options, from fine dining to casual meals, and relax in the hotel's outdoor pool, which also boasts Nile views. Additional amenities include a full-service spa, a fitness center, and meeting facilities. Personalized service ensures your stay is as comfortable as possible.

Best Area to Stay: Located on the Corniche near Tahrir Square, this hotel is a stone's throw from the Egyptian Museum and offers easy access to cultural landmarks, shopping districts, and the vibrant downtown area. Its central location makes it convenient for both leisure and business travelers.

Contact Details:
Website: The Nile Ritz-Carlton, Cairo
Phone: +20 2 25778899
Email: reservations.cairo@ritzcarlton.com

2. Kempinski Nile Hotel, Cairo
Price Range: Approx. $250–$500 per night.
Amenities: This boutique-style luxury hotel offers elegantly furnished rooms with Nile-facing balconies. The hotel features a rooftop pool, a spa offering a variety of treatments, and several dining options, including the chic Osmanly restaurant serving Ottoman-inspired cuisine. Guests also have access to a fitness center, free Wi-Fi, and 24-hour concierge service. The hotel's intimate and personalized atmosphere makes it stand out among high-end accommodations.

Best Area to Stay: Situated in the Garden City district, the Kempinski Nile Hotel is in a quieter, upscale part of downtown, yet it's within walking distance of key attractions like the Egyptian Museum and the Cairo Opera House. The serene location by the Nile adds to its charm.

Contact Details:
Website: Kempinski Nile Hotel, Cairo
Phone: +20 2 27980000
Email: reservations.cairo@kempinski.com

3. Sofitel Cairo Nile El Gezirah

Price Range: Approx. $300–$600 per night.

Amenities: This luxurious property is situated on its own private island in the Nile, offering panoramic river views from almost every room. Guests can enjoy a heated infinity pool, a spa with traditional hammams, and a variety of restaurants serving Egyptian, French, and international cuisines. The hotel also features lush gardens, making it a peaceful oasis in the heart of Cairo.

Best Area to Stay: Located on El Gezirah Island, Sofitel Cairo Nile El Gezirah provides a tranquil retreat while still being close to downtown's cultural and entertainment hotspots. The Cairo Tower and Opera House are within walking distance, and the hotel offers easy access to the city's major attractions.

Contact Details:
Website: Sofitel Cairo Nile El Gezirah
Phone: +20 2 27373737
Email: H5307@sofitel.com

4. Fairmont Nile City, Cairo
Price Range: Approx. $300–$550 per night.

Amenities: This modern and stylish hotel offers rooms with floor-to-ceiling windows showcasing stunning Nile views. Guests can indulge in the rooftop pool, relax at the luxurious Willow Stream Spa, and enjoy an impressive array of dining options, including gourmet restaurants and trendy lounges. The hotel also provides a 24-hour fitness center, free Wi-Fi, and a range of meeting facilities for business travelers.

Best Area to Stay: Fairmont Nile City is part of the Nile City Towers complex, offering guests convenient access to high-end shopping, dining, and entertainment. Its central location provides easy access to downtown landmarks and the Giza Plateau for those planning to visit the pyramids.

Contact Details:
Website: Fairmont Nile City, Cairo
Phone: +20 2 24619494
Email: nilecity@fairmont.com

5. Conrad Cairo

Price Range: Approx. $200–$400 per night.

Amenities: Conrad Cairo offers spacious rooms and suites, many with private balconies and sweeping Nile views. Guests can enjoy an outdoor pool, a 24-hour fitness center, and a variety of dining options, including an international buffet and a Lebanese specialty restaurant. The hotel also features a casino, spa services, and meeting facilities. Its luxurious yet relaxed atmosphere makes it an excellent choice for all types of travelers.

Best Area to Stay: Located in downtown Cairo along the Corniche, Conrad Cairo is close to the city's vibrant nightlife, cultural attractions, and business districts. The hotel's central location makes it a convenient base for exploring the city.

Contact Details:
Website: Conrad Cairo
Phone: +20 2 25808000
Email: reservations.cairo@conradhotels.com

Each of these luxury hotels provides an exceptional stay with unmatched Nile views, ensuring your time in Cairo is both memorable and comfortable. Whether you're looking for a historic setting, a boutique experience, or a modern retreat, these high-end accommodations cater to a variety of preferences while putting you close to the best of what downtown Cairo has to offer. From fine dining and rooftop pools to personalized service and convenient locations, you'll find everything you need for an indulgent and stress-free visit.

Mid-Range Options: Contemporary City Hotels in Downtown Cairo, Egypt

Downtown Cairo offers a vibrant mix of history, culture, and modern city life, making it a fantastic base for your visit to the Egyptian capital. If you're looking for accommodations that provide comfort, convenience, and contemporary design without breaking the bank, there are several excellent mid-range hotels to consider. These options are ideal for travelers who want a balance of style, amenities, and accessibility. Below are some of the best contemporary city hotels in Downtown Cairo.

1. Steigenberger Hotel El Tahrir
Price Range: Approx. $100–$150 per night.
Amenities: This stylish hotel features modern rooms equipped with air conditioning, flat-screen TVs, free Wi-Fi, and comfortable bedding. Guests can enjoy a complimentary breakfast buffet, a rooftop pool, a fitness center, and a full-service spa. The hotel's restaurant offers a mix of Egyptian and international cuisine, making it a convenient option for dining in.

Best Area to Stay: Located in the heart of Downtown Cairo near Tahrir Square, the hotel is steps away from the Egyptian Museum and within walking distance of public transportation, shops, and cafes. Its central location makes it ideal for both sightseeing and business travelers.

Contact Details:
Website: Steigenberger Hotel El Tahrir
Phone: +20 2 25750777
Email: reservation.tahrir@steigenberger.com

2. Novotel Cairo El Borg
Price Range: Approx. $90–$140 per night.
Amenities: This contemporary hotel offers comfortable rooms with modern furnishings, free Wi-Fi, and Nile or city views. Facilities include an outdoor pool, a fitness center, and an on-site restaurant serving a variety of dishes. The rooftop terrace is a highlight, providing stunning views of the Nile and Cairo

Tower. The hotel also offers 24-hour room service and airport shuttle services for added convenience.

Best Area to Stay: Situated on the Nile Corniche near Zamalek Island, Novotel Cairo El Borg offers easy access to Downtown Cairo and popular attractions such as the Cairo Opera House and the Egyptian Museum. Its location strikes a perfect balance between relaxation and accessibility.

Contact Details:
Website: Novotel Cairo El Borg
Phone: +20 2 27356725
Email: H6509@accor.com

3. City View Hotel
Price Range: Approx. $70–$120 per night.
Amenities: City View Hotel is a boutique-style property offering cozy, well-decorated rooms with free Wi-Fi, air conditioning, and private balconies overlooking Tahrir Square. Guests enjoy complimentary breakfast, an on-site restaurant serving traditional Egyptian dishes, and 24-hour concierge services. The friendly staff is happy to assist with tour bookings and local recommendations.

Best Area to Stay: Located directly across from the Egyptian Museum, this hotel is perfect for travelers looking to explore the heart of Cairo. Its proximity to Tahrir Square and nearby metro stations makes getting around the city easy and efficient.
Contact Details:
Website: City View Hotel

Phone: +20 2 25782123
Email: info@cityviewhotelcairo.com

4. Barcelo Cairo Pyramids Hotel
Price Range: Approx. $80–$130 per night.
Amenities: This contemporary hotel offers spacious rooms with modern decor, flat-screen TVs, free Wi-Fi, and complimentary toiletries. On-site amenities include a rooftop pool, a fitness center, and several dining options, including a buffet restaurant and a rooftop lounge with panoramic views of Cairo. The hotel also provides meeting rooms and business facilities for travelers on work trips.

Best Area to Stay: Located near the Giza district, Barcelo Cairo Pyramids Hotel is a short drive from Downtown Cairo and the iconic Giza Plateau. It's a great choice if you're looking to balance city exploration with visits to the pyramids.
Contact Details:
Website: Barcelo Cairo Pyramids
Phone: +20 2 35820070
Email: cairo@barcelo.com

5. Cairo Paradise Hotel
Price Range: Approx. $50–$80 per night.
Amenities: Cairo Paradise Hotel offers clean, spacious rooms with free Wi-Fi, flat-screen TVs, and air conditioning. Guests can start their day with a complimentary continental breakfast and take advantage of 24-hour room service. The hotel also provides a concierge desk and tour booking assistance to make your stay hassle-free.

Best Area to Stay: Located in the center of Downtown Cairo, this hotel is close to major attractions like Tahrir Square and the Egyptian Museum. It's also surrounded by local eateries and shopping streets, offering a lively and convenient atmosphere.

Contact Details:
Website: Cairo Paradise Hotel
Phone: +20 2 35781234
Email: reservations@cairoparadisehotel.com

These mid-range accommodations in Downtown Cairo provide a perfect blend of comfort, style, and affordability, ensuring you enjoy your stay without compromising on quality. Whether you're drawn to the modern amenities of international hotel chains or the charm of boutique properties, you'll find options that suit your preferences and budget. With their central locations and thoughtful services, these hotels are excellent bases for exploring Cairo's vibrant city life, iconic landmarks, and cultural treasures.

Budget Choices: Budget-Friendly Lodgings Close to Public Transport in Downtown Cairo, Egypt

Staying in Downtown Cairo gives you the best of the city's vibrant energy and easy access to major attractions, and finding budget-friendly accommodations near public transport can make your stay even more convenient. These lodgings offer excellent value for money, comfortable amenities, and a great starting point for exploring the city. Below are some of the best budget options in Downtown Cairo, perfect for travelers looking to save while staying connected to the city's sights and sounds.

1. Wake Up! Cairo Hostel
Price Range: Approx. $15–$30 per night.
Amenities: Wake Up! Cairo Hostel offers clean and bright dormitory-style and private rooms with free Wi-Fi, lockers, and air conditioning. A complimentary breakfast is served daily, and there's a communal lounge where you can meet fellow travelers. The hostel also provides 24-hour reception and a tour desk to help arrange trips around Cairo.

Best Area to Stay: Located a short walk from Ramses Railway Station and Sadat Metro Station, this hostel is ideally positioned for travelers relying on public transport. It's also close to Tahrir Square and the Egyptian Museum.

Contact Details:
Website: Wake Up! Cairo Hostel
Phone: +20 2 25781234
Email: info@wakeupcairohostel.com

2. Bella Luna Hotel
Price Range: Approx. $20–$40 per night.
Amenities: Bella Luna Hotel offers spacious rooms with private or shared bathrooms, free Wi-Fi, and air conditioning. A simple breakfast is included, and the hotel staff is available to assist with transportation and local tips. The property's

relaxed and welcoming vibe makes it a great choice for budget travelers.

Best Area to Stay: Situated near Talaat Harb Square, the hotel is within walking distance of the Sadat Metro Station and public buses, making it convenient for exploring Cairo's neighborhoods and attractions.

Contact Details:
Website: Bella Luna Hotel
Phone: +20 2 35870345
Email: reservations@bellalunahotel.com

3. New Grand Royal Hotel Cairo
Price Range: Approx. $25–$50 per night.
Amenities: This hotel offers basic but comfortable accommodations with free Wi-Fi, flat-screen TVs, and en-suite bathrooms. Guests can enjoy a daily continental breakfast and access 24-hour room service. The staff is friendly and provides assistance with travel plans and transportation bookings.

Best Area to Stay: Located near Tahrir Square, the hotel is close to Sadat Metro Station and several bus routes, giving you easy access to all parts of Cairo. The Egyptian Museum and several dining options are just a short walk away.

Contact Details:
Website: New Grand Royal Hotel Cairo
Phone: +20 2 35870987

4. Hotel Velvet 1889
Price Range: Approx. $30–$60 per night.
Amenities: Hotel Velvet 1889 offers charming rooms with a mix of modern comforts and vintage decor. Rooms include free Wi-Fi, air conditioning, and private bathrooms. Guests can start their day with a complimentary breakfast, and the 24-hour front desk staff is happy to provide directions and local recommendations.

Best Area to Stay: The hotel is conveniently located in the heart of Downtown Cairo, just steps away from the Nasser Metro Station and major bus routes. Its central location makes it easy to explore local attractions and enjoy the vibrant street life.

Contact Details:
Website: Hotel Velvet 1889
Phone: +20 2 35782123
Email: info@hotelvelvet1889.com

5. Cairo Inn
Price Range: Approx. $20–$35 per night.
Amenities: Cairo Inn features budget-friendly rooms with basic furnishings, air conditioning, and free Wi-Fi. Breakfast is included, and the hotel provides a communal lounge for guests to relax and socialize. The staff can help with booking tours and arranging transport to nearby attractions.

Best Area to Stay: The property is situated near Talaat Harb Square, just a short walk from public transport options like the Sadat Metro Station. Its central location ensures you're close to popular landmarks, restaurants, and shopping streets.

Contact Details:
Website: Cairo Inn
Phone: +20 2 35988012

These budget-friendly lodgings in Downtown Cairo provide an affordable way to enjoy the city while staying connected to public transport and major attractions. With welcoming staff, practical amenities, and prime locations, these choices ensure your trip to Cairo is both enjoyable and budget-conscious.

4.4 Zamalek
Must-See Attractions:
Cairo Tower
Cairo Tower: A Panoramic View of Egypt's Capital
The Cairo Tower is one of Cairo's most recognizable landmarks and a must-visit attraction for anyone exploring the city. Located on Gezira Island in the upscale Zamalek district, this iconic tower offers breathtaking panoramic views of Cairo and the Nile River. Its unique design, cultural significance, and prime location make it an unforgettable experience for visitors.

Location and How to Get There
The Cairo Tower is situated in Zamalek, an island in the middle of the Nile River. Its central location makes it easily accessible from many parts of the city. If you're staying in

Downtown Cairo, you can take a taxi or use ride-hailing apps like Uber or Careem for a quick and convenient ride to the tower. Public transportation options, such as buses or the metro, can get you close to the area, but you'll need to take a short taxi ride to reach the entrance. For those staying in Zamalek, the tower is within walking distance, offering a pleasant stroll through the neighborhood.

What You Will See and Do
The Cairo Tower stands at 187 meters (614 feet) and is one of the tallest structures in North Africa. As you approach the tower, its striking lattice design immediately catches your eye. Inspired by the shape of a lotus flower, the design reflects Egypt's ancient heritage while embodying modern architectural techniques.

Observation Deck
The main highlight of the Cairo Tower is its observation deck, located at the top of the structure. From here, you'll enjoy stunning 360-degree views of Cairo. On clear days, you can see major landmarks such as the Pyramids of Giza, the Nile River, and the sprawling cityscape that stretches as far as the eye can see. The deck is equipped with telescopes to help you get a closer look at specific points of interest.

Revolving Restaurant
The tower features a revolving restaurant, offering a unique dining experience with panoramic views of the city. The restaurant slowly rotates, allowing you to enjoy different perspectives while you savor a meal. The menu includes a

variety of international and Egyptian dishes, making it a great spot for a romantic dinner or a special occasion.

Viewing Experience at Night
Visiting the Cairo Tower at night is a magical experience. The city lights create a mesmerizing view, and the tower itself is beautifully illuminated. The cooler evening temperatures also make this a comfortable time to visit.

The Best Times to Visit
The Cairo Tower is open year-round, and the best time to visit depends on your preferences. If you want clear views and minimal crowds, visiting early in the morning is ideal. For those who prefer a more atmospheric experience, visiting around sunset allows you to see the city transition from day to night, with the golden light of the setting sun creating a stunning backdrop. Evenings are particularly popular for the twinkling city lights and the cooler weather, so plan ahead if you want to avoid peak crowds.

Ticket Information and Booking
Tickets to the Cairo Tower can be purchased at the entrance. The ticket price includes access to the observation deck, and there are separate charges if you choose to dine at the revolving restaurant. Discounts are available for Egyptian nationals and students with valid identification, but international visitors are welcome to enjoy the experience for a reasonable fee. There's no need to book in advance for general entry, but making a reservation for the restaurant is

recommended, especially during weekends or peak tourist seasons.

Facilities and Accessibility
The Cairo Tower is well-equipped with facilities to make your visit comfortable. Restrooms are available on-site, and there is a small gift shop where you can purchase souvenirs. The tower is accessible by elevators, making it easy for visitors of all ages and abilities to reach the observation deck and restaurant. Wheelchair users will find the tower generally accommodating, but it's a good idea to check ahead if you have specific needs.

Photography Tips and Rules
The Cairo Tower is a photographer's dream. The observation deck provides unobstructed views of Cairo, making it the perfect spot for capturing cityscapes and landmarks. For the best photos, visit during sunrise or sunset when the lighting enhances the beauty of the surroundings. If you're visiting at night, the city lights create a vibrant and dramatic effect that's equally captivating. Photography is allowed throughout the tower, but it's best to avoid using tripods during busy times to ensure a smooth flow of visitors.

Cultural and Historical Context
The Cairo Tower was completed in 1961 during the presidency of Gamal Abdel Nasser. It was designed by the Egyptian architect Naoum Shebib and built using reinforced concrete. The tower's design, inspired by the lotus flower, reflects Egypt's deep connection to its ancient history and culture. It was intended as a symbol of Egypt's post-colonial pride and

independence, standing as a modern counterpart to the Pyramids of Giza. Over the decades, the Cairo Tower has remained an important cultural and architectural landmark, serving as a venue for events and a popular attraction for both locals and tourists. Its historical significance and unique design make it an enduring icon of Cairo's skyline.

Rules, Etiquette, and Safety Tips
When visiting the Cairo Tower, it's important to follow the rules to ensure a pleasant experience for everyone. Keep your ticket with you at all times, as you may need to show it at multiple points. Dress comfortably and modestly, in line with local customs, and wear shoes suitable for walking. Be patient if there are lines for the elevators, especially during peak times, and be respectful of other visitors by keeping noise levels down.

It's also a good idea to bring a bottle of water, particularly if you're visiting during the warmer months. The observation deck is outdoors, so wear sunscreen and a hat if you're visiting during the day. If you're dining at the revolving restaurant, plan your visit to coincide with mealtime and make a reservation in advance.

Nearby Attractions
Zamalek is one of Cairo's most vibrant districts, and there's plenty to see and do near the Cairo Tower. You can visit the nearby **Gezira Arts Center**, which features art galleries and exhibitions. The **Opera House** is also close by, offering

cultural performances and events. If you enjoy walking, take a stroll along the Nile Corniche, where you can enjoy the riverside atmosphere and beautiful views.

Why You Should Visit
The Cairo Tower is more than just a tall building—it's an experience that combines stunning views, cultural significance, and a touch of luxury. It's a must-visit destination that provides a unique perspective on Cairo, allowing you to see the city in all its vastness and beauty.

Aisha Fahmy Palace: A Hidden Gem of Art and Elegance in Zamalek

The Aisha Fahmy Palace is a captivating attraction in the heart of Zamalek, Cairo, that combines history, art, and architecture. This stunning palace, once the residence of a wealthy and influential Egyptian aristocrat, is now a cultural center that hosts art exhibitions and events. A visit to Aisha Fahmy Palace offers a peaceful and inspiring experience, where you can admire both the building's historical charm and the artistic treasures within.

Location and How to Get There
Aisha Fahmy Palace is located on Gezira Island in the upscale Zamalek district, an area known for its greenery, artistic vibe, and tranquil atmosphere. Its exact address is on Mohamed Mazhar Street, making it easy to find. If you're staying in Zamalek, the palace is likely within walking distance. From other parts of Cairo, you can take a taxi or use ride-hailing apps

like Uber or Careem for a convenient trip. Public transportation options like buses and microbuses also pass through Zamalek, though they may require a short walk to reach the palace. Many visitors combine their trip to the palace with nearby attractions, such as the Cairo Tower or the Opera House, making it a perfect addition to your day.

What You Will See and Do
When you arrive at Aisha Fahmy Palace, you'll immediately notice the building's elegant design. Constructed in 1907, the palace is a prime example of early 20th-century architecture, blending European styles with Egyptian influences. The exterior features intricate carvings, beautiful balconies, and large windows that hint at the luxury inside.

The Palace Interior
Stepping inside the palace, you'll be transported to a bygone era of opulence and refinement. The interior is adorned with marble floors, carved wooden doors, and detailed ceilings. Each room showcases the wealth and taste of the palace's original owner, Aisha Fahmy, who was known for her love of art and culture. The palace itself is a work of art, with every corner offering something to admire.

Art Exhibitions
Today, Aisha Fahmy Palace serves as a cultural hub, hosting rotating art exhibitions that feature works by both Egyptian and international artists. These exhibitions span a variety of styles and mediums, from traditional paintings and sculptures to contemporary installations. Visiting during an exhibition

allows you to experience the palace as a living, breathing space that continues to inspire creativity.

Historic Furniture and Artifacts
Some rooms in the palace retain their original furniture and decorations, providing a glimpse into the lifestyle of Egypt's aristocracy in the early 20th century. Chandeliers, antique mirrors, and elegant furnishings create a sense of timeless elegance that complements the building's architectural beauty.

The Garden
Surrounding the palace is a serene garden where you can take a break from the hustle and bustle of the city. The garden features lush greenery, pathways, and seating areas, making it a perfect spot to relax after exploring the palace.

The Best Times to Visit
Aisha Fahmy Palace is open year-round, and the best time to visit depends on the exhibitions being held. Checking the schedule in advance will help you plan your visit around specific events or displays. The palace is typically open during the day, and mornings or early afternoons are ideal for enjoying the space without too many visitors. Visiting during cooler months, from October to April, is more comfortable, especially if you plan to spend time in the garden.

Ticket Information and Booking
Admission to Aisha Fahmy Palace is usually free, though some special exhibitions may require a ticket. Information about events and ticket prices can be found on the palace's

official website or social media pages. Guided tours are sometimes available, providing insights into the history of the building and its exhibits. These tours are a great way to deepen your understanding of the palace's significance.

Facilities and Accessibility
The palace offers basic facilities, including restrooms and seating areas, to ensure a comfortable visit. While the historic nature of the building may limit accessibility in some areas, efforts have been made to accommodate visitors with mobility challenges. The garden and main exhibition spaces are generally easy to navigate, but it's a good idea to contact the palace in advance if you have specific needs. Nearby cafes and restaurants in Zamalek provide additional options for refreshments and meals.

Photography Tips and Rules
Aisha Fahmy Palace is a dream location for photography enthusiasts. The intricate details of the architecture, the grandeur of the interiors, and the tranquil garden all provide excellent opportunities for capturing beautiful shots. Photography is allowed in most areas, but flash and tripods may be restricted to protect the artworks and furnishings. Be mindful of other visitors and respect any rules set by the palace staff.

Cultural and Historical Context
The palace was originally built as a private residence for Aisha Fahmy, a prominent figure in Egyptian society during the early 20th century. As the daughter of Ali Fahmy Pasha, a wealthy aristocrat, Aisha grew up surrounded by luxury and culture.

Her passion for art and her connections to Europe influenced the design and decoration of the palace, making it a showcase of elegance and sophistication.

After Aisha's passing, the palace underwent several changes before being restored and repurposed as a cultural center. Today, it stands as a testament to Cairo's rich history and commitment to preserving its artistic heritage. Visiting the palace allows you to step into a world where art and architecture come together to tell a story of creativity, beauty, and legacy.

Rules, Etiquette, and Safety Tips
When visiting Aisha Fahmy Palace, it's important to respect the space and its cultural significance. Dress modestly, in line with local customs, and avoid touching artifacts or exhibits. Keep noise levels low to maintain the serene atmosphere, especially if other visitors are enjoying the art or the gardens. If you're visiting with children, ensure they are supervised and understand the importance of preserving the space.

Nearby Attractions
Zamalek is a vibrant district with plenty to explore before or after your visit to Aisha Fahmy Palace. The nearby Cairo Tower offers stunning views of the city, while the Opera House hosts performances and events throughout the year. For a relaxing stroll, the Nile Corniche and the Gezira Sporting Club are both excellent options. Zamalek's cafes and restaurants also provide a variety of dining choices, from traditional Egyptian cuisine to international dishes.

Why You Should Visit
Aisha Fahmy Palace is more than just a historic building—it's a celebration of art, culture, and history. It's a place where the past meets the present, inviting you to discover the beauty and creativity that make Cairo such a fascinating city to explore.

The Gezira Art Center

The Gezira Art Center is one of Cairo's premier cultural institutions, located in the serene and vibrant district of Zamalek on Gezira Island. Known for its dedication to art and creativity, the center is a haven for those who want to experience Egyptian and international art in a peaceful and inspiring setting. From rotating exhibitions to permanent collections, workshops, and cultural events, the Gezira Art Center offers a wide range of experiences for visitors of all ages and interests.

Location and How to Get There
The Gezira Art Center is situated in Zamalek, an upscale neighborhood on Gezira Island in the heart of the Nile River. The district is known for its artistic and relaxed atmosphere, and the center is conveniently located near other major landmarks like the Cairo Opera House and Cairo Tower. If you're staying in Zamalek, the art center is likely within walking distance. From Downtown Cairo or other areas, you can take a taxi or use ride-hailing apps like Uber or Careem for a quick and convenient trip. For those using public transportation, buses and microbuses frequently pass near

Gezira Island, but a short taxi ride may still be needed to reach the exact location.

What You Will See and Do
The Gezira Art Center is housed in an elegant and historic building that complements the artistic works it showcases. As you step inside, you'll immediately notice the welcoming and serene environment, with natural light streaming into the exhibition halls and beautifully arranged spaces that encourage exploration and contemplation.

Art Exhibitions
The centerpiece of the Gezira Art Center is its rotating exhibitions, which feature works from both Egyptian and international artists. These exhibitions cover a wide range of artistic styles and mediums, including paintings, sculptures, photography, and multimedia installations. Each exhibit tells a unique story, offering insights into different cultural, historical, and artistic themes.

Permanent Collections
In addition to its temporary exhibits, the center houses a collection of permanent artworks that highlight the evolution of Egyptian art. These pieces provide a fascinating look at the country's artistic heritage, from traditional styles influenced by ancient Egyptian culture to modern and contemporary movements.

Workshops and Cultural Events:
The Gezira Art Center is more than just a gallery—it's a space for learning and creativity. The center regularly hosts

workshops, lectures, and cultural events, making it a hub for artistic development and community engagement. These events are open to both locals and visitors, offering a chance to learn from artists, interact with like-minded individuals, and even create your own art.

Sculpture Garden
One of the most tranquil parts of the Gezira Art Center is its sculpture garden. This outdoor space features a variety of contemporary sculptures set against lush greenery. The garden is perfect for a leisurely walk or a quiet moment of reflection, allowing you to enjoy art in a natural setting.

The Best Times to Visit
The Gezira Art Center is open throughout the year, and the best time to visit depends on the exhibitions and events taking place. To fully enjoy the experience, consider visiting in the morning or early afternoon when the center is less crowded, allowing you to explore the galleries and garden at your own pace. If you're interested in attending a specific workshop or event, check the center's schedule in advance to plan your visit. The cooler months from October to April are especially pleasant for spending time in the outdoor areas.

Ticket Information and Booking
Admission to the Gezira Art Center is often free, making it an accessible attraction for all visitors. Certain workshops or special events may have a small fee, but these are typically affordable and well worth the cost. You can find information about upcoming exhibitions, events, and ticket requirements

on the center's official website or social media pages. If you're interested in a guided tour, inquire at the front desk or check online for options.

Facilities and Accessibility
The Gezira Art Center is equipped with basic facilities to ensure a comfortable visit. Restrooms are available on-site, and there are seating areas throughout the galleries and garden where you can take a break. While the building's historic nature may limit accessibility in some areas, ramps and pathways are provided to accommodate visitors with mobility challenges. For additional assistance, it's best to contact the center in advance. Nearby cafes and restaurants in Zamalek also offer plenty of options for refreshments before or after your visit.

Photography Tips and Rules
The Gezira Art Center is a fantastic location for photography, offering a mix of indoor and outdoor settings that highlight artistic expression. The sculpture garden, in particular, is an excellent spot for capturing unique compositions and the interplay of art and nature. While photography is allowed in most areas, flash photography and tripods may be restricted to protect the artworks and ensure a smooth flow of visitors. Always check with the staff if you're unsure about specific rules.

Cultural and Historical Context
The Gezira Art Center is an integral part of Cairo's cultural landscape, located in a district long associated with creativity and intellectual pursuits. Zamalek itself has been a hub for

artists, writers, and musicians, and the center reflects this legacy through its dedication to showcasing and nurturing artistic talent. Over the years, the Gezira Art Center has hosted countless exhibitions and events that celebrate both Egyptian culture and global artistic trends. Its role as a cultural institution makes it a vital space for dialogue, education, and inspiration.

Rules, Etiquette, and Safety Tips
When visiting the Gezira Art Center, it's important to respect the space and its artworks. Avoid touching any of the exhibits and keep noise levels low to maintain the peaceful atmosphere. If you're attending a workshop or event, arrive early to secure a spot and make the most of the experience. Dress modestly, as this is customary in Egypt, and wear comfortable shoes, as you'll likely spend time walking through the galleries and garden. Be mindful of others and avoid obstructing pathways, especially if the center is busy.

Nearby Attractions
The Gezira Art Center is located in Zamalek, one of Cairo's most vibrant districts, and there are plenty of nearby attractions to explore. The Cairo Tower, offering panoramic views of the city, is just a short distance away. The Cairo Opera House, another cultural landmark, hosts performances and events throughout the year. For a relaxing stroll, the Nile Corniche and the Gezira Sporting Club are excellent options. Zamalek also boasts a variety of cafes, art galleries, and boutique shops, making it a great place to spend the day.

Why You Should Visit
The Gezira Art Center is a cultural treasure that provides a peaceful and inspiring escape from the busy streets of Cairo. Whether you're exploring its diverse exhibitions, participating in a workshop, or simply enjoying the beauty of the sculpture garden, the center offers a unique and enriching experience. It's a place where art and culture come alive, inviting you to connect with Egypt's creative spirit and discover the stories behind its artistic heritage. A visit to the Gezira Art Center is not just about viewing art—it's about immersing yourself in a space that celebrates creativity, history, and community.

Things to Do: Strolling Along the Nile, Visiting Boutiques, and Enjoying Rooftop Restaurants

Zamalek, an island situated in the Nile River at the heart of Cairo, is one of the city's most elegant and tranquil neighborhoods. Known for its leafy streets, historic architecture, and modern charm, Zamalek offers a mix of cultural, recreational, and culinary experiences that make it a favorite destination for both locals and tourists. Among the many things to do in this unique area, strolling along the Nile, visiting its distinctive boutiques, and enjoying meals at rooftop restaurants stand out as some of the most enriching activities you can experience. These activities combine relaxation, exploration, and indulgence, allowing you to connect with Zamalek's serene yet lively atmosphere.

Strolling along the Nile in Zamalek is a simple yet profoundly rewarding experience. The island's location in the middle of the river makes it an ideal place to enjoy panoramic views of the water and the city's skyline. As you walk along the Corniche, the pathway that hugs the Nile, you'll feel a sense of calm that contrasts with the bustling streets of downtown Cairo. The cool breeze from the water, the sound of boats gliding by, and the sight of traditional feluccas sailing under the evening sky create an atmosphere that is both peaceful and picturesque. Walking along the Nile at sunset is especially magical, as the changing colors of the sky reflect on the water and the city takes on a golden glow. The experience is equally enchanting at night, when the city lights illuminate the river and create a lively, festive ambiance.

As you stroll, you'll come across small parks and seating areas where you can pause to take in the scenery or watch locals enjoying their time by the river. You might see families having picnics, couples taking romantic walks, or friends gathering to chat and enjoy the view. These moments offer a glimpse into the everyday life of Cairo's residents, making your walk along the Nile feel authentic and connected to the local culture. For those who want to spend more time on the water, renting a felucca or taking a short boat ride is a fantastic way to experience the Nile from a different perspective. These traditional wooden boats are a hallmark of Egyptian life and offer a peaceful and scenic way to explore the river.

After your walk along the Nile, Zamalek's many boutiques invite you to explore the neighborhood's creative and fashionable side. The area is known for its eclectic mix of shops, ranging from high-end designer stores to small artisan studios. These boutiques offer a curated selection of clothing, jewelry, accessories, and home goods that reflect both local craftsmanship and global trends. Many of the items you'll find are unique and handmade, making them perfect for gifts or personal keepsakes. Shopping in Zamalek is not just about purchasing items—it's an opportunity to discover the artistry and creativity of Cairo's designers and makers.

Some of the most charming boutiques in Zamalek are tucked away on quiet side streets, giving them a sense of exclusivity and discovery. Walking into these stores feels like stepping into a carefully designed world, where every item is chosen with care. Whether you're browsing through elegant clothing made from fine Egyptian cotton, admiring intricate silver jewelry, or selecting a beautifully crafted piece of pottery, you'll find that each store has its own distinct personality. The shop owners are often passionate about their products and happy to share the stories behind them, adding depth and meaning to your shopping experience. Many of these boutiques also emphasize sustainability and ethical practices, making your purchases feel even more special.

After a day of walking and shopping, Zamalek's rooftop restaurants provide the perfect setting to relax and enjoy the neighborhood's culinary delights. Dining on a rooftop in Zamalek is more than just a meal—it's an experience that combines delicious food with stunning views of the city and the Nile. These restaurants are known for their stylish interiors, creative menus, and relaxed yet sophisticated ambiance. Whether you're in the mood for traditional Egyptian dishes,

Mediterranean flavors, or international cuisine, you'll find a wide variety of options to suit your taste.

The views from Zamalek's rooftop restaurants are truly spectacular, especially at night when the city lights shimmer and the Nile reflects the glow of nearby buildings. Sitting at a rooftop table with a refreshing drink and a plate of beautifully presented food, you'll feel a sense of serenity and indulgence that perfectly captures the essence of Zamalek. Many of these restaurants also offer live music or other entertainment, adding to the vibrant yet relaxed atmosphere. The combination of great food, excellent service, and breathtaking views makes rooftop dining in Zamalek a memorable highlight of any visit. Exploring Zamalek through these activities—strolling along the Nile, shopping at its unique boutiques, and enjoying meals at its rooftop restaurants—provides a well-rounded experience of this charming neighborhood. Each activity complements the others, creating a seamless journey that allows you to connect with Zamalek's natural beauty, cultural creativity, and modern elegance. Whether you're admiring the river's tranquil waters, discovering one-of-a-kind treasures in a boutique, or savoring a delicious meal with a view, you'll come away with a deeper appreciation for the neighborhood's unique character and the vibrant city of Cairo as a whole.

Accommodation Options

Luxury Stays: Boutique Hotels on Gezira Island in Zamalek, Cairo, Egypt

Gezira Island, located in the heart of the Nile and home to the upscale Zamalek district, is one of Cairo's most sought-after locations. This leafy, tranquil neighborhood offers a mix of cultural landmarks, vibrant art galleries, and luxurious accommodations. For those looking to stay in boutique hotels that offer exclusivity, charm, and personalized service, Zamalek is the perfect choice. Below are some top boutique hotel recommendations on Gezira Island to elevate your Cairo experience.

1. The Nile Art Hotel
Price Range: Approx. $250–$400 per night.
Amenities: The Nile Art Hotel combines contemporary luxury with artistic flair, featuring tastefully designed rooms adorned with local artwork. Each room offers Nile or city views, free Wi-Fi, air conditioning, and plush bedding. Guests can enjoy a complimentary gourmet breakfast, a rooftop terrace with stunning views, and an on-site gallery showcasing works from emerging Egyptian artists. The hotel also provides 24-hour concierge service and private airport transfers.

Best Area to Stay: Nestled in the heart of Zamalek, this hotel is within walking distance of the Cairo Opera House, Gezira Sporting Club, and a variety of trendy cafes and restaurants.

Its central yet serene location is ideal for exploring both cultural landmarks and the lively local scene.

Contact Details:
Website: The Nile Art Hotel
Phone: +20 2 35871234
Email: info@nilearthotel.com

2. Zamalek Palace Boutique Hotel
Price Range: Approx. $200–$350 per night.
Amenities: This charming boutique hotel offers an opulent yet intimate atmosphere, with elegant rooms featuring antique furnishings and modern amenities like free Wi-Fi, flat-screen TVs, and minibars. The property includes a lush garden courtyard, a fine dining restaurant serving Egyptian and Mediterranean cuisine, and a relaxing spa with massage services. Guests are greeted with a welcome drink and receive personalized attention throughout their stay.
Best Area to Stay: Situated in a quiet corner of Zamalek, the hotel is perfect for those who value peace and privacy while being close to cultural hotspots such as the Cairo Tower and the Museum of Modern Egyptian Art.

Contact Details:
Website: Zamalek Palace Boutique Hotel
Phone: +20 2 35791234
Email: reservations@zamalekpalacehotel.com

3. Villa Zamalek Boutique Hotel
Price Range: Approx. $180–$300 per night.

Amenities: Villa Zamalek offers a boutique hotel experience with a homey yet luxurious feel. Each suite is uniquely designed with handcrafted furnishings, spacious seating areas, and modern comforts such as Wi-Fi and air conditioning. Guests can enjoy a complimentary breakfast buffet, a cozy library, and a rooftop garden perfect for unwinding after a day of sightseeing. The staff provides personalized service and can assist with planning tours or dining reservations.

Best Area to Stay: Located near the bustling 26th of July Street, the hotel is surrounded by trendy boutiques, art galleries, and local restaurants, making it an excellent base for experiencing Zamalek's sophisticated vibe.

Contact Details:
Website: Villa Zamalek Boutique Hotel
Phone: +20 2 35672345
Email: info@villazamalek.com

4. The Gezira Boutique Retreat
Price Range: Approx. $220–$400 per night.
Amenities: This elegant retreat features spacious rooms and suites with private balconies overlooking the Nile or the lush greenery of Gezira Island. Amenities include a heated outdoor pool, a small spa offering wellness treatments, and a rooftop lounge with panoramic views. The hotel's in-house restaurant specializes in farm-to-table cuisine, and complimentary afternoon tea is served daily in the courtyard.

Best Area to Stay: Situated near the Gezira Sporting Club, this hotel is ideal for those who want to enjoy a blend of urban exploration and relaxation. The quiet surroundings make it a great retreat while remaining close to the area's cultural attractions.

Contact Details:
Website: The Gezira Boutique Retreat
Phone: +20 2 35782345
Email: reservations@geziraboutiqueretreat.com

5. La Riva Zamalek
Price Range: Approx. $200–$320 per night.
Amenities: La Riva Zamalek blends contemporary style with traditional Egyptian touches, offering beautifully designed rooms with Nile-facing balconies, free Wi-Fi, and premium bedding. The hotel features a rooftop infinity pool, a wellness spa, and an on-site bistro serving international and Egyptian dishes. Guests also have access to 24-hour room service and concierge assistance.
Best Area to Stay: Centrally located in Zamalek, La Riva is steps away from cultural institutions like the Cairo Opera House and a variety of upscale shopping and dining options. Its position on Gezira Island ensures tranquility while keeping you connected to the city's highlights.

Contact Details:
Website: La Riva Zamalek
Phone: +20 2 35980123
Email: contact@larivazamalek.com

Staying in one of Zamalek's boutique hotels on Gezira Island ensures a luxurious and peaceful experience with easy access to Cairo's cultural and historical landmarks. These accommodations provide not only comfort and elegance but also an authentic connection to the neighborhood's charm and vibrant energy. Whether you're drawn to art, fine dining, or serene Nile views, Zamalek's boutique hotels offer an unforgettable stay tailored to your preferences.

Mid-Range Options: Riverside Hotels with Modern Amenities in Zamalek, Cairo, Egypt

Zamalek, located on Gezira Island in the Nile River, is one of Cairo's most sought-after neighborhoods for its serene atmosphere, lush greenery, and vibrant cultural scene. If you're looking for mid-range hotels that offer modern amenities and stunning riverside locations, you'll find several excellent options in this area. These accommodations provide a perfect blend of comfort, convenience, and affordability, making them ideal for travelers seeking a memorable stay in Cairo. Here are some of the top choices:

1. Hilton Cairo Zamalek Residences
Price Range: Approx. $130–$200 per night.
Amenities: This stylish hotel offers modern rooms and suites with panoramic Nile views, free Wi-Fi, flat-screen TVs, and private balconies. The property features a large outdoor pool, a well-equipped fitness center, and multiple dining options, including an all-day international restaurant and a riverside

café. Guests can also enjoy 24-hour room service and concierge assistance.

Best Area to Stay: Hilton Cairo Zamalek is situated on a quiet stretch of the island, offering peace and tranquility while still being close to cultural landmarks like the Cairo Opera House and upscale restaurants in Zamalek. Its riverside location is perfect for relaxing by the Nile.

Contact Details:
Website: Hilton Cairo Zamalek Residences
Phone: +20 2 27370055
Email: reservations.zamalek@hilton.com

2. Golden Tulip Flamenco Hotel Cairo
Price Range: Approx. $100–$160 per night.
Amenities: The Golden Tulip Flamenco Hotel offers comfortable accommodations with Nile or city views, free Wi-Fi, and spacious work areas. The hotel has an on-site restaurant serving Mediterranean and international cuisine, as well as a cozy lounge bar. Meeting rooms and business facilities are also available, making it a great choice for work and leisure travelers alike.

Best Area to Stay: Located in the heart of Zamalek, the hotel is surrounded by art galleries, cafes, and boutique shops. Its proximity to the Nile Corniche and cultural attractions like the Museum of Modern Egyptian Art makes it a convenient base for exploring.

Contact Details:
Website: Golden Tulip Flamenco Hotel Cairo
Phone: +20 2 27370231
Email: info@flamencohotel.com

3. New President Hotel Zamalek
Price Range: Approx. $80–$140 per night.
Amenities: This modern hotel offers comfortable rooms with contemporary decor, free Wi-Fi, and flat-screen TVs. Guests can enjoy a complimentary breakfast buffet, a trendy rooftop bar with Nile views, and an on-site restaurant serving both Egyptian and international dishes. The hotel also provides airport shuttle services and tour booking assistance.

Best Area to Stay: New President Hotel is located in one of Zamalek's most vibrant neighborhoods, close to trendy eateries, jazz bars, and local attractions like the Cairo Tower. Its central location makes it easy to explore the island on foot.
Contact Details:
Website: New President Hotel Zamalek
Phone: +20 2 27353345
Email: contact@newpresidenthotelzamalek.com

4. Pharaohs Hotel Cairo
Price Range: Approx. $70–$120 per night.
Amenities: Pharaohs Hotel provides comfortable rooms with essential amenities, including free Wi-Fi, air conditioning, and en-suite bathrooms. Guests can enjoy a complimentary breakfast, a 24-hour front desk, and a casual on-site restaurant offering traditional Egyptian dishes. The hotel's rooftop

terrace provides a pleasant spot to relax after a day of sightseeing.

Best Area to Stay: This hotel is conveniently located near the Nile Corniche, offering easy access to nearby attractions like the Cairo Opera House and Gezira Sporting Club. Public transportation options are also within walking distance, making it a practical choice for exploring the city.

Contact Details:
Website: Pharaohs Hotel Cairo
Phone: +20 2 27351122
Email: reservations@pharaohshotel.com

5. Om Kolthoom Hotel & Tower
Price Range: Approx. $100–$170 per night.
Amenities: Named after Egypt's beloved singer, Om Kolthoom Hotel offers spacious rooms and suites with Nile views, free Wi-Fi, and modern furnishings. The property features a riverside restaurant, a coffee shop, and a fitness center. Guests can also relax at the outdoor pool or book a massage at the spa. The hotel staff provides excellent service, ensuring a comfortable stay.

Best Area to Stay: Situated along the Nile Corniche in Zamalek, this hotel offers stunning river views and is within walking distance of cultural sites, cafes, and art galleries. Its location is both scenic and practical for exploring the city.

Contact Details:
Website: Om Kolthoom Hotel & Tower

Phone: +20 2 27352100
Email: info@omkolthoomhotel.com

Each of these riverside hotels in Zamalek offers a combination of modern amenities, prime locations, and reasonable rates, making them excellent choices for mid-range travelers. Whether you're in Cairo for business or leisure, these accommodations ensure comfort, convenience, and a memorable experience with stunning views of the Nile and easy access to the best that Zamalek has to offer.

Budget Choices: Co-Living Spaces and Budget Lodgings in Zamalek, Cairo, Egypt

Zamalek, located on Gezira Island in the Nile, is known for its upscale charm, trendy cafes, and leafy streets. However, it also offers budget-friendly accommodation options that cater to travelers looking for comfort and affordability. Co-living spaces and budget lodgings in Zamalek provide excellent amenities and a community atmosphere, making them ideal for solo travelers, backpackers, or those on an extended stay. Here are some of the best choices to consider:

1. Nubian Hostel Zamalek
Price Range: Approx. $20–$40 per night for shared rooms; $50–$70 for private rooms.
Amenities: Nubian Hostel offers a vibrant and social atmosphere with clean and comfortable shared dormitories and private rooms. Amenities include free Wi-Fi, air conditioning, and a shared kitchen. A complimentary breakfast is served daily, and the common lounge area is perfect for meeting

fellow travelers. The hostel also organizes walking tours and social events, adding to its community vibe.

Best Area to Stay: Located near 26th of July Street, this hostel is surrounded by local cafes, restaurants, and art galleries. Its central location makes it easy to explore Zamalek and access public transportation for venturing into other parts of Cairo.

Contact Details:
Website: Nubian Hostel Zamalek
Phone: +20 2 27381122
Email: info@nubianhostel.com

2. Safary Hostel
Price Range: Approx. $15–$35 per night.
Amenities: This budget-friendly co-living space offers dormitory and private room options, all equipped with essential amenities like free Wi-Fi and air conditioning. Guests can enjoy a free continental breakfast and access a communal kitchen and lounge area. The hostel staff is known for being friendly and helpful, assisting with tour bookings and travel tips.

Best Area to Stay: Situated near the Zamalek Market, this hostel is within walking distance of cultural attractions, cozy cafes, and the Nile Corniche, making it a convenient base for exploring the neighborhood.
Contact Details:
Website: Safary Hostel
Phone: +20 2 27390567

Email: reservations@safaryhostel.com

3. TULIP Co-Living Space
Price Range: Approx. $25–$45 per night.
Amenities: TULIP Co-Living Space offers a modern and minimalist environment with shared and private rooms. Facilities include free high-speed Wi-Fi, a shared workspace, and a rooftop terrace for relaxation or socializing. A small on-site café serves breakfast, snacks, and coffee throughout the day. The co-living concept is perfect for digital nomads or travelers looking for a more community-driven experience.

Best Area to Stay: Located in the heart of Zamalek, TULIP is close to popular attractions like the Cairo Opera House and the Museum of Modern Egyptian Art. Its proximity to public transport makes it easy to navigate the city.

Contact Details:
Website: TULIP Co-Living Space
Phone: +20 2 27388012
Email: contact@tulipcoliving.com

4. Traveler's Nest Zamalek
Price Range: Approx. $18–$30 per night.
Amenities: This cozy and affordable guesthouse offers basic but clean accommodations with free Wi-Fi, shared bathrooms, and a communal lounge. Guests can use the shared kitchen or enjoy a complimentary breakfast provided by the staff. Traveler's Nest also offers bike rentals for exploring Zamalek and nearby areas.

Best Area to Stay: Located near the Nile Corniche, this guesthouse is an excellent choice for travelers who want to be close to Zamalek's green spaces and cultural landmarks. Its quiet yet central location provides easy access to shops and eateries.

Contact Details:
Website: Traveler's Nest Zamalek
Phone: +20 2 27379876
Email: info@travelersnestzamalek.com

5. Cairo Co-Living Hub
Price Range: Approx. $20–$50 per night.
Amenities: This trendy co-living space features stylish shared and private rooms, free Wi-Fi, and workspaces. Guests can enjoy a communal kitchen, an on-site café, and a rooftop garden with views of the Nile. Regular events like movie nights and cultural talks make it a lively place to stay.

Best Area to Stay: Cairo Co-Living Hub is located on a quiet street in Zamalek, close to public transportation and within walking distance of trendy restaurants, shops, and cultural sites. The neighborhood's serene atmosphere makes it a great spot for both work and leisure.

Contact Details:
Website: Cairo Co-Living Hub
Phone: +20 2 27381234
Email: reservations@cairocolivinghub.com

These budget-friendly co-living spaces and lodgings in Zamalek offer excellent value for travelers who want comfort, convenience, and a sense of community. Whether you're visiting for a short trip or planning an extended stay, these options provide everything you need to explore the neighborhood and enjoy Cairo's vibrant culture without straining your budget. With their central locations, welcoming atmospheres, and thoughtful amenities, these accommodations ensure a memorable stay in Zamalek.

Old Cairo (Coptic Cairo)

Must-See Attractions

The Hanging Church: A Jewel of Coptic Cairo's Heritage

The Hanging Church, also known as **St. Virgin Mary's Coptic Orthodox Church**, is one of the most iconic and historically significant landmarks in Coptic Cairo. Its unique architecture, religious importance, and long history make it a must-see attraction for visitors exploring Old Cairo. The name "Hanging Church" comes from its unique location above the gatehouse of a Roman fortress, giving it a striking appearance and a sense of mystery that draws visitors from all over the world.

Location and How to Get There

The Hanging Church is located in the heart of Coptic Cairo, a historic area in Old Cairo known for its concentration of Christian landmarks. The church is part of a larger complex that includes other significant sites like the Coptic Museum, the Church of St. Sergius and Bacchus, and the Ben Ezra Synagogue. Its exact location is within walking distance of the Mar Girgis Metro Station, making it easily accessible by public transport.

If you prefer a taxi or ride-hailing service like Uber or Careem, you can reach the church directly from most parts of Cairo, including Downtown and Zamalek. Many guided tours of Coptic Cairo include the Hanging Church as a key stop, providing transportation and insightful commentary along the way.

What You Will See and Do
The Hanging Church is a place of incredible beauty, tranquility, and historical significance. As you approach, you'll notice its distinctive facade, featuring twin bell towers and a set of stairs that lead to the entrance. Once inside, you'll find a breathtaking blend of architectural styles, religious artifacts, and spiritual ambiance that make the church a unique and unforgettable experience.

The Entrance and Courtyard:
To reach the church, you'll climb a staircase that takes you above the Roman gatehouse. This elevated position is why the church is called "hanging," as it literally rests on the ruins of the ancient Babylon Fortress. The courtyard is decorated with

religious mosaics and features a peaceful atmosphere, setting the tone for your visit.

The Interior
Inside, the church is a masterpiece of Coptic architecture. The wooden ceiling is designed to resemble the hull of Noah's Ark, symbolizing salvation, while the marble pulpit, supported by 13 slender columns, represents Jesus and the 12 Apostles. The church is adorned with intricate woodwork, icons, and stained glass windows, creating a space that feels both sacred and artistic. Take your time to admire the intricate details of the altar screen, which is inlaid with ebony and ivory and considered a fine example of Coptic craftsmanship.

Religious Icons
One of the most striking features of the Hanging Church is its collection of religious icons, some of which date back centuries. These icons depict scenes from the Bible, as well as images of saints and martyrs, providing a visual representation of Coptic Christian traditions. The icons are beautifully preserved and arranged throughout the church, offering a glimpse into the spiritual and artistic heritage of Egypt's Christian community.

Historic Significance
The Hanging Church has served as the seat of the Coptic Orthodox Pope in the past and remains a significant spiritual center for Egypt's Christian community. It has witnessed centuries of history, including periods of persecution, resilience, and renewal. Exploring the church allows you to

connect with this rich history and appreciate its role in preserving Coptic traditions.

The Best Times to Visit

The Hanging Church is open year-round, and the best time to visit is during the cooler months from October to April. Visiting in the morning is ideal, as the church is less crowded, allowing you to enjoy its peaceful atmosphere and take in the details of the architecture and artifacts. Sundays and major Christian holidays may see more activity due to religious services, so plan your visit accordingly if you prefer a quieter experience. Late afternoons can also be a pleasant time to visit, as the lighting inside the church creates a warm and serene ambiance.

Ticket Information and Booking

Entry to the Hanging Church is free, though donations are appreciated to support its maintenance and preservation. Guided tours of Coptic Cairo, which often include the Hanging Church, may charge a fee but provide added value with expert commentary and insights into the area's history. It's worth checking with local tour operators or online platforms to find tours that suit your schedule and interests.

Facilities and Accessibility

The Hanging Church is equipped with basic facilities, including restrooms and seating areas where you can rest during your visit. The steps leading to the church may pose challenges for visitors with mobility issues, but efforts have been made to improve accessibility, such as ramps and pathways in certain areas of the Coptic Cairo complex. If you have specific needs, it's advisable to contact the church or a tour operator in advance.

Photography Tips and Rules
Photography is generally allowed inside the Hanging Church, but it's important to be respectful of the space and avoid using flash, which can damage the delicate icons and decorations. The church's interior offers many opportunities for capturing stunning details, from the intricate woodwork to the beautiful altar screen. For exterior shots, the courtyard and staircase provide excellent angles that highlight the church's unique location and architecture.

Cultural and Historical Context
The Hanging Church dates back to the 3rd century CE, making it one of the oldest churches in Egypt. Its location above the Babylon Fortress reflects the early Christian community's resilience and resourcefulness during times of persecution. Over the centuries, the church has undergone renovations and expansions, each adding to its architectural and historical significance.

The church has served as a spiritual and administrative hub for Coptic Christians, hosting important events and papal ceremonies. Its history is intertwined with that of Egypt's Christian community, offering a glimpse into their traditions, struggles, and contributions to the country's cultural fabric.

Rules, Etiquette, and Safety Tips
When visiting the Hanging Church, it's important to respect its religious significance and follow the rules. Dress modestly,

covering your shoulders and knees, as a sign of respect for this sacred space. Keep your voice low, especially during services or prayers, to maintain the church's peaceful atmosphere. Avoid touching the artifacts and icons, as they are delicate and hold great spiritual value. If you're unsure about anything, don't hesitate to ask the church staff or your guide for guidance.

Nearby Attractions
The Hanging Church is part of a larger area known as Coptic Cairo, which is rich with historic and religious landmarks. After exploring the church, you can visit the **Coptic Museum**, which houses a vast collection of artifacts that tell the story of Christianity in Egypt. The **Church of St. Sergius and Bacchus**, believed to be a resting place for the Holy Family during their flight to Egypt, is another nearby attraction worth seeing. The **Ben Ezra Synagogue**, with its own fascinating history, is also within walking distance.

Why You Should Visit
The Hanging Church is more than just an architectural wonder—it's a symbol of faith, history, and cultural heritage. Whether you're drawn by its stunning design, its spiritual significance, or its role in Egypt's history, a visit to this church offers a deeply enriching experience. As you walk through its halls and admire its intricate details, you'll gain a greater appreciation for the resilience and creativity of Egypt's Christian community. A visit to the Hanging Church is an unforgettable journey into the heart of Coptic Cairo, leaving

you with a sense of awe and connection to one of the world's oldest Christian traditions.

Ben Ezra Synagogue

The Ben Ezra Synagogue is one of the most important and fascinating landmarks in Old Cairo's Coptic district. This historic site, which has roots stretching back over a millennium, is steeped in religious, cultural, and historical significance. Visiting the synagogue provides a unique opportunity to explore a vital part of Egypt's Jewish heritage while admiring its stunning architecture and learning about its incredible history.

Location and How to Get There
The Ben Ezra Synagogue is located in Coptic Cairo, close to other significant landmarks like the Hanging Church and the Coptic Museum. This makes it easy to include in your itinerary if you're exploring the area. The synagogue is just a short walk from the Mar Girgis Metro Station, making public transportation a convenient option. If you're traveling from other parts of Cairo, taxis or ride-hailing services like Uber or Careem are reliable and easy ways to reach the site. Many guided tours of Coptic Cairo include the Ben Ezra Synagogue, ensuring a hassle-free visit with added historical context.

What You Will See and Do
As you approach the Ben Ezra Synagogue, you'll notice its distinct architectural style, which reflects a blend of Jewish, Islamic, and Coptic influences. The site is serene and

welcoming, providing a quiet retreat from the busy streets of Cairo.

The Exterior and Entrance
The synagogue is housed in a historic building that was originally a Christian church before it was repurposed as a Jewish place of worship. Its unassuming exterior contrasts with the grandeur of its interior, and the entrance is marked by intricate carvings and symbols that hint at its rich history.

The Main Prayer Hall
Inside, the synagogue's prayer hall is a breathtaking space filled with intricate details. The beautifully carved wooden ceiling, marble columns, and ornate chandeliers create a sense of elegance and reverence. The bimah (raised platform) is positioned at the center, surrounded by rows of wooden pews that once accommodated worshippers. The Ark of the Covenant, which holds the Torah scrolls, is located at the eastern end and is an important focal point of the synagogue.

Historic Artifacts and Documents
The Ben Ezra Synagogue is famously associated with the discovery of the **Cairo Geniza**, a collection of ancient Jewish manuscripts that were found in a hidden storage area within the synagogue. These documents, which include religious texts, letters, and legal contracts, provide invaluable insights into the lives of Jewish communities in the medieval Islamic world. While the original manuscripts have been moved to various museums and libraries around the world, the synagogue remains a key site in understanding Jewish history.

The Geniza Story
A visit to the synagogue is incomplete without learning about the Geniza, a hidden repository where discarded Jewish texts were stored. Discovered in the late 19th century, these documents shed light on everyday life, commerce, and religion in the medieval period. The story of the Geniza is told through interpretive panels and guides at the synagogue, making it an educational experience as well as a spiritual one.

Quiet Reflection
The synagogue is no longer an active place of worship, but it retains a sacred and peaceful atmosphere. Visitors are encouraged to take a moment of quiet reflection, soaking in the history and spirituality of the site.

The Best Times to Visit
The Ben Ezra Synagogue is open year-round, and the best time to visit is during the cooler months from October to April. Arriving early in the morning or mid-afternoon allows you to explore the site without large crowds. The synagogue's tranquil ambiance is best enjoyed in a quiet setting, so visiting outside of peak hours is ideal. Combining your visit with other nearby attractions in Coptic Cairo is a great way to make the most of your day.

Ticket Information and Booking
Entry to the Ben Ezra Synagogue is included in many combined tickets for Coptic Cairo landmarks, but it's advisable to confirm the exact fees at the site or through a tour

operator. Guided tours often include the synagogue as part of a larger itinerary, providing valuable insights into its history and significance. If you're visiting independently, entry fees are typically modest, making it an affordable attraction.

Facilities and Accessibility
The synagogue is well-maintained and equipped with basic facilities to ensure a comfortable visit. Restrooms are available nearby, and seating areas allow you to rest during your exploration. While the building's historic nature may present some challenges for visitors with mobility issues, efforts have been made to improve accessibility where possible. If you have specific needs, contacting the site in advance or arranging a guided tour can help ensure a smooth visit.

Photography Tips and Rules
Photography is generally allowed inside the synagogue, though flash and tripods may be restricted to protect the delicate interiors. The ornate details of the wooden carvings, chandeliers, and columns make excellent subjects for photos. For the best results, visit during the morning or early afternoon when natural light illuminates the space, highlighting its beauty. Always check with the staff or signage for specific rules regarding photography.

Cultural and Historical Context
The Ben Ezra Synagogue has a fascinating history that reflects the diverse and multicultural heritage of Cairo. Originally a Coptic Christian church, it was sold to the Jewish community in the 9th century and became a center of Jewish worship and scholarship. Its significance grew over the centuries, not only

as a religious institution but also as a repository of Jewish culture and knowledge.

The synagogue's location in Coptic Cairo highlights the coexistence of different religious communities in the area, which has long been a melting pot of faiths and traditions. The discovery of the Cairo Geniza further cemented the synagogue's importance, connecting it to a broader narrative of Jewish life in the Islamic world.

Rules, Etiquette, and Safety Tips
When visiting the Ben Ezra Synagogue, it's important to respect its religious and historical significance. Dress modestly, covering your shoulders and knees, and maintain a quiet demeanor to preserve the peaceful atmosphere. Avoid touching any artifacts or decorations, as they are delicate and historically valuable. If you're unsure about any rules, don't hesitate to ask the staff or your guide for clarification.

Nearby Attractions
The Ben Ezra Synagogue is surrounded by several other landmarks in Coptic Cairo, making it easy to explore multiple sites in one visit. The **Hanging Church**, just a short walk away, is a stunning example of Coptic Christian architecture. The **Coptic Museum** offers a deeper dive into the history of Christianity in Egypt, with an extensive collection of artifacts and art. The nearby **Church of St. Sergius and Bacchus**, believed to have sheltered the Holy Family during their flight to Egypt, is another must-see attraction.

Why You Should Visit

The Ben Ezra Synagogue is a unique and captivating destination that offers a window into Cairo's diverse history and cultural heritage. Its beautiful architecture, fascinating history, and connection to the Cairo Geniza make it a must-visit site for anyone interested in religion, history, or art. Whether you're admiring the ornate interiors, learning about the Geniza, or simply reflecting on the peaceful ambiance, a visit to the Ben Ezra Synagogue is an unforgettable experience that enriches your understanding of Cairo's rich and complex past.

Amr Ibn Al-As Mosque

The Amr Ibn Al-As Mosque, located in Old Cairo (Fustat), is one of the most historically significant landmarks in Egypt and a must-see for anyone interested in Islamic history and architecture. Built in 641 AD, this mosque was the first to be established in Africa, making it a cornerstone of the region's Islamic heritage. Visiting this site is an enriching experience, offering a glimpse into early Islamic architecture, a serene atmosphere for reflection, and a connection to a pivotal moment in history.

Location and How to Get There
The Amr Ibn Al-As Mosque is situated in the historic district of Old Cairo, specifically in the area once known as Fustat, Egypt's first Islamic capital. The mosque is close to other important landmarks in Coptic Cairo, such as the Hanging Church and the Ben Ezra Synagogue, making it an easy addition to your itinerary.

If you're traveling by public transport, the nearest metro station is Mar Girgis, which is just a short walk from the mosque. Alternatively, taxis and ride-hailing services like Uber or Careem offer convenient and affordable ways to reach the site from anywhere in Cairo. Guided tours of Old Cairo often include the mosque as part of their itinerary, providing transportation and detailed commentary about its history and architecture.

What You Will See and Do
When you arrive at the Amr Ibn Al-As Mosque, you'll be stepping into a piece of history that has stood the test of time for over 1,300 years. The mosque has undergone numerous renovations and expansions since it was first built, but it retains its original charm and spiritual significance. Here's what you can expect during your visit:

The Exterior and Courtyard
The mosque is surrounded by high walls and features a spacious courtyard at its center, a hallmark of early Islamic architecture. As you enter, you'll notice the simple yet elegant design of the mosque, which reflects the principles of Islamic aesthetics—clean lines, geometric patterns, and a focus on function and spirituality. The courtyard is open to the sky and surrounded by arcades with beautifully crafted columns.

The Prayer Hall:
The prayer hall is the heart of the mosque and is a tranquil space for worship and reflection. The hall is supported by rows of marble columns, many of which are believed to have been repurposed from ancient Roman and Byzantine structures. This blending of styles gives the mosque a unique character and showcases the resourcefulness of early Islamic builders. The mihrab, a niche indicating the direction of Mecca, is a focal point of the prayer hall and is intricately designed.

Historic Features and Renovations
Over the centuries, the Amr Ibn Al-As Mosque has been expanded and restored multiple times, reflecting the evolving

styles and needs of different eras. While the original structure was relatively modest, later additions included minarets, domes, and decorative elements that enhanced its beauty and functionality. Exploring the mosque gives you a sense of its layered history and its enduring role as a place of worship.

Spiritual Ambiance
The mosque remains an active place of prayer, attracting worshippers and visitors alike. Its peaceful atmosphere is perfect for quiet contemplation, whether you're sitting in the courtyard, walking through the arcades, or observing the faithful at prayer. The simplicity of the design enhances its spiritual appeal, making it a space where history and devotion come together.

The Best Times to Visit
The Amr Ibn Al-As Mosque is open to visitors throughout the year, and the best time to visit depends on your preferences. If you want to experience the mosque in a serene and quiet setting, visiting early in the morning is ideal. During the cooler months from October to April, the weather is more comfortable for exploring the mosque and the surrounding area. Fridays, which are holy days in Islam, may see larger crowds due to congregational prayers, so plan your visit accordingly.

Ticket Information and Booking
There is no admission fee to enter the Amr Ibn Al-As Mosque, as it is a functioning place of worship. However, donations are appreciated to help with the upkeep of the mosque. If you're

visiting as part of a guided tour of Old Cairo, your guide will likely include the mosque in the itinerary and provide additional historical context and insights.

Facilities and Accessibility
The mosque is well-maintained and offers basic facilities for visitors, including restrooms and areas for ablution (ritual washing). While the historic nature of the building may present challenges for visitors with mobility issues, the open layout and level ground of the courtyard and prayer hall make it relatively accessible. If you have specific needs, contacting the mosque or a tour operator in advance can help ensure a smooth visit.

Photography Tips and Rules
Photography is allowed in most parts of the mosque, but it's important to be respectful of the worshippers and the sacred nature of the site. Avoid using flash photography, as it can be disruptive, and focus on capturing the beautiful architectural details, such as the columns, arches, and mihrab. The courtyard is particularly photogenic, especially in the morning or late afternoon when the light creates striking shadows and highlights.

Cultural and Historical Context
The Amr Ibn Al-As Mosque was built by Amr Ibn Al-As, the commander who led the Muslim conquest of Egypt in 641 AD. The establishment of the mosque marked the founding of Fustat, the first Islamic capital of Egypt. Originally constructed from simple materials like palm leaves and mud

bricks, the mosque was a humble yet significant symbol of the new Islamic community in Egypt.

Over the centuries, the mosque grew in size and importance, reflecting Egypt's central role in the Islamic world. It became a center for religious education, legal discussions, and community gatherings. Today, it stands as a testament to the enduring legacy of Islam in Egypt and the region's rich cultural heritage.

Rules, Etiquette, and Safety Tips
As the Amr Ibn Al-As Mosque is an active place of worship, it's important to dress modestly and behave respectfully during your visit. Women should cover their heads and wear clothing that covers their arms and legs, while men should avoid wearing shorts or sleeveless shirts. Shoes must be removed before entering the prayer hall, and plastic bags are often provided to carry them. Keep your voice low and avoid disrupting worshippers. If you're unsure about any rules or customs, don't hesitate to ask the staff or your guide for guidance.

Nearby Attractions
The Amr Ibn Al-As Mosque is located in a historically rich area with many other attractions to explore. The Coptic Museum, which showcases the history of Christianity in Egypt, is a short distance away. You can also visit the Hanging Church, the Ben Ezra Synagogue, and the Church of St. Sergius and Bacchus, all of which are significant landmarks in

Coptic Cairo. These sites together provide a comprehensive look at the religious and cultural diversity of Old Cairo.

Why You Should Visit
The Amr Ibn Al-As Mosque is more than just a historic building—it's a symbol of Egypt's Islamic heritage and a place of spiritual significance. Whether you're admiring its architectural simplicity, learning about its history, or experiencing its peaceful ambiance, a visit to this mosque offers a unique and enriching experience. It's a journey into the early days of Islam in Africa and a reminder of the enduring connections between faith, culture, and community. Visiting the Amr Ibn Al-As Mosque is a must for anyone looking to understand the deep and multifaceted history of Cairo.

Things to Do: Visiting Religious Landmarks and Coptic Museum

Old Cairo, often referred to as Coptic Cairo, is one of the most historically and spiritually rich areas in Egypt. This part of the city is a treasure trove of religious landmarks and cultural heritage, offering visitors a unique opportunity to explore sites that have played a vital role in shaping Egypt's religious and cultural identity. Among the many experiences available in Coptic Cairo, visiting its religious landmarks and the renowned Coptic Museum stands out as an enlightening journey into the past. These experiences provide a deeper understanding of the area's significance, its long history, and the ways in which different faiths have coexisted and influenced one another over the centuries.

Coptic Cairo is home to some of the most important Christian landmarks in Egypt, many of which date back to the earliest days of Christianity. As you walk through this area, you will encounter a cluster of ancient churches, each with its own story and architectural beauty. The Hanging Church, also known as the Church of the Virgin Mary, is one of the most iconic and significant sites in Coptic Cairo. Built atop the ruins of a Roman fortress, the church is named for its unique construction that appears to "hang" above the ground. Inside, the church is adorned with intricate wooden carvings, marble columns, and religious icons that reflect centuries of devotion and craftsmanship. Visiting the Hanging Church offers not only a glimpse into the architectural ingenuity of early Coptic Christians but also a chance to connect with the spiritual traditions that continue to thrive in Egypt today.

Another notable landmark is the Church of St. Sergius and Bacchus, a site deeply rooted in Christian history. According to tradition, this church was built over a crypt that served as a refuge for the Holy Family during their flight to Egypt. This connection to the story of Mary, Joseph, and Jesus makes the church a place of great reverence for both local worshippers and international visitors. As you explore the church, you will notice its simple yet beautiful design, with wooden ceilings and stone walls that convey a sense of timelessness. The crypt itself is a powerful reminder of the enduring faith and resilience of early Christians who sought to preserve their beliefs under challenging circumstances.

In addition to these churches, Coptic Cairo is also home to the Ben Ezra Synagogue, a significant site for Egypt's Jewish community. Although primarily known for its Christian landmarks, this synagogue highlights the religious diversity that has characterized the area for centuries. According to tradition, the Ben Ezra Synagogue is located on the site where baby Moses was found in the Nile River. The building's design combines Islamic and Jewish architectural elements, creating a unique aesthetic that reflects the interconnectedness of Egypt's religious heritage. Visiting the synagogue is a valuable experience for those who wish to learn about the history of Judaism in Egypt and its contributions to the country's cultural fabric.

After exploring the religious landmarks, the Coptic Museum is an essential stop to deepen your understanding of the area's history and the development of Christianity in Egypt. The museum is housed in a beautifully restored building that blends traditional Islamic and Coptic architectural styles. Inside, you will find an extensive collection of artifacts that chronicle the history of Coptic Christianity from its beginnings in the first century AD to the present day. The museum's exhibits include manuscripts, textiles, carvings, and religious icons, each providing insight into the beliefs, practices, and artistic achievements of the Coptic community.

One of the most remarkable features of the Coptic Museum is its collection of manuscripts, including some of the oldest surviving copies of biblical texts. These manuscripts are displayed in carefully designed cases that protect them from damage while allowing visitors to admire their intricate calligraphy and illuminated decorations. The museum also houses a stunning array of Coptic textiles, which were highly prized in the ancient world for their intricate patterns and vibrant colors. These textiles provide a glimpse into the daily lives of early Christians, showcasing their skills in weaving and their appreciation for beauty.

As you move through the museum, you will also encounter stone carvings and wooden panels that once adorned ancient churches and monasteries. These pieces often feature intricate designs that blend Christian symbols with motifs drawn from Egyptian and Greco-Roman traditions, illustrating the cultural exchanges that shaped Coptic art. The museum's collection of religious icons is another highlight, offering a visual representation of the faith and devotion that has sustained the Coptic community for centuries. These icons, often painted on wood and adorned with gold leaf, depict saints, angels, and biblical scenes with a sense of spirituality and grace that is deeply moving.

Visiting the religious landmarks and the Coptic Museum in Old Cairo is not just an exploration of history—it is an experience that allows you to witness the enduring legacy of faith and culture in Egypt. As you walk through the ancient streets, step into sacred spaces, and admire the artistry of the museum's exhibits, you will gain a deeper appreciation for the resilience and creativity of the Coptic community. This journey is both educational and inspiring, offering a rare opportunity to connect with a heritage that has shaped not only Egypt but also the broader history of Christianity and the region as a whole. Whether you are drawn by spiritual curiosity, historical interest, or a desire to experience the beauty of Coptic art and architecture, this experience in Old Cairo will leave you with lasting memories and a richer understanding of Egypt's diverse cultural identity.

Accommodation Options

Luxury Stays: Upscale Hotels with Cultural Ambiance in Old Cairo (Coptic Cairo), Cairo, Egypt

Old Cairo, also known as Coptic Cairo, is a historic and spiritual heart of the city, filled with centuries-old churches, synagogues, and mosques. Staying in this area offers you an unparalleled connection to Cairo's cultural and religious heritage, along with modern luxury accommodations that provide exceptional comfort and services. If you're looking for upscale hotels with a cultural ambiance, here are some of the best options to consider.

1. Marriott Mena House, Cairo
Price Range: Approx. $250–$500 per night.
Amenities: Marriott Mena House offers a luxurious experience with rooms and suites that blend modern elegance and traditional design elements. Many accommodations provide private balconies with views of the Pyramids of Giza.

Guests can enjoy a large outdoor pool, a full-service spa, and multiple dining options, including an Italian restaurant and an all-day dining venue. The property also features lush gardens, perfect for a tranquil retreat.

Best Area to Stay: Although located closer to Giza, the hotel's serene and culturally rich environment makes it a fantastic choice for travelers who want to experience Cairo's historic and iconic attractions. The nearby Pyramids provide a stunning backdrop, and it's a short drive to Coptic Cairo.
Contact Details:
Website: Marriott Mena House, Cairo
Phone: +20 2 33773222
Email: reservations.menahouse@marriott.com

2. St. Regis Cairo
Price Range: Approx. $300–$600 per night.
Amenities: This ultra-luxurious hotel offers an elegant mix of contemporary design and cultural accents, with spacious rooms and suites overlooking the Nile or city skyline. Guests have access to a world-class spa, a rooftop infinity pool, and fine dining options, including Italian and Middle Eastern cuisines. Personalized butler service ensures your stay is as comfortable as possible.

Best Area to Stay: Located along the Corniche, the St. Regis Cairo offers easy access to Old Cairo's historic sites, including the Hanging Church and Ben Ezra Synagogue. Its central location makes it an excellent base for exploring cultural landmarks and enjoying modern luxuries.

Contact Details:
Website: St. Regis Cairo
Phone: +20 2 25778899
Email: reservations.cairo@stregis.com

3. Al Masa Hotel
Price Range: Approx. $200–$350 per night.
Amenities: Al Masa Hotel offers an upscale experience with rooms designed to reflect local architectural heritage and modern comforts. Amenities include an outdoor swimming pool, a fitness center, and beautifully landscaped gardens. Guests can enjoy a complimentary breakfast buffet and dine at the on-site restaurant offering authentic Egyptian dishes.

Best Area to Stay: Located near Coptic Cairo, the hotel is convenient for exploring attractions like the Church of St. Sergius and Bacchus, the Coptic Museum, and the Amr Ibn Al-As Mosque. Its proximity to key historic sites makes it ideal for culturally inclined travelers.
Contact Details:
Website: Al Masa Hotel
Phone: +20 2 23789567
Email: info@almasahotel.com

4. Conrad Cairo
Price Range: Approx. $200–$400 per night.
Amenities: Conrad Cairo offers luxurious accommodations with Nile views, modern amenities, and an excellent cultural ambiance. Rooms are equipped with flat-screen TVs, high-speed Wi-Fi, and spacious bathrooms. The hotel features an

outdoor pool, a full-service spa, and multiple restaurants offering everything from fine dining to casual fare.

Best Area to Stay: Situated along the Nile, Conrad Cairo is a short drive to Old Cairo, making it an ideal base for exploring both cultural and modern attractions in the city.

Contact Details:
Website: Conrad Cairo
Phone: +20 2 25808000
Email: reservations.cairo@conradhotels.com

5. Villa Belle Epoque
Price Range: Approx. $250–$400 per night.
Amenities: This boutique hotel offers a luxurious and intimate atmosphere with rooms styled in early 20th-century Egyptian decor. Amenities include an outdoor pool, a garden restaurant serving organic produce, and complimentary Wi-Fi throughout the property. Villa Belle Epoque provides a unique blend of comfort and cultural sophistication, making it a standout option for discerning travelers.

Best Area to Stay: Located in Maadi, near Old Cairo, this hotel offers a peaceful retreat while being close enough to explore Coptic landmarks like the Hanging Church and the Ben Ezra Synagogue.

Contact Details:
Website: Villa Belle Epoque
Phone: +20 2 23782722

Email: contact@villabelleepoque.com

These luxury accommodations in and near Old Cairo provide an immersive experience that combines cultural ambiance with top-notch services. Whether you're drawn to the heritage-filled streets of Coptic Cairo or prefer the serene backdrop of the Nile, these hotels ensure you'll enjoy a luxurious stay while exploring one of the city's most historic areas. With personalized service, exquisite amenities, and prime locations, these options cater to travelers who want the best of Cairo's history and hospitality.

Mid-Range Options: Cozy Hotels with Easy Access to Historic Sites in Old Cairo (Coptic Cairo), Cairo, Egypt

If you're visiting Old Cairo (Coptic Cairo) and looking for accommodations that balance comfort, affordability, and convenience, there are several mid-range hotels that are perfect for your stay. These cozy properties provide modern amenities while keeping you close to the area's historic sites, ensuring you can explore landmarks like the Hanging Church, the Coptic Museum, and Ben Ezra Synagogue with ease. Here are some excellent mid-range options to consider:

1. Aton Plaza Hotel
Price Range: Approx. $70–$100 per night.
Amenities: Aton Plaza Hotel offers cozy rooms with modern furnishings, air conditioning, free Wi-Fi, and flat-screen TVs. Guests can enjoy a complimentary breakfast buffet and 24-hour room service. The hotel features a rooftop terrace with views of the surrounding area and a comfortable lounge for relaxing after a day of sightseeing.

Best Area to Stay: Located within a short walk of Coptic Cairo's historic landmarks, including the Hanging Church and the Amr Ibn Al-As Mosque, this hotel is ideal for those who want to explore the area on foot. It's also close to public transportation for easy access to other parts of Cairo.
Contact Details:
Website: Aton Plaza Hotel
Phone: +20 2 25771122
Email: info@atonplazahotel.com

2. Tulip House Coptic Cairo
Price Range: Approx. $80–$120 per night.
Amenities: This charming boutique hotel features comfortable rooms with Egyptian-inspired decor, free Wi-Fi, and en-suite bathrooms. A complimentary breakfast is served each morning, and guests can relax in the hotel's peaceful courtyard garden. The staff provides personalized service, including tour recommendations and transportation arrangements.

Best Area to Stay: Situated near the Coptic Museum, Tulip House is perfectly positioned for travelers interested in exploring Old Cairo's cultural and religious landmarks. Its quiet location offers a welcome escape from the hustle and bustle of the city.

Contact Details:
Website: Tulip House Coptic Cairo
Phone: +20 2 35870934
Email: reservations@tuliphousecopticcairo.com

3. Concorde El Salam Hotel Cairo
Price Range: Approx. $90–$130 per night.
Amenities: This mid-range hotel provides spacious rooms with air conditioning, flat-screen TVs, and free Wi-Fi. Guests can enjoy a complimentary breakfast, an outdoor pool, and a fitness center. The hotel also has an on-site restaurant serving Egyptian and international cuisine, as well as a café for light snacks and drinks.

Best Area to Stay: Located a short drive from Old Cairo, Concorde El Salam Hotel offers easy access to the district's historic sites while providing modern comforts and a relaxing atmosphere.

Contact Details:
Website: Concorde El Salam Hotel Cairo
Phone: +20 2 27771123
Email: reservations@concordecairo.com

4. Holy Land Hotel Cairo
Price Range: Approx. $75–$110 per night.
Amenities: This hotel offers clean and comfortable rooms with free Wi-Fi, air conditioning, and private balconies. Guests can enjoy a daily breakfast buffet, as well as access to an on-site restaurant serving traditional Egyptian dishes. The hotel also provides a 24-hour front desk and free parking for added convenience.
Best Area to Stay: Holy Land Hotel is located near the Mar Girgis Metro Station, making it easy to explore Old Cairo's attractions and other parts of the city. The nearby streets are filled with shops and cafes, adding to the charm of the neighborhood.

Contact Details:
Website: Holy Land Hotel Cairo
Phone: +20 2 25879012
Email: contact@holylandhotelcairo.com

5. St. George Hotel Coptic Cairo
Price Range: Approx. $85–$120 per night.
Amenities: This welcoming hotel features cozy rooms with Nile or city views, free Wi-Fi, and private bathrooms. Guests can enjoy a complimentary breakfast, a rooftop terrace, and a small fitness center. The hotel staff is known for their warm hospitality and can assist with tour bookings and transportation.

Best Area to Stay: Located in the heart of Coptic Cairo, St. George Hotel is just steps away from iconic sites like the Ben Ezra Synagogue and the Hanging Church, making it an ideal choice for history and culture enthusiasts.

Contact Details:
Website: St. George Hotel Coptic Cairo
Phone: +20 2 25788910
Email: reservations@stgeorgehotelcoptic.com

These mid-range hotels in and around Old Cairo offer a combination of comfort, affordability, and easy access to the district's historic landmarks. Whether you're exploring ancient churches, visiting museums, or enjoying the local charm, these accommodations provide everything you need for a pleasant and memorable stay in this culturally rich area of Cairo. With their prime locations and thoughtful amenities, these hotels are excellent choices for travelers looking to immerse themselves in the history of Coptic Cairo while enjoying modern conveniences.

Budget Choices: Affordable Stays for Culture Enthusiasts in Old Cairo (Coptic Cairo), Cairo, Egypt

Old Cairo (Coptic Cairo) is a treasure trove of history, culture, and spirituality, making it a prime destination for culture enthusiasts. If you're traveling on a budget, there are several affordable accommodations that provide excellent value, comfortable amenities, and proximity to the area's historic landmarks. These budget-friendly stays are perfect for exploring iconic attractions like the Hanging Church, Ben Ezra Synagogue, and the Coptic Museum without stretching your travel budget. Here are some excellent choices:

1. Mesho Inn Hostel
Price Range: Approx. $15–$30 per night.
Amenities: Mesho Inn Hostel offers clean and basic accommodations, with free Wi-Fi, air conditioning, and shared or private bathrooms. Guests are provided with complimentary breakfast and have access to a communal kitchen. The hostel's friendly staff can help arrange tours and provide useful travel tips.

Best Area to Stay: Located near the Mar Girgis Metro Station, Mesho Inn is within easy walking distance of Coptic Cairo's main attractions, including the Coptic Museum and the Hanging Church. The convenient location makes it ideal for culture enthusiasts exploring the area.

Contact Details:
Website: Mesho Inn Hostel

Phone: +20 2 27381234
Email: info@meshoinnhostel.com

2. Holy Family Hotel
Price Range: Approx. $20–$40 per night.
Amenities: Holy Family Hotel provides budget-friendly rooms with free Wi-Fi, air conditioning, and private or shared bathrooms. Guests can enjoy a simple breakfast each morning and access a rooftop terrace with views of the surrounding area. The hotel also offers a small library and a lounge for relaxing after a day of sightseeing.

Best Area to Stay: Situated near the Church of St. Sergius and Bacchus, this hotel is perfect for those wanting to immerse themselves in the spiritual and historical essence of Coptic Cairo. Public transport options are nearby, allowing easy access to other parts of the city.

Contact Details:
Website: Holy Family Hotel
Phone: +20 2 25781122
Email: reservations@holyfamilyhotel.com

3. Cairo Moonlight Hostel
Price Range: Approx. $18–$35 per night.
Amenities: This cozy hostel offers both dormitory and private rooms with essential amenities such as free Wi-Fi, comfortable bedding, and air conditioning. A complimentary breakfast is served daily, and the property has a shared lounge area and a

24-hour reception desk. Guided tours of Coptic Cairo can also be arranged through the hostel.

Best Area to Stay: Cairo Moonlight Hostel is located close to Tahrir Square, providing easy access to Old Cairo via public transport. Its central location also allows you to explore the surrounding neighborhoods and enjoy local eateries.

Contact Details:
Website: Cairo Moonlight Hostel
Phone: +20 2 27379876
Email: info@cairomoonlighthostel.com

4. Traveler's Joy Guesthouse
Price Range: Approx. $25–$45 per night.
Amenities: Traveler's Joy Guesthouse provides budget-friendly accommodations with private rooms featuring air conditioning, free Wi-Fi, and simple furnishings. A light breakfast is included, and there is a small kitchen available for guests to prepare meals. The guesthouse also has a communal lounge for socializing or planning your day.

Best Area to Stay: Located in the heart of Coptic Cairo, this guesthouse is within walking distance of the area's historic churches and synagogues. Its proximity to Mar Girgis Metro Station makes it easy to explore further afield.

Contact Details:
Website: Traveler's Joy Guesthouse
Phone: +20 2 35870987

Email: contact@travelersjoyguesthouse.com

5. New Cairo Budget Inn
Price Range: Approx. $20–$35 per night.
Amenities: This budget inn offers clean, no-frills accommodations with free Wi-Fi, air conditioning, and private bathrooms. Guests can enjoy a daily breakfast and take advantage of the 24-hour front desk. The property also offers free maps and guidance for exploring Old Cairo.

Best Area to Stay: New Cairo Budget Inn is located near the entrance to Coptic Cairo, making it a convenient choice for exploring attractions like the Coptic Museum, the Hanging Church, and Ben Ezra Synagogue.

Contact Details:
Website: New Cairo Budget Inn
Phone: +20 2 25781234
Email: reservations@newcairobudgetinn.com
These affordable accommodations provide a great base for culture enthusiasts exploring Old Cairo. With their proximity to historic sites, comfortable amenities, and reasonable prices, these options ensure that you can focus on enjoying the area's rich history and cultural charm without worrying about your budget. Whether you prefer a hostel, guesthouse, or budget hotel, you'll find something to suit your needs and enhance your stay in Coptic Cairo.

CHAPTER 3

ITINERARIES FOR EVERY TRAVELER

How To Craft Your Desired Itinerary

Crafting your own travel itinerary is one of the most rewarding parts of planning a trip. It allows you to create a journey that reflects your interests, priorities, and pace. Cairo, with its immense variety of attractions and experiences, is the perfect destination to design a personalized adventure. Taking the time to craft an itinerary that suits your preferences ensures that every moment of your visit is meaningful and aligned with what excites and inspires you most. This guide will provide practical advice on how to build an itinerary tailored to your taste, with the flexibility to adjust as needed.

The first step to creating the best itinerary for yourself is understanding what type of traveler you are. Think about what interests you most—whether it's history, food, shopping, outdoor activities, or a mix of everything. Reflect on how you prefer to spend your days. Do you enjoy packing in as many sights as possible, or do you prefer a slower pace, taking time to soak in the atmosphere of each place? Being clear about what excites you will help you prioritize the experiences that matter most.

Next, start by gathering information about Cairo's main attractions and the hidden gems you might not have heard of before. Research the historical landmarks, vibrant markets, cultural experiences, and scenic spots the city has to offer. Write down the ones that catch your interest. For example, if history fascinates you, include places like the Great Pyramids, the Egyptian Museum, and the Citadel. If local culture appeals to you, explore areas like Khan El Khalili Bazaar or Al-Moez Street. For food lovers, don't miss Cairo's renowned street food spots and traditional restaurants. The goal is to create a list of possibilities without worrying yet about how to fit them all in.

Once you have a list, think about how much time you have for your trip. Be realistic about how many places you can visit each day without feeling rushed. Cairo is a large, bustling city, and getting around can take time. Factor in transportation, meal breaks, and some downtime to relax. A good rule of thumb is to group attractions that are close to each other so you can save time traveling between them. For example, you might dedicate a day to exploring the Giza Plateau, where the Great Pyramids, the Sphinx, and the Solar Boat Museum are all located, while another day can be spent in Islamic Cairo, visiting the Citadel and nearby mosques.

Budgeting is another important aspect of crafting your itinerary. Think about how much you want to spend on activities, food, transportation, and accommodations. Some attractions may require entry fees, while others are free to explore. Knowing the costs ahead of time helps you allocate your resources wisely and avoid surprises. For travelers on a tight budget, Cairo offers plenty of affordable experiences, such as enjoying a walk along the Nile or exploring local markets. If you're willing to splurge, consider guided tours, private transportation, or upscale dining experiences.

Flexibility is key to a well-crafted itinerary. While it's helpful to have a plan, it's equally important to leave room for spontaneity. You might discover an intriguing café, a lively street performance, or a friendly local who recommends a place you hadn't heard of. Allowing time for unplanned moments makes your trip more enjoyable and memorable. Your itinerary should serve as a guide, not a rigid schedule.

Another crucial element to consider is the time of year you're visiting. Cairo's weather can influence your plans. Summers are hot, so you might want to schedule outdoor activities for early mornings or late afternoons. Winters are mild and more comfortable for sightseeing throughout the day. Check for local holidays or events that could affect opening hours or crowd levels at popular attractions. This information helps you avoid unnecessary stress and ensures you get the most out of your visit.

As you refine your plan, use tools like maps, apps, and a detailed itinerary planner to organize your days. Mark the locations of attractions, transportation routes, and places to eat. Having this information at your fingertips makes navigating the city much easier. To save time and energy, consider pre-booking tickets for popular attractions or arranging transportation in advance.

Finally, remember that the best itinerary is the one that reflects your unique preferences and interests. Whether you want to dive into Cairo's rich history, explore its vibrant culture, or simply enjoy the local food and atmosphere, your trip should be about what matters most to you. With thoughtful planning, you can create a journey that feels personal and fulfilling, filled with experiences that you'll cherish long after you leave. By taking the time to craft your own itinerary, you gain the freedom to explore Cairo on your own terms. With the help of the 14-page itinerary planner included with this guide, you'll have all the tools you need to organize your thoughts, prioritize your activities, and create a plan that ensures every day is filled with excitement and discovery. This is your chance to design a trip that is as unique and unforgettable as the city of Cairo itself. Start planning today and prepare to experience the adventure of a lifetime.

Bonus: 14-Day Itinerary Planner

To make trip planning even easier, we've included a 14-Day Itinerary Planner that you can access by scanning the QR code below. This comprehensive planner helps you organize your trip day by day, with suggested activities, meal stops, and insider tips for each region of Cairo.

What You'll Find in the Planner:
- A fully customizable template for 14 days.
- Space to jot down your own notes and preferences.

Scan the QR code to get started and enjoy the convenience of having your perfect Cairo trip at your fingertips!

How to Access the Planner

Follow these simple steps to scan the QR code and access your itinerary planner:

1. Open Your Camera

Use your smartphone or tablet's camera app. Most modern devices automatically detect QR codes without additional apps.

2. Scan the QR Code

Point your camera at the QR code, ensuring the full code is visible within the frame. Hold your device steady until a notification or link appears on your screen.

3. Tap the Link
Once the QR code is recognized, a link will pop up. Tap the link, and it will take you directly to the page where the planner can be accessed.

4. Download or Print
One the planner page, download the file to your device. You can either save it for future use or print it immediately to start customizing your itinerary.

3-Day Itinerary for Cairo, Egypt: A Solo Traveler's Guide

Cairo, Egypt's bustling capital, offers a mix of ancient history, vibrant culture, and modern city life. A 3-day visit gives you enough time to experience its must-see attractions, savor local flavors, and explore its dynamic neighborhoods. This itinerary is designed to balance sightseeing and relaxation, ensuring a memorable trip. Practical tips for transportation, costs, and meals are included to help you navigate Cairo confidently as a solo traveler.

Day 1

Morning: The Great Pyramids and the Sphinx
What to See: Start your adventure at the Giza Plateau, home to the iconic Great Pyramids and the Sphinx. Arrive early to beat the crowds and enjoy the cooler morning hours.

Transportation: Take a taxi or Uber from central Cairo. Approximate cost: EGP 150–200 ($5–7). Shared minivans are also available for a lower cost but may take longer.

Entry Fees: EGP 240 ($8) for general admission; additional fees for access to the Great Pyramid or the Solar Boat Museum.

Tip: Wear comfortable walking shoes and bring a hat, sunscreen, and water.

Lunch: Traditional Egyptian Cuisine
Where to Eat: Head to Felfela in Giza for dishes like koshari (a mix of rice, lentils, and pasta) or grilled meats. Average cost: EGP 100–150 ($3–5).

Recommendation: Try the Egyptian falafel with tahini sauce.
Afternoon: The Solar Boat Museum

What to See: Visit this museum near the Great Pyramid to view a reconstructed ancient Egyptian boat used for pharaohs' journeys in the afterlife.

Entry Fee: EGP 100 ($3).
Transportation: Walking distance from the pyramids.
Evening: Nile River Cruise

What to Do: Enjoy a relaxing evening with a dinner cruise on the Nile, complete with traditional music and a tanoura dance show.

Cost: EGP 400–600 ($13–20), depending on the cruise.

Tip: Book in advance through reputable companies or your hotel.

Day 2

Morning: The Egyptian Museum
What to See: Discover an extensive collection of artifacts, including treasures from King Tutankhamun's tomb. Allocate 2–3 hours for a thorough visit.

Entry Fee: EGP 200 ($6); additional fees for photography or access to the Mummy Room.

Transportation: Located in Tahrir Square, easily accessible by taxi, Uber, or metro. Metro fare: EGP 5 ($0.20).

Tip: Arrive when the museum opens to avoid crowds.

Lunch: Local Delights
Where to Eat: Try Abou Tarek, famous for its koshari. Cost: EGP 50–80 ($2–3).

Tip: Opt for a light meal to keep your energy up for the afternoon.

Afternoon: Islamic Cairo and the Citadel of Salah El-Din
What to See: Visit the Citadel, a historic fortress featuring the stunning Mohammed Ali Mosque with panoramic views of Cairo.

Entry Fee: EGP 180 ($6).

Transportation: A short taxi or Uber ride from Tahrir Square. **Cost**: EGP 50–70 ($2–3).

Tip: Dress modestly, especially if visiting mosques.

Evening: Khan El Khalili Bazaar
What to Do: Stroll through Cairo's most famous market, where you can shop for spices, jewelry, and souvenirs. Don't forget to haggle!

Dinner: Enjoy tea and traditional Egyptian pastries at El Fishawi Café in the heart of the bazaar. Cost: EGP 50–100 ($2–4).

Day 3

Morning: Coptic Cairo
What to See: Explore the Hanging Church, Ben Ezra Synagogue, and the Coptic Museum to delve into Egypt's Christian history.

Entry Fee: Most sites are free; the Coptic Museum charges EGP 100 ($3).
Transportation: Take the metro to Mar Girgis station for EGP 5 ($0.20).

Tip: Allocate 2–3 hours to fully explore the area.

Lunch: Authentic Egyptian Meal

Where to Eat: Eat at Sobhy Kaber, a popular spot for traditional Egyptian dishes like grilled kofta and molokhia (green soup).
Cost: EGP 150–200 ($5–7).

Afternoon: Al-Azhar Park
What to Do: Spend a relaxing afternoon at this beautifully landscaped park, with views of the Citadel and Islamic Cairo's skyline.

Entry Fee: EGP 30 ($1).

Tip: Bring a book or enjoy a refreshing drink at one of the park's cafes.

Evening: Dinner with a View
What to Do: Wrap up your trip with dinner at the rooftop restaurant of the Nile Ritz-Carlton, overlooking the city skyline.
Cost: EGP 400–600 ($13–20) for a memorable meal.

Transportation: Take a taxi or Uber back to your accommodation. Cost: EGP 50–80 ($2–3).

7-Day Itinerary

Cairo is a city steeped in history and culture, offering a unique blend of ancient wonders, bustling markets, and modern attractions. This 7-day itinerary is designed to help you explore the city's highlights at a comfortable pace while balancing sightseeing with relaxation. Practical details, transportation tips, and meal recommendations are included to ensure you feel confident navigating Cairo as a solo traveler.

Day 1: Arrival and Exploring Downtown Cairo

Morning: Arrive and settle into your hotel. Rest and prepare for an exciting week ahead.

Afternoon: Stroll around **Tahrir Square** and visit the **Egyptian Museum** to explore ancient artifacts, including treasures from King Tutankhamun's tomb.

Entry Fee: EGP 200 ($6); additional fees for the Mummy Room.

Transportation: Uber or taxi to Tahrir Square; cost: EGP 50–80 ($2–3).

Evening: Enjoy a traditional Egyptian dinner at **Abou Tarek**, famous for koshari. Cost: EGP 80–120 ($3–4).

Day 2

Morning: Visit the **Giza Plateau** to see the Great Pyramids, the Sphinx, and the Solar Boat Museum.

Entry Fee: EGP 240 ($8) for general admission; additional fees for pyramid interiors or the Solar Boat Museum.

Transportation: Uber or taxi from central Cairo; cost: EGP 150–200 ($5–7).

Tip: Arrive early to avoid crowds and wear comfortable walking shoes.

Afternoon: Have lunch at **Felfela Giza**, offering Egyptian classics. Cost: EGP 100–150 ($3–5).

Evening: Optional **Sound and Light Show** at the pyramids.
Cost: EGP 350–450 ($11–15).

Day 3: Islamic Cairo and the Citadel

Morning: Explore **Islamic Cairo**, starting with the **Citadel of Salah El-Din** and the **Mohammed Ali Mosque**.

Entry Fee: EGP 180 ($6).

Transportation: Taxi or Uber; cost: EGP 50–80 ($2–3).

Afternoon: Visit **Sultan Hassan Mosque** and **Al-Rifa'i Mosque**, located nearby. Allocate 1–2 hours for both.
Entry Fee: Combined ticket for EGP 100 ($3).
Lunch: Enjoy local dishes at **El Fishawi Café** in Khan El Khalili bazaar. Cost: EGP 50–100 ($2–4).

Evening: Shop for souvenirs at **Khan El Khalili Bazaar** and soak in the lively atmosphere.

Day 4: Coptic Cairo

Morning: Explore **Coptic Cairo**, including the **Hanging Church**, **Ben Ezra Synagogue**, and the **Coptic Museum**.

Entry Fee: EGP 100 ($3) for the museum; other sites are free.

Transportation: Take the metro to Mar Girgis station; cost: EGP 5 ($0.20).

Afternoon: Have lunch at a local café in the area, such as **Kazaz**, for light Egyptian fare. Cost: EGP 70–120 ($2–4).

Evening: Relax in **Al-Azhar Park**, a beautifully landscaped space with stunning views of the Cairo skyline.

Entry Fee: EGP 30 ($1).

Dinner: Dine at **Citadel View Restaurant** inside the park. Cost: EGP 200–300 ($7–10).

Day 5: Day Trip to Saqqara and Memphis

Morning: Take a day trip to **Saqqara** to see the Step Pyramid and explore **Memphis**, the ancient capital of Egypt.

Entry Fee: EGP 200 ($6) for Saqqara; EGP 80 ($2.50) for Memphis.

Transportation: Book a private car or tour; cost: EGP 400–700 ($13–23).

Tip: Bring water and snacks for the trip.

Lunch: Stop at a nearby local eatery offering grilled meats and Egyptian bread. Cost: EGP 120–150 ($4–5).

Evening: Return to Cairo and enjoy a relaxed evening at your hotel or explore a nearby café.

Day 6

Morning: Visit the **Cairo Tower** for panoramic views of the city.

Entry Fee: EGP 200 ($6).

Transportation: Uber or taxi; cost: EGP 50–80 ($2–3).

Afternoon: Explore the trendy neighborhood of **Zamalek**, known for its art galleries, boutiques, and riverside cafes.

Lunch: Try **Zooba**, a modern take on Egyptian street food. Cost: EGP 120–180 ($4–6).

Evening: Take a felucca ride on the Nile to unwind and enjoy the sunset.
Cost: EGP 300–500 ($10–16) for a private boat.

Day 7: Shopping and Farewell

Morning: Spend your final morning shopping at **City Stars Mall** or **Mall of Arabia** for modern and traditional items.

Transportation: Uber or taxi; cost: EGP 150–200 ($5–7).

Lunch: Enjoy a farewell meal at **Sequoia**, a stylish restaurant overlooking the Nile in Zamalek. Cost: EGP 300–500 ($10–16).

Afternoon: Visit any attractions you missed or relax before your departure.

Evening: Head to the airport. Transportation options include Uber or pre-arranged shuttle; cost: EGP 200–300 ($7–10).

14-Day Itinerary: Cairo and Beyond (Luxor, Alexandria, and Aswan)

Egypt offers an extraordinary blend of ancient wonders, vibrant cities, and breathtaking landscapes. This 14-day itinerary is designed to help you experience the highlights of Cairo, Luxor, Alexandria, and Aswan, with a comfortable mix of exploration and downtime. It provides detailed guidance on transportation, costs, and activities, making it perfect for solo travelers looking to navigate Egypt confidently.

Day 1-3

Day 1: Arrival and Introduction to Cairo
Morning: Arrive in Cairo and check into your hotel. Rest and adjust after your journey.

Afternoon: Explore **Tahrir Square** and visit the **Egyptian Museum** to marvel at treasures from King Tutankhamun's tomb.

Entry Fee: EGP 200 ($6).

Transportation: Uber from your accommodation; cost: EGP 50–80 ($2–3).

Evening: Dine at **Abou Tarek**, known for its authentic koshari. Cost: EGP 80–120 ($3–4).

Day 2

Morning: Visit the **Great Pyramids**, the **Sphinx**, and the **Solar Boat Museum**.

Entry Fee: EGP 240 ($8) for general access; additional fees for pyramid interiors.

Transportation: Uber or private taxi; cost: EGP 150–200 ($5–7).

Afternoon: Lunch at **Felfela** in Giza. Cost: EGP 100–150 ($3–5).

Evening: Optional **Sound and Light Show** at the pyramids. **Cost**: EGP 350–450 ($11–15).

Day 3

Morning: Explore the **Citadel of Salah El-Din** and the **Mohammed Ali Mosque**.

Entry Fee: EGP 180 ($6).

Afternoon: Wander through **Khan El Khalili Bazaar** and have lunch at **El Fishawi Café**.

Evening: Relax at **Al-Azhar Park** for sunset views.

Day 4-5

Morning: Take a train from Ramses Station to Alexandria (approx. 2.5 hours).

Cost: EGP 100–150 ($3–5).

Afternoon: Visit the **Bibliotheca Alexandrina** and **Pompey's Pillar**.

Entry Fee: EGP 80 ($2.50).

Evening: Enjoy seafood at **Fish Market Restaurant** by the harbor. Cost: EGP 200–300 ($7–10).

Day 5: Exploring Alexandria
Morning: Tour the **Catacombs of Kom El Shoqafa** and **Qaitbay Citadel**.

Entry Fee: EGP 100 ($3) for the catacombs; EGP 80 ($2.50) for the citadel.

Afternoon: Relax at the **Corniche** and have lunch at **Trianon Café**.

Evening: Return to Cairo by train.

Day 6-9

Day 6: Travel to Luxor
Morning: Take a flight or an overnight train to Luxor.
Cost: Flight approx. $100; train approx. EGP 300–400 ($10–13).
Afternoon: Check into your hotel and relax.

Evening: Stroll along the **Corniche** or visit **Luxor Temple** at sunset.

Day 7: West Bank Wonders
Morning: Explore the **Valley of the Kings**, including Tutankhamun's tomb.

Entry Fee: EGP 240 ($8) for general access; additional EGP 300 ($10) for Tutankhamun's tomb.

Afternoon: Visit **Hatshepsut's Temple** and the **Colossi of Memnon**.

Transportation: Book a private guide or taxi; cost: EGP 500–700 ($16–23).

Day 8: East Bank Gems
Morning: Visit **Karnak Temple**, one of Egypt's largest temple complexes.

Entry Fee: EGP 200 ($6).

Afternoon: Have lunch at **Sofra Restaurant**, serving traditional Egyptian food.

Evening: Relax at your hotel or enjoy a felucca ride on the Nile.

Day 9: Optional Hot Air Balloon Ride
Morning: Take a sunrise hot air balloon ride over Luxor's temples and landscapes.

Cost: Approx. $100.

Afternoon: Fly or take a train to Aswan.

Day 10-12

Day 10: Discover Aswan
Morning: Visit the **Philae Temple** and the **Aswan High Dam**.

Entry Fee: EGP 200 ($6) for Philae; EGP 50 ($2) for the dam.

Afternoon: Explore the **Nubian Museum**.

Evening: Dine at **El Dokka Restaurant**, offering views of the Nile.

Day 11: Abu Simbel
Morning: Take an early-morning trip to **Abu Simbel** (approx. 3 hours by car).

Entry Fee: EGP 240 ($8).

Transportation: Book a tour or private transfer; cost: $50–$80.

Day 12: Relaxation
Morning: Visit the **Elephantine Island** and **Nubian villages**.
Evening: Take a train or flight back to Cairo.

Day 13-14

Day 13: Modern Cairo
Morning: Visit the **Cairo Tower** for panoramic views.

Afternoon: Explore the **Museum of Islamic Art**.
Evening: Enjoy dinner at **Sequoia** in Zamalek.

Day 14: Departure
Morning: Shop for souvenirs at **Khan El Khalili** or a modern mall.

Afternoon: Relax before your flight.

CHAPTER 4

SHOPPING AND SOUVENIRS

Khan El Khalili Bazaar: The Heart of Cairo's Souks

Khan El Khalili Bazaar is one of the most famous and oldest marketplaces in Cairo, known as the heart of the city's shopping and cultural experience. A visit to this bustling souk is a journey through time, offering a glimpse into Cairo's vibrant history, traditional craftsmanship, and local lifestyle. Situated in the heart of Islamic Cairo, this bazaar has been a hub of trade, culture, and interaction since the 14th century. It was originally established as a caravanserai, a place where merchants would gather to trade goods and rest. Over the centuries, it has transformed into a vibrant marketplace that attracts locals and tourists alike.

Walking through Khan El Khalili is like stepping into a world where the past and present coexist. The narrow, winding alleys are lined with shops and stalls that sell a wide variety of goods, from traditional Egyptian souvenirs to handcrafted items that showcase the country's artistry. The architecture of the bazaar itself is captivating, with intricate designs, ornate facades, and historic buildings that speak of its rich heritage. The atmosphere is lively and colorful, with the sounds of traders calling out to customers, the scents of spices and perfumes filling the air, and the sight of vibrant displays of goods creating an unforgettable sensory experience.

One of the most popular items to purchase at Khan El Khalili is jewelry. Gold and silver pieces, many of which are handcrafted, can be found in abundance. Some items are intricately designed with traditional Egyptian motifs, making them not just beautiful adornments but also meaningful keepsakes. There are also shops specializing in brassware, where you can find lanterns, trays, and other decorative items that are meticulously engraved and polished, reflecting the skill of the artisans. These brass items are particularly popular because they capture the essence of Egyptian aesthetics and are often used to add a touch of elegance to homes.

For those interested in textiles, the bazaar offers a range of options, including handwoven scarves, tablecloths, and clothing made from high-quality Egyptian cotton. These items are lightweight and easy to pack, making them perfect for travelers looking for practical yet meaningful souvenirs. You will also find shops selling colorful rugs and carpets, which are often hand-knotted and made from natural materials. These pieces are a testament to the rich textile tradition of Egypt and make for unique additions to any home.

Spices and herbs are another highlight of shopping at Khan El Khalili. The aromatic stalls display a variety of colorful spices, from cumin and coriander to turmeric and chili powder. Many of these spices are grown in Egypt and are known for their quality and flavor. Purchasing spices here is an excellent way to take a piece of Egypt's culinary tradition back home. In addition to spices, you can find dried herbs, teas, and essential oils, all of which make wonderful gifts for friends and family.

Perfumes and essential oils are another specialty of the bazaar. Egypt has a long history of perfume-making, and many shops in Khan El Khalili continue this tradition. Visitors can find a wide array of fragrances, from floral scents to exotic blends, often sold in beautifully crafted glass bottles. These perfumes are usually oil-based, making them more concentrated and long-lasting than alcohol-based perfumes. Shopkeepers often encourage customers to try different scents, and many shops can create custom blends based on individual preferences.

No trip to Khan El Khalili is complete without exploring the stalls selling traditional Egyptian souvenirs such as papyrus paintings, miniature statues, and replicas of ancient artifacts. Papyrus, a material used by ancient Egyptians for writing and art, is often adorned with hand-painted images of hieroglyphics, gods, and pharaohs. These pieces make for meaningful and educational souvenirs. Additionally, many shops sell alabaster and stone carvings, which are replicas of ancient Egyptian relics. These items are carefully crafted to resemble artifacts found in museums, making them a popular choice for history enthusiasts.

When shopping at Khan El Khalili, it's important to be prepared for bargaining. Haggling is a common practice in Egyptian markets, and many shopkeepers expect it. While it may feel intimidating at first, it's considered part of the experience. Start by offering a price lower than what you're willing to pay, and negotiate until you reach a fair deal. Shopkeepers are usually friendly and willing to engage in lighthearted negotiations, making it a fun and interactive process.

Aside from shopping, Khan El Khalili is also an excellent place to experience Cairo's vibrant café culture. One of the most famous establishments in the bazaar is El Fishawi, a café that has been serving customers for over 200 years. Known as the "Café of Mirrors," it is a popular spot for locals and tourists to enjoy a cup of Egyptian tea or coffee while soaking in the atmosphere of the bazaar. The café's traditional seating and historic charm make it a must-visit spot. Many other cafes in the area offer shisha (water pipes) and a variety of drinks, providing a relaxing break from the hustle and bustle of shopping.

The best time to visit Khan El Khalili is in the late afternoon or early evening when the bazaar comes alive with activity. The cooler temperatures make it more comfortable to walk around, and the dim lighting adds a magical ambiance to the marketplace. While the bazaar can get crowded, especially during weekends and holidays, the lively atmosphere is part of its charm.

Navigating the bazaar can feel overwhelming due to its maze-like layout, but that's part of the adventure. It's recommended to allow yourself plenty of time to wander and explore without a strict agenda. Many of the best finds are tucked away in smaller alleys or hidden shops that you might stumble upon by chance. If you're looking for specific items, don't hesitate to ask shopkeepers for directions—they're usually happy to help. Khan El Khalili Bazaar is more than just a shopping destination; it's an immersive cultural experience. It offers a window into Cairo's rich history, vibrant traditions, and the artistry of its people. Whether you're looking for unique souvenirs, handcrafted goods, or simply a memorable adventure, Khan El Khalili is a must-visit spot that will leave a lasting impression.

Local Markets for Spices, Perfumes, and Textiles

Cairo, with its rich cultural heritage and bustling atmosphere, is a paradise for shoppers looking to immerse themselves in the local flavors, scents, and textures of Egypt. For centuries, the city has been a hub of trade, with markets and bazaars that offer a wide range of goods crafted by skilled artisans and traders. Among the many treasures you can find in Cairo, local markets specializing in spices, perfumes, and textiles stand out as vibrant reflections of Egypt's traditions and daily life. Visiting these markets is not just about shopping—it's about experiencing the essence of Egyptian culture through its sights, smells, and textures.

One of the most compelling aspects of shopping for spices in Cairo is the sensory journey it provides. Egyptian cuisine heavily relies on an array of spices that are not only essential for flavor but also hold cultural and historical significance. Markets like the spice souks in Islamic Cairo and stalls near

Khan El Khalili Bazaar are brimming with colorful displays of spices piled high in pyramids. These stalls are a feast for the senses, with the vibrant reds of paprika, the golden hues of turmeric, and the earthy tones of cumin and coriander. The air is filled with the aroma of these spices, which often draws shoppers in before they even see the displays.

Spices such as cardamom, cinnamon, and cloves are particularly sought after, as they are integral to many Egyptian dishes, desserts, and beverages. Sumac, with its tangy flavor, and za'atar, a blend of thyme, sesame seeds, and sumac, are popular options for travelers looking to bring a taste of Egypt back home. Many traders are knowledgeable and happy to explain the uses of different spices or recommend blends for cooking specific dishes. Some even create custom spice mixes based on your preferences, providing a personal touch to your shopping experience. Most spices are sold by weight, allowing you to purchase as little or as much as you need.

Perfumes are another highlight of Cairo's shopping experience, as Egypt has a long history of perfume-making that dates back to ancient times. Perfume shops in the city often double as small workshops where oils are blended and bottled. Unlike the alcohol-based perfumes commonly found in the West, Egyptian perfumes are typically made from essential oils, which make them more concentrated and long-lasting. These oils are derived from natural ingredients such as roses, jasmine, and sandalwood, many of which are grown in Egypt. Perfume shops in Cairo, especially those around Khan

El Khalili, offer a wide range of scents, from light and floral to rich and exotic.

One of the unique features of shopping for perfumes in Cairo is the opportunity to create a custom blend. Many shops allow you to select your preferred base oils and work with the shopkeeper to craft a personalized fragrance. This hands-on experience adds a layer of intimacy and creativity to your purchase, making it a meaningful souvenir. The bottles themselves are often works of art, made from intricately designed glass that reflects the skill of local artisans. Whether you're buying a custom perfume or a pre-made scent, the perfume market in Cairo offers a truly memorable experience. Textiles are another treasure that shoppers can find in Cairo's local markets. Egyptian cotton, renowned for its quality and softness, is one of the most sought-after products for visitors. Markets in Islamic Cairo, such as Souq al-Khayamiyya (the Tentmakers' Bazaar), are excellent places to explore a variety of textiles. The Tentmakers' Bazaar is particularly famous for its handcrafted appliqué work, where colorful fabrics are stitched together to create intricate patterns and designs. These pieces are often used as wall hangings, cushion covers, or table runners, making them versatile and unique souvenirs.

In addition to cotton, you'll find a range of other textiles, including scarves, shawls, and traditional garments like galabeyas. The scarves and shawls are often made from materials like silk or wool, and they come in an array of colors and patterns. Many of these items are handwoven, which adds to their authenticity and charm. Traders are usually open to explaining the origins and methods used to produce their textiles, giving you a deeper appreciation for your purchase. If you're looking for something truly special, you can even find handmade carpets and rugs in some markets, crafted using techniques passed down through generations.

Shopping in Cairo's markets for spices, perfumes, and textiles is not just about the products—it's about the experience of engaging with local traders and learning about their crafts. Bargaining is an essential part of the market culture in Cairo and is expected in most transactions. While this may feel unfamiliar to some travelers, it's considered a normal and even enjoyable part of shopping in Egypt. Start by offering a price lower than what you're willing to pay, and negotiate until both you and the trader reach a fair agreement. Most shopkeepers are friendly and approachable, making the bargaining process a lively and interactive experience.

It's important to set aside ample time for your visit to these markets, as exploring them can be an all-day affair. The maze-like alleys and the sheer variety of goods available mean that you'll likely spend hours wandering, discovering new items, and chatting with traders. Carry cash in small denominations, as many shops do not accept credit cards, and be prepared to navigate through crowded spaces, especially during peak hours.

The best times to visit Cairo's markets are in the morning or late afternoon when the temperatures are cooler, and the crowds are thinner. Make sure to dress comfortably and wear shoes suitable for walking. Bringing a reusable bag or backpack is also a good idea, as it allows you to carry your purchases easily. If you're unsure where to find specific markets or items, don't hesitate to ask locals or your hotel staff for recommendations—they're often happy to help.

Shopping for spices, perfumes, and textiles in Cairo is more than just a retail experience—it's an opportunity to connect with the city's culture, history, and people. Each item you purchase tells a story, whether it's a jar of saffron that adds flavor to your meals, a bottle of jasmine oil that reminds you of the city's fragrant air, or a handmade scarf that reflects the artistry of Egyptian textiles. These markets are places where tradition and creativity come alive, offering you not only unique souvenirs but also memories that will stay with you long after your visit.

Unique Souvenirs: Papyrus, Jewelry, and Egyptian Art

Cairo is a city filled with opportunities to find unique souvenirs that reflect the rich culture, history, and artistry of Egypt. Among the most sought-after items for travelers are papyrus, jewelry, and Egyptian art, each representing different facets of the country's heritage and craftsmanship. Shopping for these items in Cairo is more than just a transaction; it is an experience that allows you to connect with the traditions and stories that have shaped Egyptian culture over thousands of years.

Papyrus is one of the most iconic souvenirs you can buy in Cairo, deeply rooted in the country's ancient history. Papyrus was the first material used for writing in ancient Egypt, made from the papyrus plant that grew along the banks of the Nile River. Today, skilled artisans continue this tradition by crafting authentic papyrus sheets, which are often adorned with hand-painted designs. These designs typically feature scenes from Egyptian mythology, depictions of gods and pharaohs, or hieroglyphic inscriptions. Buying papyrus is not only a way to own a piece of history but also an opportunity to appreciate the detailed artistry that goes into each piece.

When shopping for papyrus, it is essential to distinguish authentic items from imitations. Genuine papyrus has a textured surface with visible horizontal and vertical fibers, giving it a unique feel and appearance. It is also flexible and durable, unlike imitation papyrus made from banana leaves or other materials, which can feel brittle or overly smooth. Many shops in Cairo, particularly those near the Giza Pyramids and in the Khan El Khalili Bazaar, offer papyrus paintings. Some even demonstrate the traditional process of making papyrus, allowing you to see how the plant is transformed into the material used for artwork. Prices for papyrus vary depending on the size and complexity of the design, but it is generally affordable and makes an excellent gift or keepsake.

Jewelry is another popular souvenir in Cairo, offering a chance to own pieces that reflect Egypt's rich traditions and symbolism. Egyptian jewelry often incorporates motifs inspired by ancient mythology, such as the Eye of Horus, the scarab beetle, or the ankh symbol, each carrying its own meaning. The Eye of Horus is believed to offer protection, the scarab beetle represents rebirth and transformation, and the ankh symbolizes life and eternity. These motifs are commonly featured in necklaces, bracelets, earrings, and rings, making the jewelry not only beautiful but also meaningful.

Gold and silver jewelry are particularly prized in Cairo, with goldsmiths and silversmiths known for their skill and attention to detail. The gold used in Egyptian jewelry often has a higher karat value, giving it a richer and more vibrant color. Silver pieces are also popular and are sometimes adorned with gemstones or enamel work for added elegance. Many shops offer custom designs, allowing you to create a piece that is uniquely yours. Prices for jewelry vary depending on the material, design, and craftsmanship, but bargaining is common, and you can often secure a good deal.

When purchasing jewelry in Cairo, it is essential to shop at reputable stores or markets to ensure you are buying genuine items. Khan El Khalili Bazaar is a great place to start, with its numerous jewelry shops offering a wide selection of designs. Additionally, there are modern jewelry boutiques in areas like Zamalek and Downtown Cairo that combine traditional motifs with contemporary styles. Whether you prefer a simple silver bracelet or an intricate gold necklace, Egyptian jewelry makes a lasting souvenir that you can wear and cherish for years to come.

Egyptian art is another category of souvenirs that captures the country's unique cultural identity. This art can take many forms, from paintings and sculptures to handcrafted items that reflect traditional techniques. Many artists in Cairo draw inspiration from ancient Egyptian themes, using symbols, colors, and imagery that evoke the grandeur of the pharaohs. You can find paintings depicting scenes from the Nile, portraits of deities, or abstract interpretations of hieroglyphs, each telling a story of Egypt's history and spirituality.

Sculptures and carvings are also popular, often made from materials like alabaster, basalt, or bronze. These pieces can range from small figurines to larger statues and are meticulously crafted to resemble ancient artifacts. Common subjects include replicas of famous statues, such as the bust of Nefertiti or the statue of Ramses II, as well as representations of animals like cats, which held a sacred place in Egyptian culture. These sculptures make for striking decorative pieces that add a touch of history and elegance to any home.

For those interested in more modern interpretations, Cairo is home to a thriving contemporary art scene. Many galleries and workshops, particularly in neighborhoods like Zamalek, showcase the work of local artists who blend traditional influences with modern techniques. This includes everything from abstract paintings to mixed-media installations, offering a fresh perspective on Egyptian culture. Buying contemporary art not only supports local talent but also allows you to take home a piece that reflects the dynamic creativity of modern Egypt.

Shopping for Egyptian art, whether traditional or contemporary, is an immersive experience. Many workshops and galleries are open to visitors, giving you the chance to meet the artists and learn about their creative processes. This personal connection adds depth to your purchase, making it more than just a transaction. Prices for art vary widely, depending on the medium, size, and artist, but there is something to suit every budget, from affordable prints to one-of-a-kind masterpieces.

When shopping for souvenirs like papyrus, jewelry, and Egyptian art, it's important to allocate enough time to explore your options fully. Markets like Khan El Khalili can be busy and overwhelming, so patience is key. Take the time to browse different shops, compare prices, and engage with the traders, who are often happy to share stories about their products and their cultural significance. Bargaining is a common practice, especially in markets, so don't hesitate to negotiate for a fair price.

These souvenirs are not just items to bring back home—they are pieces of Egypt's history, culture, and artistry. Each one carries a story, whether it's the meticulous craftsmanship of a papyrus painting, the symbolic meaning of a piece of jewelry, or the creative expression of a local artist. By choosing these unique items, you are not only taking home a reminder of your trip but also supporting the traditions and talents that make Cairo such a remarkable destination.

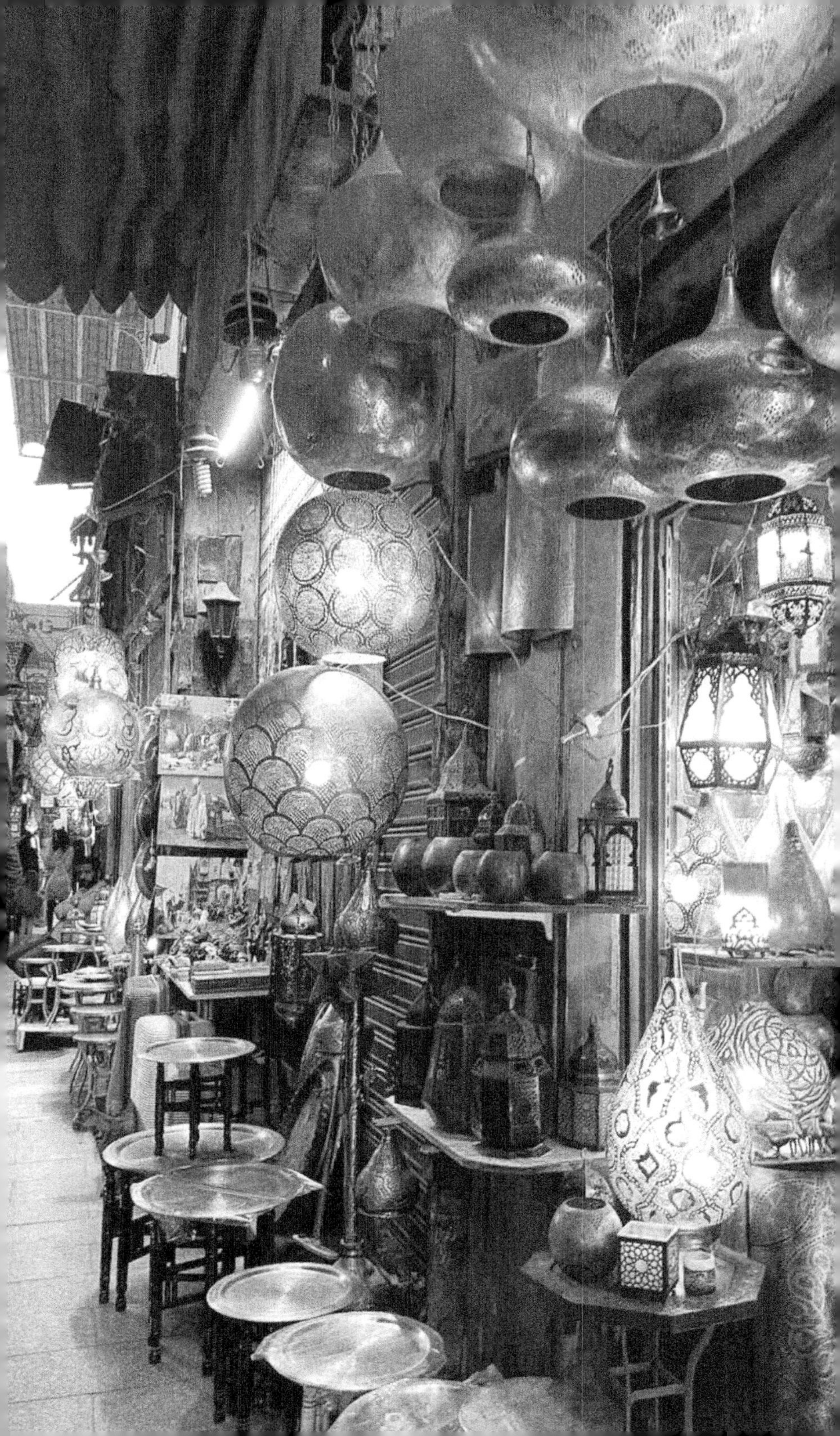

CHAPTER 5

CUISINE AND DINING IN CAIRO

Traditional Egyptian Dishes You Must Try

Cairo, Egypt, is a city where history, culture, and flavor blend seamlessly, creating a dining experience that is as vibrant and diverse as the city itself. Egyptian cuisine is rooted in traditions that go back thousands of years, reflecting the agricultural richness of the Nile Valley and the culinary influences of neighboring regions. Three dishes, in particular, stand out as staples of traditional Egyptian dining: koshary, fattah, and ful medames. These dishes are not only popular among locals but are also a must-try for anyone visiting Cairo. They provide a window into the daily life and heritage of Egypt through flavors that are simple yet deeply satisfying.

Koshary is often considered Egypt's national dish and is a favorite among locals and tourists alike. This hearty and affordable meal is a perfect example of how Egyptian cuisine is built on a foundation of accessible ingredients and creative combinations. Koshary is made by layering rice, lentils, and macaroni, which are then topped with a tangy tomato sauce, crispy fried onions, and a drizzle of garlic vinegar. For an added kick, many people like to sprinkle chili sauce on top, adjusting the level of spice to their preference. Despite its humble ingredients, koshary is a dish that delivers a complex and satisfying flavor profile, with the tanginess of the tomato sauce balancing the richness of the onions and the hearty base of rice and lentils.

Koshary is widely available in Cairo, with countless koshary shops serving this beloved dish. It is often served in generous portions, making it a filling meal that is perfect for lunch or dinner. One of the best places to try koshary is at Abou Tarek, a renowned restaurant in downtown Cairo that has been serving the dish for decades. At koshary shops, you'll notice that the dish is typically assembled to order, ensuring that each element is fresh and the flavors are perfectly balanced. Eating koshary is not just about the food—it's also about the communal atmosphere of the restaurants, where you can see locals enjoying their meals and feel a sense of connection to Cairo's bustling daily life.

Fattah is another traditional dish that holds a special place in Egyptian cuisine, particularly during festive occasions and celebrations. It is a dish that showcases the importance of bread, rice, and meat in Egyptian cooking. Fattah consists of layers of crispy bread pieces, rice, and slow-cooked meat, all brought together with a tangy garlic and vinegar tomato sauce. The combination of textures—from the softness of the rice to the crispiness of the bread—and the richness of the meat make fattah a dish that is both comforting and indulgent.

Fattah is often served during religious celebrations, such as Eid al-Adha, when families gather to share a meal together. In restaurants, fattah is usually prepared with lamb or beef, but variations exist depending on regional preferences and availability. The dish is typically served in a large platter, making it ideal for sharing with friends or family. To truly appreciate fattah, it's worth visiting a traditional Egyptian restaurant where the dish is prepared using time-honored methods. The meat is often cooked slowly to ensure it is tender and flavorful, and the bread is fried or toasted to achieve the perfect crunch. Fattah is a dish that speaks to the importance of communal dining in Egyptian culture, as it is meant to be shared and enjoyed in the company of others.

Ful medames is perhaps one of the oldest and most iconic dishes in Egyptian cuisine. Made from fava beans that are slow-cooked until they reach a creamy consistency, ful medames is a dish that is both simple and versatile. It is typically seasoned with olive oil, lemon juice, garlic, and cumin, but the toppings can vary widely depending on personal preferences. Common additions include chopped onions, tomatoes, parsley, and chili peppers. Ful medames is often served with fresh pita bread, which is used to scoop up the beans and soak up the flavorful juices.

In Cairo, ful medames is a staple breakfast dish, enjoyed by people from all walks of life. It is commonly sold at street stalls and small eateries, where it is served piping hot alongside plates of pickled vegetables and hard-boiled eggs. The dish's popularity stems from its nutritional value and affordability, making it a favorite among students, workers, and families alike. Ful medames is not just a meal; it is a ritual that reflects the rhythm of daily life in Cairo. Many locals have their favorite spots for ful, and the dish is often accompanied by lively conversations and the clinking of glasses filled with hot tea.

What makes ful medames particularly special is its role in uniting people across different backgrounds. Whether you're eating it at a street stall or a fine-dining restaurant, the essence of the dish remains the same: a humble yet satisfying meal that nourishes both the body and the soul. Some of the best places to try ful medames in Cairo include Gad, a popular chain of Egyptian eateries, and local food carts where the dish is prepared fresh every morning. Watching the vendor ladle the beans into bowls and sprinkle on the seasonings is an experience in itself, as it highlights the simplicity and charm of Egyptian street food culture.

As you explore Cairo's culinary scene, these three dishes—koshary, fattah, and ful medames—will give you a deep appreciation for the flavors and traditions that define Egyptian cuisine. They are more than just food; they are symbols of the country's history, hospitality, and resourcefulness. Each dish tells a story, from the origins of koshary as a working-class meal to the festive significance of fattah and the timeless appeal of ful medames. By trying these dishes, you are not only tasting Egypt's rich culinary heritage but also participating in a tradition that has been passed down through generations. Dining in Cairo is an adventure that connects you to the heart of the city and its people, making your visit unforgettable.

Street Food Hotspots and Market Snacks

Cairo's street food scene is a vibrant and essential part of the city's culture, offering an authentic way to experience the flavors of Egypt. Walking through Cairo's streets, you'll find an abundance of food stalls, carts, and small shops where vendors prepare fresh, flavorful dishes right before your eyes. These street food hotspots and market snacks are not just about quick and affordable meals; they are a reflection of Egypt's culinary traditions, showcasing the ingenuity of local cooks who transform simple ingredients into delicious creations. Exploring street food in Cairo allows you to engage with the city's lively atmosphere, meet friendly locals, and taste the essence of Egyptian cuisine.

One of the most popular street foods in Cairo is **taameya**, which is the Egyptian version of falafel. Made from fava beans rather than chickpeas, taameya has a softer texture and a unique flavor. The mixture is seasoned with fresh herbs like parsley and coriander, along with garlic and spices, giving it a vibrant green interior. The patties are fried to golden perfection and often served in pita bread with tahini sauce, pickles, and fresh vegetables. Taameya is a favorite breakfast item and can be found at nearly every street corner. Vendors typically prepare the falafel fresh, frying it in large pans as customers line up for their morning meal. This makes taameya not only delicious but also incredibly affordable, with a sandwich costing just a few Egyptian pounds.

Another must-try street food is **koshary**, which is both a national dish and a street food staple. Many locals grab a bowl of koshary from small street-side shops during lunch hours. The dish consists of rice, lentils, macaroni, and chickpeas layered together and topped with a tangy tomato sauce, crispy fried onions, and a drizzle of garlic vinegar. Vendors often allow customers to customize their koshary by adding more sauce, chili, or vinegar to suit their taste. Watching the vendor skillfully assemble the layers is part of the experience, and the hearty portion sizes make koshary an incredibly satisfying meal. Some of the best koshary stalls in Cairo, like Koshary El Tahrir, have been serving this dish for generations, maintaining the same quality and flavor that keeps people coming back.

Ful medames is another iconic Egyptian dish that can be enjoyed as a street food snack. It consists of slow-cooked fava beans seasoned with olive oil, lemon juice, garlic, and cumin. Ful is often served in small bowls and accompanied by freshly baked pita bread, which is used to scoop up the beans. Many vendors also offer toppings like diced tomatoes, onions, parsley, or hard-boiled eggs, allowing customers to personalize their meal. Ful carts are a common sight in Cairo, especially in the early mornings when people gather to enjoy this nourishing dish before starting their day. The simplicity of ful, combined with its rich, comforting flavor, makes it a timeless favorite.

For those with a sweet tooth, Cairo's street food scene offers a variety of delectable snacks. One such treat is **konafa**, a dessert made from shredded phyllo dough soaked in sweet syrup and filled with cream, nuts, or cheese. Konafa is prepared on small griddles at street stalls, with vendors expertly shaping the dough into thin layers before adding the filling and cooking it until golden brown. The result is a dessert that is both crispy and indulgently sweet. Another popular dessert is **basbousa**, a semolina cake soaked in syrup and often topped with almonds or coconut. These treats are widely available in markets and bakeries, providing a delightful way to end a meal or satisfy a craving while exploring the city.

Street vendors also sell savory snacks that are perfect for eating on the go. One such snack is **sambousek**, which are small, deep-fried pastries filled with minced meat, cheese, or vegetables. They are crispy on the outside and flavorful on the inside, making them a convenient option for a quick bite. Another popular item is **hawawshi**, a type of Egyptian stuffed bread filled with spiced ground beef or lamb and baked until crispy. Hawawshi is often cooked in traditional ovens, giving it a smoky flavor that enhances its appeal.

Cairo's markets are an excellent place to explore a variety of street food options while immersing yourself in the city's vibrant atmosphere. The **Khan El Khalili Bazaar** is not only a hub for shopping but also a haven for food lovers. Vendors here sell everything from fresh juices and roasted nuts to traditional sweets and snacks. A refreshing drink to try is **sugarcane juice**, which is pressed fresh on the spot and served cold, offering a sweet and energizing boost as you navigate the busy streets. You'll also find stalls selling **roasted sweet potatoes**, a simple yet delicious snack that is especially popular during the cooler months.

The **Attaba Market** is another hotspot for street food, known for its affordable prices and wide variety of offerings. This bustling market is frequented by locals and is a great place to sample authentic Egyptian snacks like **kebda iskandarani**, which is a spiced liver dish typically served in sandwiches. Vendors at Attaba also sell fresh fruits, nuts, and seeds, making it a great spot to pick up healthy snacks for later.

One of the joys of exploring Cairo's street food scene is the opportunity to interact with the vendors themselves. Many of these vendors have been in the business for decades, inheriting recipes and techniques from their families. They are often eager to share stories about their food and offer recommendations on how best to enjoy it. This personal connection adds depth to the experience, turning a simple meal into a memorable encounter.

Navigating Cairo's street food scene requires a sense of adventure and an open mind. While the city's vibrant streets can be overwhelming at first, they are also filled with hidden gems waiting to be discovered. To ensure a safe and enjoyable experience, look for vendors with busy stalls, as this is usually a sign of fresh and high-quality food. Carry small bills and coins for easier transactions, as most street vendors operate on a cash-only basis. Finally, embrace the spontaneity of street food dining—whether you're sitting on a makeshift bench or standing by a cart, the flavors and atmosphere are sure to leave a lasting impression.

Cairo's street food and market snacks are more than just a way to satisfy hunger; they are an integral part of the city's culture and identity. Each bite tells a story of tradition, resilience, and community, making street food one of the most authentic ways to experience the heart of Cairo. From the comforting flavors of ful medames to the sweet indulgence of konafa, the city's culinary offerings are as diverse and dynamic as its streets, inviting you to savor every moment of your journey.

Top Restaurants and Nile-Side Dining Experiences

Cairo, Egypt, is not only a city steeped in history but also a culinary haven offering a wide variety of dining experiences. From authentic Egyptian fare to international cuisine, Cairo's restaurant scene is a reflection of its rich cultural heritage and modern cosmopolitan flair. Among its many dining options, the city is particularly renowned for its top-tier restaurants and unique Nile-side dining experiences. These venues provide a perfect blend of exceptional food, breathtaking views, and memorable atmospheres, making dining in Cairo a highlight of any visit.

For those seeking a fine dining experience that captures the essence of Egypt, many restaurants in Cairo specialize in traditional dishes prepared with care and precision. Places like Abou El Sid are celebrated for their authentic Egyptian cuisine served in an ambiance that evokes the charm of a bygone era. At Abou El Sid, you can savor dishes such as molokhia, a flavorful soup made from jute leaves, or fattah, a layered dish of crispy bread, rice, and slow-cooked meat topped with a tangy garlic tomato sauce. The restaurant's decor, featuring antique furnishings and dim lighting, creates a cozy and nostalgic setting that enhances the dining experience. It's a place where locals and visitors come together to enjoy the rich flavors of Egypt, paired with excellent service and a warm, welcoming atmosphere.

Another gem in Cairo's culinary landscape is Zooba, a modern take on Egyptian street food that has gained a loyal following for its creative yet authentic menu. Zooba's offerings include dishes like taameya (Egyptian falafel), koshary, and ful medames, presented in a contemporary style without losing their traditional essence. The restaurant's vibrant decor and casual setting make it an inviting spot for a relaxed meal. Whether you're dining at one of its branches in Downtown Cairo or Zamalek, Zooba provides a fresh perspective on classic Egyptian cuisine, making it a must-visit for food enthusiasts.

For an elevated dining experience, Cairo also boasts several upscale restaurants that combine exquisite cuisine with stunning views of the Nile. Pier 88, located on a floating platform in Zamalek, offers a sophisticated menu that blends Mediterranean and international flavors. Known for its chic ambiance and exceptional service, Pier 88 is a favorite among locals and tourists alike. Dishes such as seafood risotto, beef fillet, and freshly prepared pasta showcase the restaurant's commitment to quality and flavor. Dining here is as much about the food as it is about the experience, with the gentle sway of the Nile adding a serene and romantic touch to your evening.

If you're looking for a truly unique Nile-side dining experience, the Nile Ritz-Carlton's rooftop restaurant is an excellent choice. Offering panoramic views of the city and the river, the restaurant combines luxury with a relaxed atmosphere. The menu features a mix of Middle Eastern and international dishes, with options ranging from grilled meats to fresh salads and indulgent desserts. The setting is perfect for a leisurely dinner as the sun sets over Cairo, bathing the city in warm hues and casting a golden glow over the water. The attentive service and carefully curated menu make this dining spot a standout option for special occasions or simply enjoying the beauty of Cairo.

Another noteworthy Nile-side venue is Sequoia, located in Zamalek at the tip of Gezira Island. Sequoia is known for its open-air design, offering diners unobstructed views of the Nile while they enjoy a menu inspired by Mediterranean and Egyptian cuisines. Popular dishes include mezza platters, grilled seafood, and freshly baked bread. The restaurant's ambiance, enhanced by soft lighting and comfortable seating, creates a relaxed yet elegant dining experience. Sequoia is particularly popular in the evenings when the river's reflection adds a magical quality to the setting, making it a perfect spot for both casual dinners and celebratory gatherings.

Cairo's dining scene also caters to those seeking international flavors, with a variety of restaurants offering cuisines from around the world. For Italian food lovers, Vivo at the Nile Ritz-Carlton is a top choice, known for its authentic dishes crafted with imported ingredients and prepared by skilled chefs. The restaurant's refined decor and river views add to the dining experience, making it an excellent option for a special night out. Similarly, Osmanly at the Kempinski Nile Hotel provides a taste of Ottoman-inspired cuisine, with dishes like lamb kofta, Turkish-style kebabs, and baklava. The restaurant's intimate setting and focus on traditional flavors make it a favorite among those looking to explore regional culinary influences.

For a more casual yet equally memorable experience, Cairo's floating restaurants are a unique way to enjoy a meal while cruising along the Nile. These boats offer a range of dining options, from buffet-style meals to à la carte menus featuring Egyptian and international dishes. The gentle motion of the boat combined with the city's illuminated skyline creates a peaceful and picturesque backdrop for your meal. Many of these cruises also include live entertainment, such as traditional music or tanoura dance performances, adding an extra layer of cultural immersion to your dining experience.

Cairo's markets and local eateries also play an important role in the city's culinary identity, offering affordable and authentic meals that capture the spirit of Egyptian food culture. Places like Gad and El Tawab are known for their hearty dishes served in a no-frills setting. Here, you can enjoy classics like shawarma sandwiches, stuffed vine leaves, or grilled chicken, all prepared with fresh ingredients and bold flavors. These eateries provide a glimpse into the daily lives of Cairo's residents, where food is not just nourishment but a source of connection and community.

Dining in Cairo is an adventure that goes beyond the food on your plate. It's an opportunity to explore the city's rich heritage, experience its diverse flavors, and enjoy the warmth of its hospitality. Whether you're indulging in a gourmet meal at a luxury restaurant, savoring street food at a bustling market, or enjoying a quiet dinner by the Nile, each dining experience in Cairo offers a unique perspective on the city's vibrant culture. The variety and quality of Cairo's culinary offerings ensure that every meal is a memorable part of your journey, leaving you with a deeper appreciation for Egypt's rich traditions and contemporary flair.

LYALY AL SHARQ ليالي الشرق

CHAPTER 6

DAY TRIPS FROM CAIRO

Saqqara

A day trip from Cairo to Saqqara is a journey into one of the most significant and fascinating chapters of ancient Egyptian history. Saqqara, located about 30 kilometers (19 miles) south of Cairo, is home to the Step Pyramid of Djoser, a structure that holds immense historical and architectural importance. This pyramid is not only the centerpiece of the Saqqara necropolis but also a landmark that marks the transition from simple burial mounds to the grand pyramid structures that Egypt is famous for today. A visit to Saqqara offers a chance to explore a site that predates the Great Pyramids of Giza, providing unique insights into the evolution of ancient Egyptian architecture, culture, and burial practices.

The Step Pyramid of Djoser was constructed during the 27th century BCE under the reign of Pharaoh Djoser, who was the second king of Egypt's Third Dynasty. Designed by Imhotep, the pharaoh's chief architect, this pyramid is considered the world's first large-scale stone structure. Unlike the smooth-sided pyramids that were built later, the Step Pyramid consists of six stepped layers that rise to a height of approximately 60 meters (197 feet). The design of the pyramid was revolutionary for its time, as it transitioned from the use of mudbrick to limestone, laying the foundation for the construction of the iconic pyramids that followed in later dynasties.

Visiting the Step Pyramid is a deeply enriching experience, as it allows you to appreciate the ingenuity and ambition of ancient Egyptian builders. The pyramid was originally conceived as a mastaba, a flat-roofed rectangular structure, but Imhotep expanded the design by stacking additional layers on top, creating the step-like appearance that gives the pyramid its name. This innovative approach not only transformed the way royal tombs were constructed but also demonstrated the advanced understanding of engineering and design possessed by the ancient Egyptians. The limestone blocks used in the construction were quarried locally, and their precise placement reflects the skill and organization of the workforce involved.

Surrounding the Step Pyramid is a vast complex of courtyards, temples, and enclosures, which were built to serve various ceremonial and religious purposes. The enclosure wall that surrounds the pyramid is made of finely cut limestone and features decorative panels and false doors, which were believed to allow the king's spirit to move freely between the physical and spiritual worlds. One of the highlights of the complex is the South Tomb, which is thought to have been built for symbolic reasons rather than as an actual burial site. Its intricate carvings and detailed reliefs are a testament to the artistry of the period.

As you explore the Saqqara necropolis, you will notice that the site is not limited to the Step Pyramid alone. Saqqara served as a burial ground for Memphis, the ancient capital of Egypt, for thousands of years, and it contains a rich array of tombs, pyramids, and monuments spanning various dynasties. Among these are the Pyramid of Unas, which features the Pyramid Texts, the oldest known religious inscriptions in the world. These texts provide invaluable insights into ancient Egyptian beliefs about the afterlife and the journey of the soul.

Another notable site within Saqqara is the Tomb of Ti, a beautifully decorated mastaba that belonged to a high-ranking official during the Fifth Dynasty. The tomb's walls are adorned with detailed scenes depicting daily life in ancient Egypt, including farming, fishing, and religious rituals. These vivid carvings offer a glimpse into the lives of ordinary people as well as the customs and traditions of the time. The artistry and precision of the carvings are remarkable, making the tomb a must-see for anyone interested in ancient Egyptian art.

Getting to Saqqara from Cairo is relatively straightforward. Many visitors choose to hire a private car or taxi for the day, which provides flexibility and convenience. The drive takes approximately 45 minutes to an hour, depending on traffic. Alternatively, you can book a guided tour that includes transportation, which is a great option if you want to learn more about the history and significance of the site from an experienced Egyptologist. Once you arrive at Saqqara, you will need to purchase an entry ticket, which costs around EGP 200 for general access. Additional tickets may be required for specific tombs or pyramids within the site.

When visiting Saqqara, it is important to wear comfortable walking shoes and bring plenty of water, as the site covers a large area and involves a fair amount of walking. The terrain can be uneven, so it's advisable to watch your step and take your time as you explore. The best time to visit is in the early morning or late afternoon when the temperatures are cooler, and the light is ideal for photography. The golden hues of the desert and the striking geometry of the Step Pyramid create a stunning backdrop for capturing memorable photos.

A visit to Saqqara is not complete without taking a moment to reflect on the legacy of Imhotep, the architect of the Step Pyramid. Imhotep was later deified as a god of wisdom and medicine, a rare honor for a non-royal figure. His contributions to Egyptian architecture and engineering left an indelible mark on history, and the Step Pyramid stands as a lasting testament to his genius.

Exploring Saqqara is a journey through time, offering a deeper understanding of the origins of pyramid construction and the cultural and spiritual practices of ancient Egypt. The site's historical significance, combined with its architectural wonders and artistic treasures, makes it an essential destination for anyone visiting Cairo. Whether you are a history enthusiast, an architecture aficionado, or simply a curious traveler, a day trip to Saqqara provides a rich and rewarding experience that will leave you with a profound appreciation for the achievements of one of the world's greatest civilizations.

Dahshur

A day trip to Dahshur from Cairo is an incredible opportunity to explore some of the most fascinating and historically significant pyramids in Egypt, the Bent Pyramid and the Red Pyramid. Located about 40 kilometers (25 miles) south of Cairo, Dahshur is part of the expansive Memphis necropolis and is less crowded than other pyramid sites, offering a quieter and more immersive experience. These pyramids provide a unique glimpse into the architectural evolution that eventually led to the construction of the iconic Pyramids of Giza, making Dahshur a must-visit destination for anyone interested in ancient Egyptian history and engineering.

The Bent Pyramid is one of the most remarkable structures in Dahshur and holds a special place in the history of pyramid construction. Built during the reign of Pharaoh Sneferu, the first king of the Fourth Dynasty, around 2600 BCE, the Bent Pyramid represents a significant step in the transition from step-sided pyramids to the smooth-sided pyramids that became the hallmark of ancient Egypt. Its unique shape, with a noticeable change in angle partway up its sides, has made it an architectural curiosity for centuries.

The pyramid's distinctive appearance is believed to be the result of an adjustment made during its construction. Initially, the pyramid was designed with steep sides rising at an angle of approximately 54 degrees. However, as construction progressed, structural issues became apparent, likely due to the weight of the limestone blocks and the instability of the foundation. To address this, the angle of the upper portion was reduced to 43 degrees, giving the pyramid its bent appearance. This modification not only ensured the stability of the structure but also provided valuable lessons for future pyramid builders. The Bent Pyramid is notable for its well-preserved outer casing of Tura limestone, which still covers much of its surface. This casing gives visitors a rare opportunity to see how the pyramids originally looked before centuries of erosion and stone removal. Unlike most other pyramids, where the outer casing has been stripped away, the Bent Pyramid offers a glimpse into the ancient Egyptians' meticulous craftsmanship. The pyramid also features two entrances—one on the northern face and another on the western side—both of which lead to a series of internal passageways and chambers.

Nearby, the Red Pyramid stands as another testament to Sneferu's architectural ambition. It is considered the first successful attempt at building a true smooth-sided pyramid and is named after the reddish hue of the limestone blocks used in its construction. The Red Pyramid, also known as the North Pyramid, is the third-largest pyramid in Egypt, with a height of approximately 105 meters (344 feet) and a base length of about 220 meters (722 feet). Its shape and proportions served as a prototype for the Great Pyramid of Giza, which was built by Sneferu's son, Pharaoh Khufu.

Unlike the Bent Pyramid, the Red Pyramid has a uniform angle of 43 degrees from base to apex, indicating that the lessons learned from the structural challenges of the Bent Pyramid were successfully applied. The pyramid's internal layout is relatively simple, featuring a long descending passageway that leads to two antechambers and a burial chamber. Visitors to the Red Pyramid can enter the pyramid and explore its interior, which is an unforgettable experience. The burial chamber, with its high corbelled ceiling, showcases the ingenuity of ancient Egyptian engineers in distributing the weight of the structure to prevent collapse.

One of the most striking aspects of visiting Dahshur is the sense of serenity and space. Unlike the more popular Giza Plateau, which can be crowded with tourists and vendors, Dahshur offers a peaceful environment where you can appreciate the grandeur of the pyramids without distractions. The surrounding desert landscape enhances the site's timeless beauty, allowing you to immerse yourself in the history and mystery of ancient Egypt.

Getting to Dahshur from Cairo is relatively easy and can be done by private car, taxi, or as part of a guided tour. The drive takes approximately one to one-and-a-half hours, depending on traffic. Many visitors choose to combine a trip to Dahshur with visits to nearby sites such as Saqqara and Memphis, creating a full day of exploration. Admission to Dahshur is affordable, with tickets costing around EGP 80–100 for general access. Additional fees may apply if you choose to enter the pyramids, but the experience is well worth the cost.
When visiting Dahshur, it is important to come prepared for the desert environment. Wear comfortable walking shoes and lightweight clothing, and bring plenty of water to stay hydrated. The site is exposed to the elements, so sunscreen, a hat, and sunglasses are recommended to protect yourself from

the sun. The best time to visit is in the early morning or late afternoon when the temperatures are cooler, and the lighting is ideal for photography.

Exploring the Bent and Red Pyramids is not just about admiring their architectural achievements; it is also an opportunity to reflect on the innovations and challenges faced by the ancient Egyptians as they perfected their pyramid-building techniques. These structures stand as monuments to human ingenuity and determination, offering a tangible connection to a civilization that continues to inspire awe and fascination.

A visit to Dahshur is an essential addition to any trip to Cairo, providing a deeper understanding of the development of pyramid construction and the legacy of Pharaoh Sneferu. The Bent and Red Pyramids are not only impressive feats of engineering but also symbols of the ambition and creativity that defined ancient Egypt. Whether you are a history enthusiast, an architecture aficionado, or simply a curious traveler, Dahshur promises an unforgettable experience that will leave you with a profound appreciation for one of the world's greatest civilizations.

Fayoum Oasis: Waterfalls, Lakes, and Wildlife

A day trip from Cairo to Saqqara, Dahshur, and the Fayoum Oasis offers a journey through Egypt's fascinating history, breathtaking landscapes, and unique wildlife. Each destination holds its own treasures, from ancient pyramids to serene waterfalls and diverse ecosystems. This trip allows you to explore the cultural and natural wonders of Egypt, making it a perfect excursion for travelers seeking a mix of history, adventure, and tranquility.

The first stop on this journey is Saqqara, an archaeological site located about 30 kilometers south of Cairo. Saqqara is home to the Step Pyramid of Djoser, the earliest large-scale stone structure in the world, built during the Third Dynasty around 2650 BCE. Designed by the renowned architect Imhotep, the Step Pyramid is a testament to the ingenuity of ancient Egyptian builders. Unlike the smooth-sided pyramids at Giza, the Step Pyramid features a series of stepped layers, which mark the transition from mastaba tombs to more complex pyramid designs. Surrounding the pyramid is a vast funerary complex with courtyards, shrines, and decorated tombs that provide insights into the beliefs and practices of ancient Egypt. Beyond the Step Pyramid, Saqqara is a vast necropolis containing numerous tombs and pyramids from different periods of Egyptian history. The Pyramid of Unas, for example, features the Pyramid Texts, the oldest known religious writings in the world. Nearby, the Mastaba of Ti showcases detailed carvings that depict scenes of daily life, such as farming, fishing, and religious ceremonies. These artistic works reveal not only the spiritual beliefs of the time but also the everyday activities of ancient Egyptians, offering a well-rounded view of their civilization.

From Saqqara, the journey continues to Dahshur, a quieter yet equally significant site located a short drive away. Dahshur is known for the Bent Pyramid and the Red Pyramid, both built during the reign of Pharaoh Sneferu in the Fourth Dynasty. The Bent Pyramid, with its distinctive angled sides, represents an experimental phase in pyramid construction. Initially designed with steep sides, the pyramid's angle was adjusted during construction to prevent structural issues, resulting in its unique bent appearance. Nearby, the Red Pyramid stands as the first successful smooth-sided pyramid, showcasing the advancements made in architectural techniques. Its reddish limestone blocks give it its name, and visitors can explore its interior chambers, which provide a glimpse into the engineering brilliance of the ancient builders.

After exploring these ancient wonders, the trip shifts to the Fayoum Oasis, a lush and verdant region located approximately 100 kilometers southwest of Cairo. The Fayoum Oasis is a striking contrast to the arid desert landscapes surrounding it, offering a tranquil retreat filled with natural beauty and rich biodiversity. The oasis is fed by the Bahr Youssef, a canal that channels water from the Nile River, and is dotted with lakes, waterfalls, and fertile farmland.

One of the highlights of the Fayoum Oasis is Wadi El Rayan, a protected area known for its stunning waterfalls, which are a rare sight in Egypt. The Wadi El Rayan Waterfalls connect two man-made lakes and are surrounded by sand dunes and rocky terrain, creating a picturesque setting that attracts both locals and tourists. The area is perfect for relaxation, picnics, and photography, as well as outdoor activities like hiking and sandboarding. The sound of the cascading water combined with the serene desert backdrop makes it an unforgettable experience.

Another gem in the Fayoum Oasis is Lake Qarun, one of the oldest natural lakes in the world. This large saltwater lake is a haven for birdwatchers, as it serves as a refuge for numerous migratory bird species. Flamingos, herons, and kingfishers are commonly spotted here, making it a paradise for nature enthusiasts. The lake also provides opportunities for fishing and boating, allowing visitors to engage with the natural surroundings in a peaceful and enjoyable way.

For those interested in wildlife and geology, the Valley of the Whales (Wadi Al-Hitan) is a must-visit site within the Fayoum region. This UNESCO World Heritage Site is home to some of the most well-preserved fossilized remains of ancient whales, which date back millions of years. The fossils provide valuable evidence of the transition of whales from land-dwelling mammals to marine creatures. The valley is an open-air museum where visitors can walk along marked trails and view these extraordinary fossils in their natural setting.

The Fayoum Oasis is also rich in cultural and historical landmarks. The area is dotted with ancient ruins, including the Temple of Sobek, dedicated to the crocodile god, and the Medinet Madi temple complex, which dates back to the Middle Kingdom. These sites offer a glimpse into the religious and cultural practices of ancient Egypt, adding a historical dimension to the natural beauty of the oasis.

The drive back to Cairo from the Fayoum Oasis provides an opportunity to reflect on the day's adventures. From the ancient architectural feats of Saqqara and Dahshur to the natural splendor of the Fayoum Oasis, this trip encompasses the diverse landscapes and legacies that define Egypt. It is a journey that not only deepens your appreciation for the country's rich history but also highlights its natural treasures and ecological diversity.

Traveling to these sites from Cairo is best done with a private car or as part of a guided tour, ensuring convenience and flexibility. The roads are well-maintained, and the journey offers scenic views of the Egyptian countryside. Admission fees to the sites are reasonable, and guided tours often include knowledgeable Egyptologists who can provide deeper insights into the significance of each location. When planning your trip, it is advisable to start early in the morning to make the most of your time and avoid the midday heat.

This day trip from Cairo to Saqqara, Dahshur, and the Fayoum Oasis is a well-rounded experience that combines history, culture, and nature. It offers a chance to explore lesser-known sites that are just as captivating as Egypt's more famous landmarks, making it an essential addition to any itinerary. Whether you are marveling at the ancient pyramids, enjoying the tranquility of the oasis, or discovering the unique wildlife of the region, this journey promises to leave you with lasting memories and a deeper connection to the wonders of Egypt.

CHAPTER 7

OUTDOOR ACTIVITIES AND NATURE SPOTS

Exploring Al-Azhar Park

Al-Azhar Park in Cairo is a stunning green space that stands as a symbol of transformation and renewal in the heart of a historic city. It is one of the largest and most beautifully landscaped parks in the Middle East, offering a serene escape from the hustle and bustle of Cairo's streets. Opened in 2005, the park covers 30 hectares (about 74 acres) and is a masterpiece of urban development that has become a cherished destination for both locals and tourists. Its location, overlooking some of the oldest parts of Islamic Cairo, makes it not just a natural retreat but also a place of cultural and historical significance.

The park was created on what was once a garbage dump, a neglected area that had accumulated debris and waste for centuries. Its transformation into a lush, well-maintained garden was a project led by the Aga Khan Trust for Culture as part of a larger initiative to restore and enhance the historic fabric of Cairo. This ambitious project not only revitalized the area but also provided a much-needed green space for the city's residents, many of whom live in densely populated neighborhoods with limited access to parks or recreational areas. Today, Al-Azhar Park is celebrated as a model of urban renewal and environmental stewardship.

When you enter Al-Azhar Park, you are immediately struck by its beauty and tranquility. The park is meticulously designed, with winding pathways, manicured lawns, and a variety of trees, shrubs, and flowers. It is a place where nature and architecture come together harmoniously, creating a setting that is both peaceful and visually stunning. The layout of the park includes water features such as fountains and small lakes, which add to the sense of calm and provide a cooling effect, especially during the warmer months. The sound of water trickling through fountains, combined with the scent of blooming flowers, makes the park a sensory delight.

One of the highlights of Al-Azhar Park is the breathtaking views it offers. The park is situated on a hill, giving visitors panoramic vistas of Cairo's skyline. From here, you can see iconic landmarks such as the Citadel of Saladin, with its imposing walls and the majestic Mohammed Ali Mosque. The view extends across the old city, with its minarets and domes rising above the densely packed buildings, creating a scene that is both historic and picturesque. As the sun sets, the city is bathed in golden light, and the illuminated monuments take on a magical quality, making the park an ideal spot for photography or simply enjoying the beauty of Cairo.

Al-Azhar Park is not just a place for relaxation but also a hub for cultural and recreational activities. It hosts concerts, art exhibitions, and festivals throughout the year, showcasing both traditional and contemporary Egyptian culture. These events add a vibrant energy to the park and provide visitors with an opportunity to experience the richness of Cairo's artistic and musical heritage. For families, the park offers play areas for children, making it a popular destination for picnics and weekend outings. Couples often visit the park for romantic walks, while groups of friends gather to enjoy the serene surroundings.

For those interested in dining, the park features several restaurants and cafes that cater to a range of tastes. The most notable is the Citadel View Restaurant, which, as the name suggests, offers spectacular views of the Citadel and the surrounding cityscape. The restaurant serves a mix of Egyptian and international dishes, allowing visitors to enjoy a delicious meal while taking in the scenery. The park also has smaller cafes where you can grab a coffee or a light snack, making it easy to spend several hours exploring and relaxing without needing to leave.

The history surrounding Al-Azhar Park adds another layer of interest to the experience. The park is located in an area that is rich in Islamic heritage, with several important historic sites nearby. The park itself is named after Al-Azhar Mosque, one of the oldest and most significant mosques in Cairo, known for its role as a center of learning and spirituality. Just outside the park, you can explore the Darb al-Ahmar neighborhood, which is home to beautifully restored monuments, mosques, and madrasas (Islamic schools) that date back to the Fatimid and

Mamluk periods. Walking through this area gives you a sense of the deep history and cultural richness that defines Cairo.

Accessibility to Al-Azhar Park is straightforward, making it a convenient destination for visitors. The park is located near the center of Cairo, and it can be reached by taxi, private car, or public transportation. The entrance fee is modest, and the revenue generated is used for the park's maintenance and community development projects in the surrounding neighborhoods. This self-sustaining model ensures that the park remains a clean, safe, and welcoming space for all.

When planning a visit to Al-Azhar Park, it is worth considering the best time to go. Early mornings and late afternoons are ideal, as the weather is cooler, and the lighting is perfect for enjoying the views or taking photographs. Evenings are also a great time to visit, as the park takes on a different ambiance with its illuminated pathways and fountains. Whether you prefer a quiet stroll, a family outing, or a cultural event, Al-Azhar Park offers something for everyone.

Nile Cruises and Evening Felucca Rides

A Nile cruise or an evening felucca ride in Cairo offers an unforgettable way to experience one of the world's most iconic rivers. The Nile is more than just a waterway; it has been the lifeline of Egypt for thousands of years, shaping the country's history, culture, and daily life. Whether you choose a luxurious cruise or a traditional felucca ride, these activities provide a unique perspective on Cairo and an opportunity to connect with the river that has defined the region for millennia.

Nile cruises in Cairo typically range from a few hours to a full evening experience, making them a popular choice for both tourists and locals seeking relaxation and entertainment. These cruises often include dinner, live performances, and panoramic views of the city's skyline. Many cruise boats are designed with comfort and elegance in mind, featuring spacious decks, air-conditioned interiors, and fine dining options. As you glide along the river, you can enjoy a freshly prepared meal, which often includes a variety of Egyptian and international dishes. The setting is enhanced by soft music, creating a tranquil atmosphere that allows you to unwind while taking in the sights.

What makes a Nile cruise truly special is the view of Cairo from the water. The river offers a vantage point that showcases the city's vibrant mix of old and new. On one side, you may see the towering modern buildings and hotels that define the city's cosmopolitan character, while on the other, the minarets of historic mosques rise above the skyline, reminding you of Cairo's deep cultural heritage. As night falls, the city lights reflect on the water, creating a magical and almost dreamlike ambiance.

Most Nile cruises also include entertainment, which is an integral part of the experience. Traditional performances such as belly dancing, tanoura spinning (a type of Sufi dance), and live music are often featured. These shows celebrate Egyptian culture and add a festive element to the evening. Watching the graceful movements of the dancers or the colorful spinning skirts of the tanoura performers is a captivating experience that immerses you in the artistic traditions of Egypt. Some cruises even offer interactive segments, encouraging guests to join in the dancing or learn about the history behind the performances.

For those seeking a more traditional and intimate experience, an evening felucca ride is an excellent choice. Feluccas are wooden sailboats that have been used on the Nile for centuries, and they remain an iconic symbol of the river. Unlike the larger, motorized cruise boats, feluccas rely on the power of the wind, making the ride quieter and more serene. The absence of engines allows you to fully appreciate the sounds of the river, from the gentle lapping of the water against the boat to the occasional call of a bird flying overhead.

An evening felucca ride is perfect for those who want a peaceful escape from the noise and activity of the city. The boats are typically operated by experienced sailors who guide the felucca along the calm waters, creating a smooth and relaxing journey. As you sit back and enjoy the ride, you can take in the natural beauty of the Nile and its surroundings. The soft glow of the setting sun casts a warm light over the river, while the cool evening breeze adds to the sense of tranquility. It's a moment of stillness that feels worlds away from the bustling streets of Cairo.

Feluccas are often decorated with colorful fabrics and cushions, adding a touch of charm to the experience. Many operators allow you to bring your own snacks or beverages, making it easy to enjoy a casual meal or a cup of tea while you sail. Whether you're traveling with friends, family, or as a couple, the intimate setting of a felucca creates a memorable and personal connection to the Nile.

Navigating the Nile by felucca also provides a closer connection to Cairo's history. The river has been a central part of life in Egypt for thousands of years, serving as a source of sustenance, transportation, and inspiration. As you sail, you can imagine the countless generations who have relied on the Nile, from ancient civilizations to modern-day communities. The experience is both humbling and enriching, giving you a deeper appreciation for the river's enduring significance.

Whether you choose a cruise or a felucca ride, both experiences are enhanced by the practical convenience they offer. Most cruises and felucca rides depart from central locations in Cairo, such as the areas near the Corniche, making them easily accessible. Cruises typically require advance booking, especially during peak tourist seasons, while feluccas can often be rented on the spot. Prices for both options vary depending on the duration, inclusions, and level of luxury, but there are choices to suit a wide range of budgets. A felucca ride is generally more affordable, making it an excellent option for travelers looking for a budget-friendly activity.

When planning your Nile experience, it's important to consider the time of day. Evening cruises and felucca rides are particularly popular because they allow you to enjoy the cooler temperatures and the enchanting atmosphere of the river at night. The soft lighting and reflections on the water create a serene environment that is perfect for relaxation or quiet conversation. For those who prefer a daytime experience, some cruises and felucca operators offer morning or afternoon options, which provide clearer views of the city and its landmarks.

A Nile cruise or felucca ride is more than just an activity—it's an opportunity to engage with one of the most iconic and enduring elements of Egyptian culture. The river has shaped the identity of Egypt in countless ways, and experiencing it firsthand allows you to connect with its history, beauty, and significance. Whether you're enjoying a lavish dinner on a cruise or quietly sailing on a felucca, the Nile offers a sense of timelessness that leaves a lasting impression. It's an experience that combines relaxation, culture, and natural beauty, making it an essential part of any visit to Cairo.

Desert Safari Adventures

A desert safari adventure in Egypt is a thrilling and unforgettable way to explore the vast and awe-inspiring landscapes that define much of the country. The deserts of Egypt are not just endless stretches of sand; they are regions of immense natural beauty, historical significance, and cultural richness. Taking part in a desert safari allows you to experience the stark yet captivating scenery, ancient geological formations, and the unique lifestyle of the Bedouin people who have thrived in these harsh conditions for centuries. This activity is as much about adventure as it is about discovering the heart of Egypt's natural environment and heritage.

One of the most popular areas for desert safaris is the White Desert, located in the Western Desert about 500 kilometers southwest of Cairo. This area is renowned for its surreal chalk rock formations, which have been sculpted by wind erosion over thousands of years. These natural sculptures take on strange and striking shapes, resembling everything from mushrooms and animals to abstract forms. The contrast between the pure white limestone and the golden sands creates an otherworldly landscape that is breathtaking to behold. The White Desert is particularly magical at sunrise and sunset when the soft light accentuates the contours and textures of the rocks, casting dramatic shadows and bathing the entire area in warm hues.

Another must-visit location for desert safaris is the Black Desert, which lies near the White Desert. The Black Desert gets its name from the layer of volcanic rocks and dark stones that cover its surface, creating a stark and dramatic appearance. The combination of black hills rising from the sandy plains gives the landscape a unique and almost mystical quality. Exploring the Black Desert often involves climbing some of these hills for panoramic views of the surrounding area, offering a sense of the vastness and tranquility of the desert.

The Bahariya Oasis is a common starting point for safaris to the White and Black Deserts. This oasis, with its palm groves and natural springs, provides a stark contrast to the arid desert surroundings. It is a place where you can learn about the traditional ways of life in the desert and enjoy the hospitality of the local communities. Many desert safari tours begin with a visit to Bahariya, allowing you to experience both the lush greenery of the oasis and the stark beauty of the surrounding deserts.

Desert safaris in Egypt often include visits to unique geological sites, such as the Crystal Mountain. This small ridge, located between Bahariya and the White Desert, is made of quartz crystals that sparkle in the sunlight, making it a fascinating stop for travelers. The site is a natural marvel, and many visitors enjoy taking photographs or collecting small pieces of quartz as souvenirs. Nearby, the Agabat Valley is another highlight, with its dramatic limestone formations, golden sand dunes, and rugged terrain that showcases the diversity of Egypt's desert landscapes.

For those seeking a more adventurous experience, the Great Sand Sea, located near the Siwa Oasis, is a vast expanse of rolling sand dunes that stretch as far as the eye can see. This area is perfect for activities such as dune bashing, sandboarding, and quad biking, which offer a mix of adrenaline and fun. Dune bashing, in particular, involves riding in a 4x4 vehicle over the steep and undulating dunes, providing an exhilarating and unforgettable experience. Sandboarding, on the other hand, allows you to glide down the slopes of the dunes on a specially designed board, combining the thrill of snowboarding with the beauty of the desert.

Desert safaris are also an opportunity to immerse yourself in the culture and traditions of the Bedouin people, who have lived in harmony with the desert for generations. Many tours include a visit to a Bedouin camp, where you can learn about their customs, taste traditional food, and listen to their stories and music. Bedouin meals often feature freshly baked bread, grilled meats, and flavorful stews, all prepared using traditional methods. Sharing a meal with the Bedouins under the open sky is a memorable experience that offers a glimpse into their way of life and their deep connection to the desert.

Spending a night in the desert is another highlight of many safari tours. Camping under the stars allows you to experience the desert's quiet beauty and its dramatic transformation from day to night. The absence of city lights means that the night sky is filled with countless stars, creating a breathtaking view that is perfect for stargazing. Many travelers describe this as one of the most magical moments of their trip, as the stillness and vastness of the desert create a sense of peace and wonder.

Safety and comfort are key considerations during a desert safari, and reputable tour operators take great care to ensure that visitors have a safe and enjoyable experience. Professional guides are knowledgeable about the terrain and are equipped to handle the challenges of the desert environment. They provide all necessary equipment, such as tents, sleeping bags, and food, and ensure that vehicles are well-maintained and capable of navigating the rugged terrain. It is important to choose a licensed and experienced tour operator to ensure a high standard of safety and service.

When planning a desert safari, it is important to dress appropriately for the desert climate. Loose, lightweight clothing made of breathable fabrics is ideal for staying cool during the day while providing protection from the sun. A wide-brimmed hat, sunglasses, and sunscreen are essential to shield yourself from the intense sunlight. At night, temperatures can drop significantly, so it is advisable to bring a warm jacket or sweater. Comfortable, sturdy footwear is also important, as exploring the desert often involves walking on uneven terrain.

A desert safari in Egypt is more than just an adventure; it is an opportunity to connect with the natural world and discover the timeless beauty of the desert. The experience of exploring these vast and varied landscapes, learning about the culture and history of the region, and marveling at the geological wonders is both enriching and inspiring. Whether you are seeking excitement, tranquility, or a deeper understanding of Egypt's heritage, a desert safari promises an unforgettable journey into the heart of one of the world's most captivating environments.

CHAPTER 8

CAIRO'S HIDDEN GEMS

Al-Moez Street

Al-Moez Street, located in the heart of Islamic Cairo, is one of the most remarkable and historically significant streets in the city. Walking through this area is like stepping back in time, as every corner is filled with stunning examples of Islamic art, architecture, and culture. The street is a living museum that showcases Cairo's rich history and its role as a center of Islamic civilization for centuries. For anyone interested in history, architecture, or culture, a visit to Al-Moez Street is an essential experience that provides a deeper understanding of Cairo's unique heritage.

The history of Al-Moez Street dates back to the Fatimid era when it was established as the main thoroughfare of Cairo, which was then the capital of the Fatimid Caliphate. Named after the Fatimid Caliph Al-Moez Li-Din Allah, the street was originally designed to serve as the center of administration, trade, and religious life in the city. Over the centuries, successive dynasties, including the Ayyubids, Mamluks, and Ottomans, contributed to the street's development, building mosques, madrasas (Islamic schools), sabils (water fountains), and palaces that still stand today.

The unique charm of Al-Moez Street lies in its ability to blend history with modern life. As you walk along the street, you will see a mix of ancient monuments, bustling bazaars, and local residents going about their daily activities. The street is a vibrant and dynamic space where the past and present coexist in harmony. The carefully restored facades of the historic buildings reflect the architectural styles of different periods, showcasing the intricate craftsmanship and artistic traditions of Islamic Cairo.

One of the most striking features of Al-Moez Street is the sheer number of historic landmarks that line its path. Among the most notable is the Qalawun Complex, a magnificent ensemble of structures that includes a mosque, a madrasa, and a mausoleum. Built in the 13th century by Sultan Al-Mansur Qalawun, the complex is renowned for its elaborate decorations, including carved stone, inlaid wood, and colorful mosaics. The mausoleum, in particular, is considered one of the finest examples of Mamluk architecture and is often compared to the grandeur of the Alhambra in Spain.

Another highlight of the street is the Al-Aqmar Mosque, which is one of the oldest mosques in Cairo. Built during the Fatimid period, the mosque is known for its unique façade, which features intricate geometric patterns and calligraphy. The design of the mosque reflects the Fatimid emphasis on symbolism and religious expression, making it a fascinating site for those interested in Islamic art and architecture. Despite its relatively small size, the Al-Aqmar Mosque holds great historical and cultural significance.

As you continue your walk along Al-Moez Street, you will come across the Sultan Al-Ghuri Complex, a striking example of Mamluk architecture from the early 16th century. This complex includes a mosque, a madrasa, and a khanqah (Sufi lodge), all built around a central courtyard. The architecture of the complex is characterized by its symmetry, intricate stonework, and decorative tilework. The site is also known for its evening cultural performances, where visitors can enjoy traditional music and dance in a historic setting.

Al-Moez Street is also home to a number of sabil-kuttabs, which are unique structures that served as both water dispensers and Quranic schools. These buildings were designed to provide free drinking water to passersby while also offering a space for education. The Sabil-Kuttab of Abdel Rahman Katkhuda is a particularly beautiful example, with its richly decorated façade and intricately carved woodwork. These structures reflect the philanthropic and educational values of Islamic society, adding another layer of meaning to the street's history.

Walking along Al-Moez Street also offers the opportunity to explore its vibrant markets and shops. The street is a hub for traditional crafts, including textiles, jewelry, pottery, and leather goods. Local artisans often display their work in small stalls, allowing visitors to purchase unique souvenirs and learn about the techniques used to create them. The markets are a sensory delight, filled with the sounds of merchants calling out their wares, the aroma of spices and incense, and the colorful displays of goods.

In addition to its architectural and cultural treasures, Al-Moez Street is a place where you can experience the warmth and hospitality of Cairo's residents. The street is alive with activity, from families strolling in the evening to groups of friends gathering at cafes to enjoy tea and conversation. Many of the cafes and restaurants along the street serve traditional Egyptian dishes, offering a chance to sample local flavors in an authentic setting. Popular options include koshary, a hearty mix of rice, lentils, and pasta, and feeter, a flaky pastry that can be filled with sweet or savory ingredients.

Visiting Al-Moez Street is a rewarding experience at any time of day, but the atmosphere is particularly magical in the evening. The street is beautifully lit, with soft lights illuminating the facades of the historic buildings and creating a warm and inviting ambiance. Many visitors choose to visit during this time to enjoy the cooler temperatures and the vibrant energy of the street at night.

To make the most of your visit to Al-Moez Street, it is recommended to join a guided tour led by a knowledgeable Egyptologist or historian. These tours provide valuable context and insights into the history and significance of the street's landmarks, helping you appreciate the rich heritage of Islamic Cairo. Alternatively, you can explore the street on your own, taking the time to admire the details of the architecture and soak in the atmosphere.

Al-Moez Street is easily accessible from other parts of Cairo and is located near several other historic sites, including the

Khan El Khalili Bazaar and the Al-Azhar Mosque. Its central location makes it a convenient addition to any itinerary, whether you are exploring the city for a day or a week. The street's combination of history, culture, and community makes it a must-visit destination that offers a deep and authentic connection to Cairo's past and present.

The Cave Church of St. Simon

The Cave Church of St. Simon, located in the Mokattam Hills of Cairo, is a hidden gem that showcases a blend of history, faith, and remarkable artistry. It is not just a place of worship but also a site of cultural and spiritual significance that offers a deeper understanding of Cairo's diverse religious heritage. Visiting this church, which is carved into the natural rock of the Mokattam Hills, provides a unique experience that is both awe-inspiring and humbling.

The Cave Church of St. Simon is part of the Monastery of St. Simon the Tanner, a large complex that serves as the spiritual center for Cairo's Zabbaleen community. The Zabbaleen, often referred to as Cairo's garbage collectors, are a marginalized Christian community that has played a vital role in managing the city's waste for decades. Despite their challenging living conditions, the Zabbaleen have created a strong and resilient community centered around their faith, and the Cave Church stands as a testament to their devotion and perseverance.

The history of the Cave Church dates back to the 1970s when the Zabbaleen moved to the Mokattam area after being relocated by the government. As their community grew, they sought a place to gather and worship. The natural caves in the Mokattam Hills provided an ideal location for building a church that could accommodate large numbers of people. Over time, the church was expanded and transformed into the impressive structure it is today. The main church, named after St. Simon the Tanner, can hold over 20,000 worshippers, making it the largest church in the Middle East.

St. Simon the Tanner, for whom the church is named, is a revered figure in Coptic Christian tradition. According to legend, he was a pious and humble man who lived during the 10th century and worked as a tanner of hides. He is best known for his role in a miracle that is said to have saved the Christian community in Cairo. The story goes that the Fatimid Caliph Al-Mu'izz challenged the Christian Patriarch to prove the truth of the Gospel by moving the Mokattam Mountain. St. Simon, through his prayers and faith, was able to accomplish this miraculous feat, leading to the mountain's movement and the salvation of the Christian community.

The church itself is a marvel of engineering and artistry. Carved directly into the limestone cliffs of the Mokattam Hills, the church features a large amphitheater-style design that allows for excellent visibility and acoustics. The interior is adorned with stunning carvings and sculptures that depict biblical scenes, stories from the life of St. Simon, and symbols of the Christian faith. These intricate works of art were created by talented local artists and craftsmen, and they add to the spiritual atmosphere of the church. The use of natural rock as both a structural element and a canvas for art gives the church a raw and organic beauty that is unlike any other place of worship in Cairo.

One of the most striking features of the Cave Church is its expansive frescoes and carvings, which cover the walls and ceilings of the church. These artworks are not only visually stunning but also serve as a form of storytelling, illustrating important moments from the Bible and the history of the Coptic Church. The attention to detail in these carvings is extraordinary, with each figure and scene brought to life through the skilled use of light, shadow, and texture. The artworks are illuminated by natural light that filters through openings in the rock, creating a serene and contemplative atmosphere.

Visiting the Cave Church offers more than just an opportunity to admire its architecture and art; it also provides insight into the lives and faith of the Zabbaleen community. The church is a central part of their spiritual and social life, hosting regular services, religious festivals, and community events. Despite their hardships, the Zabbaleen have maintained a strong sense of identity and faith, and their resilience is reflected in the care and dedication they have put into building and maintaining the church.

Getting to the Cave Church can be an adventure in itself, as it is located in an area that is not typically frequented by tourists.

The Mokattam Hills are situated in southeastern Cairo, and the church is accessed through the Zabbaleen settlement. Visitors often hire a private car or join a guided tour to reach the church, as public transportation options are limited. The journey to the church provides a glimpse into the daily lives of the Zabbaleen, with their homes, workshops, and recycling operations visible along the way. While the area may appear chaotic at first glance, it is a place of industry and community where every corner is filled with activity and purpose.

The best time to visit the Cave Church is during the day when natural light enhances the beauty of the carvings and the surrounding landscape. The church is open to visitors of all faiths, and there is no entrance fee, though donations are welcome and go toward the maintenance of the church and support for the Zabbaleen community. It is important to dress modestly and respect the sanctity of the space, as it is an active place of worship.

For those interested in exploring more of the area, the Monastery of St. Simon also includes several smaller chapels and religious sites, each with its own unique history and character. The complex is surrounded by the rugged beauty of the Mokattam Hills, which provide a dramatic backdrop to the church and monastery. The views from the hills are also worth taking in, as they offer a sweeping panorama of Cairo's skyline.

A visit to the Cave Church of St. Simon is a profoundly moving experience that combines spirituality, history, and art in a setting of extraordinary natural beauty. It is a place that inspires reflection and admiration, not only for its physical grandeur but also for the strength and faith of the community that built it. For anyone exploring Cairo's hidden gems, the Cave Church is an essential destination that reveals a lesser-known but deeply meaningful aspect of the city's rich cultural and religious heritage.

Zabbaleen Garbage City

Zabbaleen Garbage City, located in the Mokattam district of Cairo, offers a truly unique and fascinating perspective on urban resilience, environmental sustainability, and human ingenuity. This area is home to the Zabbaleen community, a group of predominantly Coptic Christians who have lived and worked in Cairo's waste management sector for generations. Though the term "Garbage City" may seem unappealing at first glance, a closer look reveals an inspiring story of resourcefulness, community spirit, and a way of life that has evolved around the art of recycling.

The Zabbaleen, whose name translates to "garbage people," play an essential role in Cairo's waste management system. For decades, they have been responsible for collecting and sorting the city's trash, recycling a remarkable percentage of what they collect. Unlike modern waste disposal systems that often rely on mechanized processes, the Zabbaleen employ manual methods to separate and repurpose waste. Their efficiency in recycling is impressive, with estimates suggesting that they recycle up to 80% of the waste they collect—far higher than many industrialized nations.

Garbage City itself is a bustling and vibrant area, characterized by its narrow streets lined with homes, workshops, and piles of sorted waste. Walking through the area, you can see the intricate system the Zabbaleen have developed for managing waste. Each household specializes in processing specific types of materials, such as plastic, metal, paper, or glass. The work is labor-intensive and often involves the entire family, with skills and techniques passed down through generations. Despite the challenges they face, the Zabbaleen take great pride in their work and their contribution to keeping Cairo clean.

What makes Garbage City particularly unique is its dual identity as both a place of work and a close-knit community. The Zabbaleen have built a strong social fabric, centered around their shared faith, traditions, and commitment to their work. The community's religious life is anchored by the Cave Church of St. Simon, a massive church carved into the cliffs of the Mokattam Hills. This church serves as a spiritual and cultural hub for the Zabbaleen, hosting regular services, festivals, and gatherings that strengthen their sense of identity and solidarity.

A visit to Garbage City offers a rare opportunity to witness this way of life up close. It is an eye-opening experience that challenges preconceived notions about waste, recycling, and the people who work in this field. The area provides valuable insights into the global issue of waste management and highlights the potential for community-driven solutions to environmental challenges. Visitors are often struck by the resourcefulness and ingenuity of the Zabbaleen, who have turned what many would consider a problem into a livelihood. One of the most striking aspects of Garbage City is the scale and organization of the recycling operations. Large piles of sorted waste are stored in designated areas, waiting to be processed further or sold to buyers. For example, plastic bottles are shredded into small flakes, which can be melted down and repurposed into new products. Paper is bundled and sold to mills for recycling, while metals are cleaned and sent to factories for reuse. The Zabbaleen have also embraced innovative approaches to recycling, such as using organic waste to produce compost or biogas.

Despite its significance, Garbage City faces many challenges. The work is physically demanding and often carried out in difficult conditions, with limited access to protective equipment or modern facilities. The community has also struggled with social stigma and marginalization, as their association with waste has led to discrimination and a lack of recognition for their contributions. However, the Zabbaleen have shown remarkable resilience in the face of these challenges, and their story is one of determination and perseverance.

In recent years, efforts have been made to support the Zabbaleen and improve their living and working conditions. Non-governmental organizations (NGOs) and social enterprises have partnered with the community to provide education, healthcare, and technical training. These initiatives aim to empower the Zabbaleen and enhance their capacity to manage waste sustainably. Additionally, the government has started to recognize the importance of the Zabbaleen's role in Cairo's waste management system and has taken steps to formalize their work and integrate them into the broader economy.

Visiting Garbage City requires an open mind and a willingness to look beyond the surface. While the area may initially appear chaotic and overwhelming, it is a place of immense cultural and environmental importance. Tours of Garbage City, often led by local guides or NGOs, provide an in-depth look at the community's work and way of life. These tours are not only informative but also help raise awareness about the Zabbaleen's contributions and the challenges they face.

When visiting, it is important to approach the experience with respect and sensitivity. The Zabbaleen are proud of their work and their community, and visitors should be mindful of their privacy and dignity. Taking photos without permission or treating the area as a spectacle can be intrusive and disrespectful. Instead, focus on learning from the experience and engaging with the community in a meaningful way.

Garbage City is more than just a place—it is a living example of human adaptability and the power of community. It challenges conventional ideas about waste and recycling, demonstrating that even the most unassuming materials can have value when approached with creativity and determination. The Zabbaleen's story is one of hope and inspiration, showing how people can find solutions to complex problems through collaboration and ingenuity.

For those exploring Cairo's hidden gems, a visit to Garbage City offers a perspective that is both humbling and enlightening. It is a reminder of the interconnectedness of our actions and the importance of sustainability in today's world. By witnessing the Zabbaleen's work and learning about their contributions, visitors can gain a deeper appreciation for the challenges and opportunities of living in harmony with our environment.

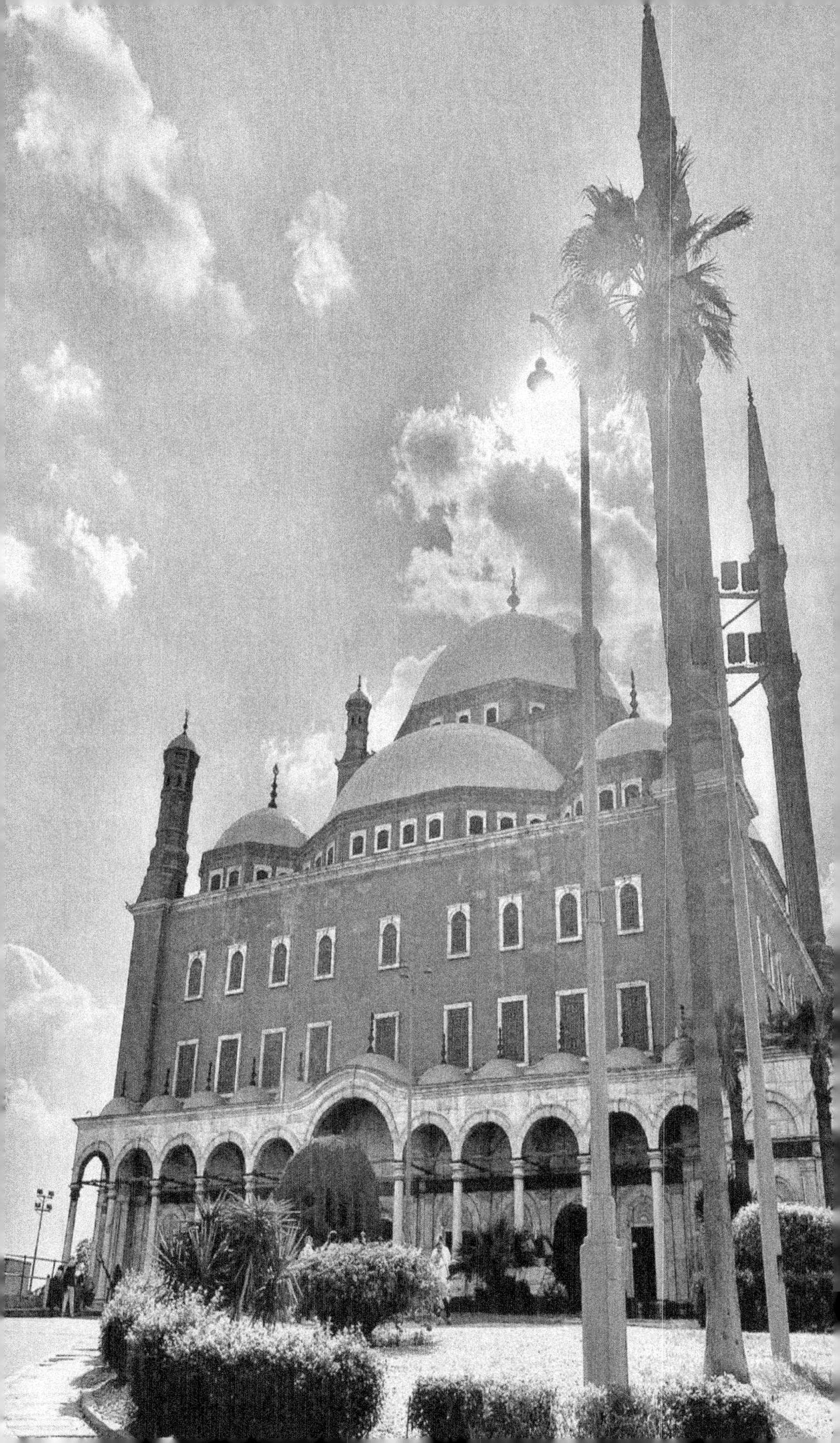

CHAPTER 9

CULTURAL EXPERIENCES AND HISTORY

Attending a Sufi Dance Performance

Attending a Sufi dance performance in Cairo is a deeply captivating cultural experience that offers a profound glimpse into the spiritual and artistic heritage of Egypt. This mesmerizing performance, often referred to as tanoura, is not merely a dance but a meditative and devotional expression of Sufi mysticism. It is rooted in the centuries-old traditions of the Sufi order, which emphasize the pursuit of spiritual enlightenment and the connection between the human soul and the divine. Witnessing a Sufi dance performance allows you to immerse yourself in this rich and meaningful tradition, gaining insight into the intersection of religion, music, and art in Egyptian culture.

The tanoura dance derives its name from the brightly colored, multi-layered skirts worn by the performers. These skirts are a defining feature of the dance and play a crucial role in the visual and symbolic aspects of the performance. As the dancers spin gracefully, their skirts flare out in vibrant patterns, creating a kaleidoscopic effect that is both hypnotic and awe-inspiring. The movements of the dance are deliberate and purposeful, symbolizing the spiritual journey of the soul as it seeks unity with the divine. Each spin represents the cyclical nature of life and the continuous search for meaning and connection.

The setting for a Sufi dance performance is as important as the dance itself. In Cairo, one of the most popular venues for experiencing this art form is the Wekalet El Ghouri, a beautifully preserved Mamluk-era building located near the bustling Khan El Khalili Bazaar. This historic venue provides an intimate and atmospheric backdrop for the performance, with its intricate architecture and soft lighting enhancing the mystical ambiance. The setting transports you to a different time, allowing you to fully appreciate the depth and beauty of the tradition.

The performance typically begins with an introduction by a group of musicians, who play traditional instruments such as the oud (a stringed instrument similar to a lute), the ney (a type of flute), and various percussion instruments. The music is an integral part of the experience, as it sets the tone and guides the rhythm of the dance. The melodies are deeply evocative, blending hauntingly beautiful tunes with rhythmic patterns that build in intensity as the performance progresses. The music itself is a form of devotion, with its repetitive and entrancing qualities designed to elevate both the performers and the audience to a state of spiritual reflection.

As the music swells, the dancers enter the stage, dressed in their distinctive costumes. The primary dancer, known as the dervish, takes center stage and begins to spin in a counterclockwise direction, following the rhythm of the music. The act of spinning is not merely a physical movement but a meditative practice that allows the dancer to transcend the material world and focus entirely on the divine. The dervish's movements are smooth and controlled, demonstrating incredible skill and discipline. Despite the rapid spinning, the dancer maintains perfect balance and composure, embodying the spiritual harmony that the dance seeks to achieve.

One of the most striking aspects of the tanoura dance is the symbolic use of the dancer's costume. The layers of the skirt represent different aspects of existence, such as the physical body, the soul, and the universe. As the dancer spins, the swirling patterns of the skirt create a visual representation of cosmic energy and unity. In some performances, the dervish removes layers of the skirt during the dance, symbolizing the shedding of earthly attachments and the journey toward spiritual enlightenment. The colors and designs of the skirts often carry additional symbolic meanings, reflecting themes of harmony, balance, and divine order.

Throughout the performance, the connection between the dancer and the music becomes increasingly evident. The rhythm of the music mirrors the dancer's movements, creating a seamless interplay between sound and motion. This synchronization reflects the Sufi belief in the unity of all things, where every element of existence is interconnected and harmonized. The audience, too, becomes part of this dynamic, as the energy of the performance resonates deeply, evoking a sense of awe and introspection.

The spiritual significance of the Sufi dance extends beyond its visual and auditory appeal. It is a form of dhikr, a Sufi practice that involves the repetition of prayers, chants, or movements as a way of remembering and drawing closer to God. The dance embodies this practice through its repetitive spinning, which mirrors the act of turning one's heart and mind toward the divine. For the Sufi dervish, the dance is both a personal and communal act of devotion, offering a path to spiritual fulfillment and connection.

Attending a Sufi dance performance in Cairo is not just an opportunity to witness a beautiful art form but also a chance to engage with a profound aspect of Egyptian and Islamic culture. The experience provides a window into the spiritual traditions that have shaped the region for centuries, offering a deeper appreciation for the values of harmony, unity, and devotion that underpin Sufism. It is a reminder of the power of art and music to transcend cultural and religious boundaries, fostering a shared sense of wonder and connection among people from all walks of life.

To fully appreciate the performance, it is helpful to approach it with an open mind and a willingness to explore its deeper meanings. The dance is not meant to be merely entertaining but to inspire reflection and a sense of connection to something greater than oneself. Many visitors describe the experience as meditative and transformative, leaving them with a lasting sense of peace and inspiration.
Practical details for attending a Sufi dance performance in Cairo include planning your visit to coincide with scheduled

performances, as they typically take place on specific evenings. Tickets can often be purchased in advance, either online or at the venue, and it is advisable to arrive early to secure a good seat. The performances are suitable for all ages and are accessible to both locals and tourists, making them a welcoming and inclusive experience.

Exploring Egypt's Coptic Heritage

Exploring Egypt's Coptic heritage is an enlightening journey through one of the oldest Christian communities in the world. The Copts, who are the indigenous Christian people of Egypt, have a history that traces back to the earliest days of Christianity, making their culture and traditions an integral part of the country's rich tapestry. Delving into Coptic heritage offers a deeper understanding of Egypt's religious, historical, and cultural evolution, as well as an appreciation for the resilience and faith of this ancient community.

Coptic Christianity has its roots in the first century AD, with the arrival of St. Mark the Evangelist, who is believed to have brought Christianity to Egypt. As one of the first Christian communities, the Copts played a significant role in shaping early Christian theology, monastic traditions, and art. Despite centuries of challenges, including periods of persecution and social marginalization, the Copts have preserved their identity, faith, and traditions. Today, their heritage is evident in the numerous churches, monasteries, and cultural artifacts scattered throughout Egypt, many of which can be explored in Cairo.

One of the most iconic places to begin your exploration of Coptic heritage is Old Cairo, also known as Coptic Cairo. This area is home to some of the most significant Coptic landmarks, each offering a unique glimpse into the community's history and spiritual life. Walking through the narrow streets of Coptic Cairo feels like stepping back in time, as the ancient buildings and serene atmosphere transport you to a bygone era.

The Hanging Church, also known as the Church of the Virgin Mary, is one of the most famous landmarks in Coptic Cairo. Built in the 3rd century AD, it is called the Hanging Church because it was constructed on top of the southern gate of the Roman Fortress of Babylon. This architectural marvel appears to "hang" above the ground, supported by wooden beams. Inside, the church is adorned with intricate woodwork, beautiful icons, and marble inlays, reflecting the artistic and spiritual devotion of the Copts. The church also serves as the seat of the Coptic Orthodox Pope, underscoring its importance as a center of faith and leadership.

Another essential stop is the Church of St. Sergius and Bacchus, one of the oldest churches in Egypt. This church holds great religious significance, as it is believed to have been built over the site where the Holy Family—Mary, Joseph, and the infant Jesus—took refuge during their flight to Egypt. The crypt, which is considered the exact location of their stay, is a sacred site for Christian pilgrims. The church's simplicity and historical resonance make it a deeply moving place to visit, offering a sense of connection to the early days of Christianity.

Adjacent to these churches is the Coptic Museum, which houses one of the most extensive collections of Coptic art and artifacts in the world. The museum provides a comprehensive overview of Coptic history, showcasing items such as ancient manuscripts, textiles, carvings, and metalwork. Each piece tells a story of the Copts' faith, creativity, and resilience, highlighting their contributions to Egypt's cultural heritage. Walking through the museum's galleries, you can trace the evolution of Coptic art and gain a deeper appreciation for its unique blend of Egyptian, Greco-Roman, and Christian influences.

Monasticism is another vital aspect of Coptic heritage, and Egypt is considered the birthplace of Christian monasticism. The Coptic monks of the 4th century laid the foundation for monastic traditions that spread throughout the Christian world. While many of Egypt's historic monasteries are located outside Cairo, such as the Monastery of St. Anthony and the Monastery of St. Paul in the Eastern Desert, some are easily accessible from the capital. These monasteries offer a glimpse into the ascetic lifestyle and spiritual practices of the monks, who dedicated their lives to prayer, contemplation, and community service.

The Coptic calendar, liturgical practices, and festivals also provide insight into the community's spiritual and cultural life. Major Coptic celebrations, such as Christmas (celebrated on January 7) and Easter, are marked by unique traditions, including special prayers, hymns, and feasts. The Coptic liturgy, conducted in the ancient Coptic language, is a rich and solemn expression of faith that has remained largely unchanged for centuries. Attending a Coptic service or festival offers a rare opportunity to witness these traditions firsthand and experience the deep spirituality of the community.

The challenges faced by the Coptic community throughout history have shaped their identity and contributed to their enduring resilience. From the Arab conquest in the 7th century to modern times, the Copts have navigated periods of marginalization while maintaining their faith and cultural heritage. Their ability to adapt and thrive in the face of adversity is a testament to their strength and determination, and exploring their history provides valuable lessons about perseverance and unity.

Beyond Old Cairo, traces of Coptic heritage can be found in other parts of the city. The Mokattam Hills, for example, are home to the Cave Church of St. Simon the Tanner, a massive church carved into the cliffs and a spiritual center for the Zabbaleen community. This unique site demonstrates the community's ingenuity and deep faith, as well as their commitment to creating a sacred space that reflects their identity.

Exploring Egypt's Coptic heritage is not only a journey through history but also an opportunity to engage with the living traditions of a vibrant community. The Copts' contributions to art, architecture, theology, and social life are an integral part of Egypt's identity, and their story is one of faith, resilience, and cultural richness. Whether you are visiting the ancient churches of Old Cairo, learning about monastic traditions, or admiring Coptic art, this exploration offers a deeper understanding of Egypt's diverse and multifaceted heritage.

Festivals and Religious Events in Cairo

Festivals and religious events in Cairo are an integral part of the city's cultural identity, reflecting its rich history, diverse communities, and deep spiritual traditions. Attending these events or learning about them offers a unique window into the lives, beliefs, and customs of the people who call Cairo home. These occasions are not only significant for their religious and cultural meanings but also for the ways they bring people together in celebration, reflection, and unity. From Islamic and Christian observances to secular festivities, Cairo's calendar is filled with vibrant events that highlight the city's heritage and communal spirit.

One of the most widely celebrated festivals in Cairo is Ramadan, the Islamic holy month of fasting, prayer, and reflection. During this time, the city transforms into a lively and spiritual hub. From sunrise to sunset, Muslims abstain from food, drink, and other physical needs as an act of devotion and self-discipline. As the sun sets each day, families and communities come together for iftar, the meal that breaks the fast. The streets of Cairo come alive with activity as food vendors, cafes, and restaurants set up colorful displays to offer traditional dishes like koshary, lentil soup, and konafa. Decorative lanterns known as *fanous* illuminate the city, creating a festive atmosphere that is both spiritual and communal. Late into the night, people gather for tarawih prayers at mosques, with the sound of Quranic recitations filling the air.

Eid al-Fitr, the festival that marks the end of Ramadan, is another major event in Cairo. This three-day celebration begins with a special prayer held at mosques and open spaces across the city. Families dress in their finest clothes, exchange gifts, and share elaborate meals. The joy of the occasion is palpable as children receive *eidiya* (small sums of money given as gifts), and homes are filled with the aroma of sweet pastries like kahk. Public spaces such as parks and entertainment venues are bustling with families enjoying outings, and the sense of community and generosity is evident everywhere.

Eid al-Adha, the Festival of Sacrifice, is another significant Islamic event observed in Cairo. Commemorating the willingness of Prophet Ibrahim (Abraham) to sacrifice his son in obedience to God, this festival is marked by the ritual sacrifice of animals such as sheep, goats, or cows. The meat is distributed among family, friends, and those in need, symbolizing charity and compassion. During Eid al-Adha, Cairo's mosques hold special prayers, and the city is filled with the sounds of greetings and laughter as people gather to celebrate.

For Egypt's Coptic Christian community, Christmas and Easter are the most important religious events. Coptic

Christmas, celebrated on January 7, is a solemn and joyous occasion that begins with the Midnight Mass held at churches across Cairo, including the historic Hanging Church and the Cathedral of St. Mark in Abbassia. Following the Mass, families come together to enjoy festive meals that often include traditional dishes like *fatta*, a hearty dish of bread, rice, and meat. Easter, known as *Pascha* in the Coptic tradition, is preceded by Holy Week, a period of reflection and prayer. The celebrations culminate in the Easter Vigil, a deeply spiritual service filled with hymns and prayers.

Another unique festival in Cairo is Sham El-Nessim, an ancient Egyptian holiday that has been celebrated for thousands of years. This springtime festival, which falls on the Monday after Coptic Easter, is a secular event that marks the arrival of spring. Families and friends gather in parks, along the Nile, and in other outdoor spaces to enjoy picnics and traditional foods like salted fish (*feseekh*), green onions, and colored eggs. The festival is a testament to Egypt's enduring connection to its Pharaonic past and its ability to blend traditions from different eras.

Moulid festivals are another fascinating aspect of Cairo's cultural life. These events celebrate the birthdays of saints, prophets, or revered figures in both Islamic and Christian traditions. One of the most prominent moulids is the Moulid of Sayyidna al-Hussein, held in honor of the grandson of the Prophet Muhammad. This event takes place in the area surrounding the Al-Hussein Mosque, where thousands of devotees gather for days of prayers, processions, and festivities. The atmosphere is electric, with Sufi chanting, traditional music, and colorful decorations creating a sense of spiritual exuberance. Christian moulids, such as the Moulid of the Virgin Mary, are celebrated with equal devotion, often involving processions, hymns, and the lighting of candles.

The Cairo International Film Festival is another event that highlights the city's cultural vibrancy. While not religious in nature, this prestigious festival draws filmmakers, actors, and cinephiles from around the world. Held annually, the festival showcases a wide range of films, from thought-provoking dramas to experimental works, offering a platform for creative expression and cultural exchange.

The Cairo Opera House frequently hosts performances and events that celebrate Egypt's artistic heritage. From classical music concerts to ballets and traditional dance shows, these events provide a glimpse into the country's rich cultural tapestry. Special performances are often organized during national holidays or commemorative events, adding to the festive spirit of the city.

Festivals and religious events in Cairo are not only about celebration but also about creating a sense of belonging and continuity. These occasions provide opportunities for people to come together, express their faith, and honor their traditions. They also reflect the city's diversity, with events that cater to different religious and cultural communities coexisting harmoniously. For visitors, participating in or observing these festivals is a chance to connect with Cairo's soul, experiencing the warmth, hospitality, and deep-rooted traditions that define the city.

The rhythm of life in Cairo is shaped by these events, each adding a layer of meaning and richness to the city's cultural landscape. From the spiritual devotion of Ramadan to the joyous picnics of Sham El-Nessim, Cairo's festivals and religious events offer a vivid and authentic glimpse into the lives of its people. They remind us of the importance of community, tradition, and shared experiences in creating a sense of identity and belonging.

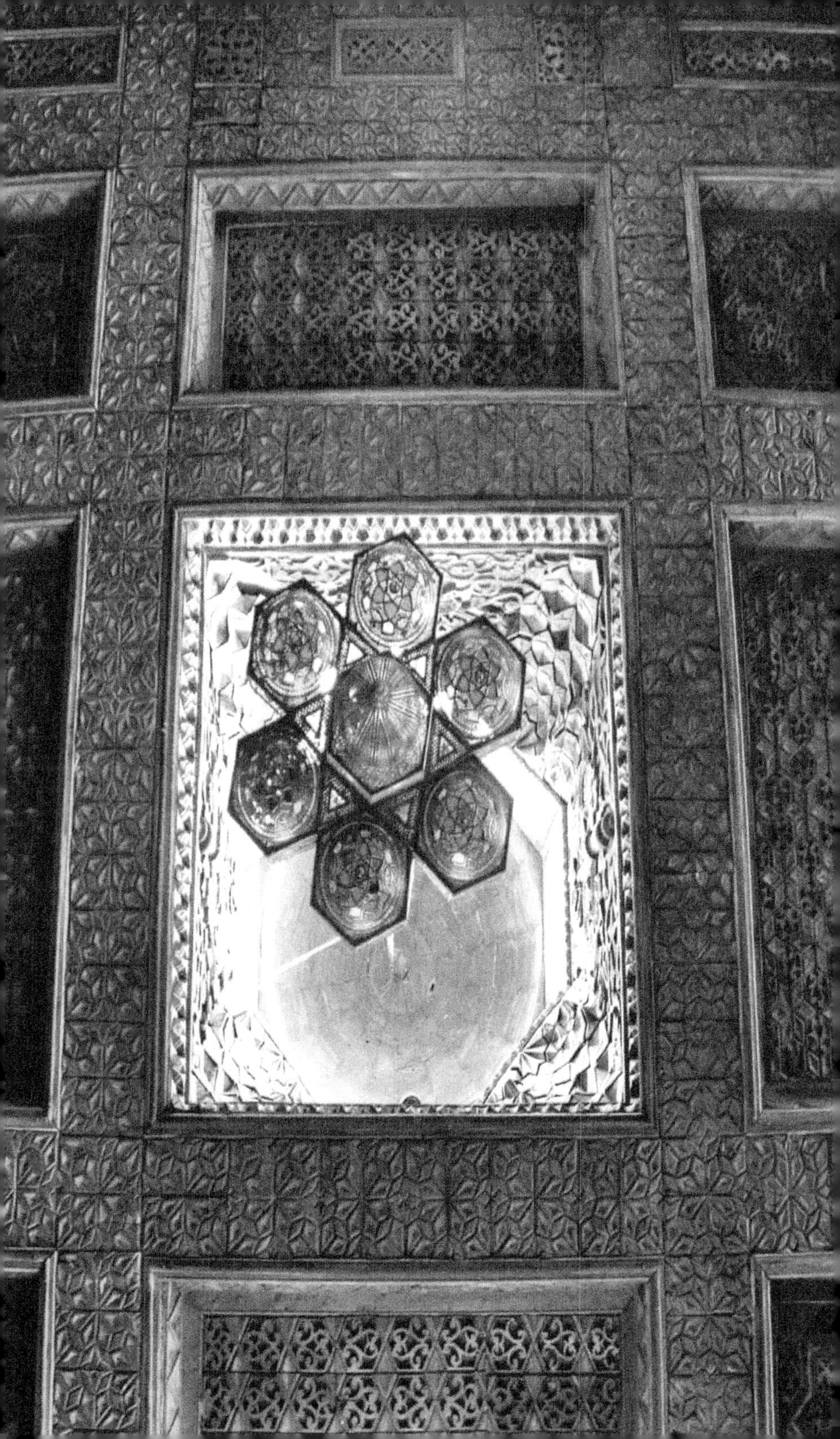

CHAPTER 10

PRACTICAL TIPS AND RESOURCES

Essential Packing List for Cairo

Packing for a trip to Cairo, Egypt, requires careful thought and preparation to ensure you have everything you need for a comfortable and enjoyable visit. Cairo is a city that blends history, culture, and modern life, offering a wide variety of experiences, from exploring ancient pyramids to navigating bustling markets. The weather, cultural norms, and types of activities you plan to do all play a role in determining what to pack. This essential packing list will help you prepare for your trip so that you can make the most of your time in Cairo while staying comfortable and respectful of local customs.

When it comes to clothing, it is important to consider both the climate and the cultural norms of Egypt. Cairo experiences hot weather for much of the year, with temperatures often reaching over 30°C (86°F) in the summer months. Lightweight, breathable fabrics like cotton and linen are ideal for staying cool during the day. Long-sleeved shirts and long pants are recommended not only to protect your skin from the sun but also to show respect for local cultural standards, particularly when visiting religious sites. Women may also find it helpful to pack a few loose-fitting maxi dresses or skirts that provide comfort and coverage. While Cairo is a relatively cosmopolitan city, modest dressing is appreciated, especially in more traditional areas.

Sun protection is another essential consideration when packing for Cairo. The city receives plenty of sunlight throughout the year, so you will need to protect yourself from the sun's intense rays. A wide-brimmed hat or a lightweight scarf can provide shade for your face and neck. Sunglasses with UV protection are a must to shield your eyes from glare, especially when exploring outdoor sites like the Giza Plateau. Sunscreen with a high SPF is critical to prevent sunburn, and it is advisable to choose a water-resistant formula that lasts throughout the day.

Footwear is an important aspect of your packing list because you are likely to spend a significant amount of time walking. Comfortable, sturdy shoes are essential, especially if you plan to visit historical sites like the pyramids, the Egyptian Museum, or the Citadel. Closed-toe shoes, such as sneakers or lightweight hiking shoes, are ideal for uneven terrain and dusty conditions. If you prefer sandals, opt for ones with good arch support and straps to keep them secure. Avoid packing shoes with thin soles or heels, as they may not be practical for walking on cobblestone streets or sandy paths.

Since Cairo is known for its bustling bazaars and crowded streets, a secure and practical bag is a necessity. A crossbody bag with a sturdy strap is a good option, as it allows you to keep your belongings close while leaving your hands free. Look for a bag with multiple compartments to organize essentials like your wallet, phone, and travel documents. If you are carrying a camera or other valuables, consider using an anti-theft bag with features like lockable zippers or RFID-blocking pockets.

Packing for your health and hygiene is equally important. Cairo's tap water is not safe for drinking, so it is advisable to bring a reusable water bottle with a built-in filter to stay hydrated. This can save you money and reduce plastic waste compared to buying bottled water. Hand sanitizer and wet wipes are useful for maintaining cleanliness, especially after handling cash or using public facilities. A small first-aid kit is recommended, including basics like adhesive bandages, pain relievers, antiseptic cream, and any personal medications you may need. Over-the-counter remedies for common travel issues, such as an upset stomach or allergies, can also be helpful.

Electronics and travel accessories should also be carefully chosen. Egypt uses the European-style two-prong plug (Type C or Type F), so you will need a universal travel adapter to charge your devices. Power banks are useful for keeping your phone charged, especially during long days of sightseeing. If you plan to take photos or videos, ensure that you bring extra memory cards and batteries for your camera. A lightweight tripod or selfie stick can be handy for capturing shots of landmarks without needing assistance from others.

Documents and money are critical items to organize before your trip. Ensure that your passport is valid for at least six months from your date of entry into Egypt and that you have obtained any necessary visas. Print out copies of your passport, travel insurance, and booking confirmations, and store them separately from the originals. Cash is widely used in Cairo, particularly in markets and smaller shops, so bring some Egyptian pounds for everyday expenses. ATMs are common in the city, but it is a good idea to have some cash on hand when you arrive. Credit cards are accepted in larger establishments, but they may not be as widely used in smaller, local venues.

Cultural sensitivity is an important aspect of visiting Cairo, and packing a few additional items can help you blend in and show respect. For women, a lightweight scarf is a versatile accessory that can be used to cover your head or shoulders when visiting mosques or conservative areas. Men may also want to bring a button-up shirt and lightweight pants for similar occasions. A small notebook and pen can be useful for jotting down addresses, translations, or tips from locals, particularly if you encounter language barriers.

For those who plan to explore the rich history and culture of Cairo, guidebooks and travel apps can be valuable resources. A pocket-sized guidebook with maps and key phrases can be a helpful companion during your adventures. If you prefer digital resources, download apps that provide offline maps, language translation, and information about attractions.

Finally, consider packing a few items for your comfort and enjoyment. Earplugs or noise-canceling headphones can be useful for blocking out city noise or ensuring a good night's sleep. A lightweight travel pillow and eye mask are helpful for long flights or bus journeys. If you enjoy journaling or reading, bring a notebook or an e-reader to document your experiences or pass the time during quiet moments.

By carefully selecting and organizing your packing list, you can ensure a smooth and enjoyable trip to Cairo. Each item you bring will play a role in enhancing your comfort, convenience, and overall experience, allowing you to focus on discovering the wonders of this extraordinary city. Whether you are marveling at ancient monuments, exploring lively markets, or enjoying the hospitality of the locals, being well-prepared will make your journey all the more memorable.

Useful Travel Phrases in Arabic

Learning a few essential travel phrases in Arabic before visiting Cairo, Egypt, can significantly enhance your experience. Even if you are not fluent, making the effort to communicate in the local language shows respect for the culture and often results in warmer interactions with locals. Arabic is the official language of Egypt, and while English is widely spoken in tourist areas, knowing some basic Arabic phrases can help you navigate situations, especially when dealing with taxi drivers, market vendors, or in more traditional neighborhoods. This guide provides a comprehensive list of useful phrases, their meanings, and how they can be applied during your trip.

One of the first phrases every traveler should learn is "As-salamu alaykum" (السلام عليكم), which means "Peace be upon you." This is a universal greeting in Arabic and is commonly used when meeting someone or entering a shop or home. It is polite to respond with "Wa alaykum as-salam" (وعليكم السلام), meaning "And peace be upon you too." This simple exchange sets a friendly and respectful tone for your interactions.

When introducing yourself or expressing gratitude, phrases like "Shukran" (شكراً), meaning "Thank you," and "Afwan" (عفواً), meaning "You're welcome," are essential. These words can be used in various situations, from thanking someone for directions to expressing appreciation for a meal. For a more formal way to say thank you, you can use "Shukran jazeelan" (شكراً جزيلا), which translates to "Thank you very much."

Politeness is highly valued in Egyptian culture, so knowing how to say "Please" and "Excuse me" can go a long way. "Min fadlak" (من فضلك) means "Please" when addressing a man, while "Min fadlik" (من فضلك) is used for a woman. To say "Excuse me," you can use "Law samaht" (لو سمحت) for a man or "Law samahti" (لو سمحتي) for a woman. These phrases are useful for getting someone's attention or asking for help.

When navigating the city, it is helpful to know how to ask for directions or clarify your destination. Phrases like "Ayna..." (أين...) mean "Where is..." and can be followed by the name of a place, such as "Ayna al-mat'am?" (أين المطعم؟), meaning "Where is the restaurant?" or "Ayna al-hammam?" (أين الحمام؟), meaning "Where is the bathroom?" Another useful phrase is

"Kam yuba'd?" (كم يبعد؟), which means "How far is it?" These phrases can help you communicate with taxi drivers, hotel staff, or passersby.

If you plan to shop in Cairo's famous markets, learning numbers and phrases for bargaining is essential. Numbers in Arabic are straightforward once you familiarize yourself with them. For example, "Wahid" (واحد) is one, "Ithnayn" (إثنان) is two, and "Thalatha" (ثلاثة) is three. To ask "How much is this?" you can say "Bikam hadha?" (بكم هذا؟) or "Bikam hadhihi?" (بكم هذه؟) for feminine objects. Vendors may respond in Arabic, so knowing the numbers or asking them to write down the price can be helpful.

When dining out, you might need phrases related to ordering food or drinks. To say "I want" or "I would like," you can use "Ureed" (أريد). For example, "Ureed shay" (أريد شاي) means "I would like tea." To ask for water, you can say "Ureed maa'" (أريد ماء). If you want to inquire about the menu, you can say "Hal hunak qaa'ima lil-akl?" (هل هناك قائمة للطعام؟), meaning "Is there a menu?"

If you need assistance, knowing how to ask for help is invaluable. The phrase "Hal mumkin musa'ada?" (هل ممكن مساعدة؟) means "Can you help me?" You can follow this with a specific request, such as "Hal mumkin musa'ada fi al-muwasalat?" (هل ممكن مساعدة في المواصلات؟), meaning "Can you help with transportation?" To indicate urgency, you can use "Ana muhtaaj musa'ada!" (أنا محتاج مساعدة!), meaning "I need help!"

For social interactions, basic phrases like "Kayfa halak?" (كيف حالك؟), meaning "How are you?" when addressing a man, or "Kayfa halik?" (كيفَ حالك؟) for a woman, can help you start conversations. Responses such as "Ana bekhair" (أنا بخير), meaning "I am fine," or "Alhamdulillah" (الحمد لله), meaning "Thank God," are commonly used.

In case of emergencies, knowing how to communicate your needs is critical. To call for help, you can say "Najda!" (نجدة!), meaning "Help!" or "Musta'jil!" (مستعجل!), meaning "Emergency!" If you need to contact the police, you can say "Ayn al-shurta?" (أين الشرطة؟), meaning "Where is the police?" It is also helpful to know phrases like "Hal hunak tabib?" (هل هناك طبيب؟), meaning "Is there a doctor?"

Learning a few additional phrases for daily interactions can also be beneficial. For example, "Ma'a al-salama" (مع السلامة) means "Goodbye," while "Sabah al-khayr" (صباح الخير) means "Good morning." To say "Good evening," you can use "Masa' al-khayr" (مساء الخير). These greetings and farewells are simple yet effective ways to connect with people.

Finally, understanding local customs and etiquette goes hand in hand with language. Egyptians are known for their hospitality and friendliness, and even a small effort to speak Arabic can lead to meaningful connections. Practice these phrases before your trip, and don't hesitate to use them during your stay. Locals often appreciate the effort, and your willingness to learn can open doors to unforgettable experiences in Cairo.

Staying Connected: Internet and Mobile Data Options

Staying connected during your visit to Cairo, Egypt, is an essential aspect of ensuring a smooth and enjoyable trip. Whether you need to navigate the city, keep in touch with loved ones, or access important travel information, having reliable internet and mobile data is invaluable. Cairo, as a bustling metropolis, offers a range of options to stay connected, from local SIM cards to Wi-Fi services, catering to the needs of both short-term visitors and long-term travelers. Understanding the available options, their costs, and how to access them can help you make an informed decision and avoid unnecessary hassles during your trip.

One of the most practical and cost-effective ways to stay connected in Cairo is by purchasing a local SIM card. Egypt has several major telecom providers, including Vodafone Egypt, Orange Egypt, Etisalat Misr, and WE. These companies offer prepaid SIM cards that are widely available at the airport, in major shopping centers, and at retail outlets throughout the city. Purchasing a local SIM card is a straightforward process, but you will need to present your passport for registration as part of Egypt's telecommunications regulations. Once registered, you can choose from a variety of prepaid plans that include mobile data, call minutes, and text messages.

Local SIM cards are an excellent choice for travelers who want uninterrupted internet access and the ability to make local calls. Data packages are generally affordable, with options ranging from small daily plans to large monthly bundles. For example, a 2GB data plan may cost around 50 EGP (approximately $3 USD), while larger packages with 10GB or more can range between 150-300 EGP ($10-$20 USD), depending on the provider and the specific plan. Most providers also offer add-ons that allow you to top up your data if you run out before your plan expires.

To ensure a smooth experience, it is advisable to check the network coverage and data speeds of the provider you choose. Vodafone and Orange are often praised for their widespread coverage and reliable service, especially in urban areas like Cairo. However, if you plan to travel to more remote regions of Egypt, it is worth inquiring about the provider with the best coverage for your intended destinations.

If you do not want to purchase a local SIM card, another option is to use Wi-Fi, which is widely available in Cairo. Most hotels, cafes, and restaurants offer free Wi-Fi to their customers. Many larger establishments provide strong and reliable connections, making it easy to check emails, browse the web, or use messaging apps. However, it is important to note that public Wi-Fi networks can vary in quality, and some may have limited bandwidth or slower speeds during peak hours. For sensitive transactions, such as online banking or accessing personal accounts, it is advisable to use a secure virtual private network (VPN) to protect your data from potential security risks.

For travelers who rely heavily on internet connectivity, portable Wi-Fi devices, often called pocket Wi-Fi, are an excellent solution. These devices can be rented or purchased before or during your trip and provide a personal hotspot for your smartphone, tablet, or laptop. They are especially useful for groups or families traveling together, as multiple devices can connect to the same hotspot. Portable Wi-Fi devices are available from local telecom providers or specialized rental companies, with daily rental rates typically ranging from $5-$10 USD. Data limits and speeds vary depending on the plan, so it is important to choose a package that meets your needs.

Another option to consider is using your home country's roaming service, although this is often the most expensive choice. Many international carriers offer roaming packages for Egypt, which allow you to use your existing phone number and data plan while abroad. While convenient, roaming charges can be significantly higher than local options, with costs for data usage, calls, and texts quickly adding up. If you decide to use roaming, it is worth checking with your provider for specific rates and any available international packages that can help reduce costs.

In addition to these options, Cairo's tech-friendly environment also includes co-working spaces and business lounges that cater to remote workers and digital nomads. These spaces typically offer high-speed internet, comfortable workstations, and amenities like printing services and meeting rooms. They can be a great option if you need a quiet and professional setting to get some work done while staying connected.

When choosing how to stay connected in Cairo, it is important to consider your specific needs and usage habits. If you plan to use navigation apps, stream videos, or stay active on social media, a local SIM card with a generous data plan is likely the best option. On the other hand, if your internet needs are limited to occasional browsing or checking emails, relying on Wi-Fi at your hotel or favorite café may suffice.

To maximize your connectivity, it is also helpful to download offline maps and essential apps before your trip. Google Maps, for example, allows you to download maps of Cairo for offline use, which can be a lifesaver when navigating areas with limited connectivity. Apps like Uber or Careem (a popular ride-hailing service in Egypt) also work seamlessly with mobile data and can help you get around the city with ease.

Lastly, staying connected in Cairo is not just about accessing the internet or making calls—it is also about ensuring that your devices are charged and ready to use. Carrying a portable power bank can be invaluable, especially during long days of sightseeing when access to power outlets may be limited. A power bank with a capacity of at least 10,000mAh is recommended to keep your devices charged throughout the day.

CONCLUSION

Cairo is a city like no other—a living, breathing tapestry of ancient wonders, vibrant culture, and warm hospitality. From the awe-inspiring majesty of the Great Pyramids and the Sphinx to the intricate charm of Islamic architecture and the timeless stories of Coptic heritage, Cairo invites you to step into a world where history and modernity intertwine seamlessly. This is a place where you can explore bustling markets overflowing with treasures, cruise along the serene Nile as the city lights twinkle, and savor the rich flavors of Egyptian cuisine in every bite.

As you wander the lively streets of Cairo, every corner reveals something unique. Whether it's the melodic call to prayer echoing through the air, the laughter of families enjoying Sham El-Nessim, or the rhythmic whirling of a Sufi dancer's tanoura, Cairo captivates all your senses. You can lose yourself in the vibrant alleys of Khan El Khalili Bazaar, marvel at the craftsmanship of ancient artifacts in the Egyptian Museum, or find tranquility in the green oasis of Al-Azhar Park. No matter your interests, Cairo offers experiences that are as diverse as they are unforgettable.

Now is the perfect time to turn your dream of exploring Cairo into a reality. This guide has equipped you with everything you need to plan your journey—from understanding local customs to navigating the city's many layers of history, culture, and adventure. You have the tools to embrace every moment, from savoring authentic koshary at a street-side eatery to standing in the shadow of the ancient pyramids, feeling the weight of centuries beneath your feet. Let this guide be your companion, helping you uncover hidden gems, find the best places to stay, and create a journey tailored to your style.

As you prepare to embark on this incredible adventure, imagine the memories waiting to be made—the sun setting over the Nile as you enjoy an evening felucca ride, the vibrant energy of Cairo's streets, and the feeling of stepping into a temple that has stood for thousands of years. Cairo is more than just a destination; it is an experience that stays with you long after you leave. It is a place where the past whispers its stories and the present hums with life, offering a journey that is both enriching and exhilarating.

Pack your bags, book your ticket, and let the wonders of Cairo welcome you. This city promises not just a trip, but an unforgettable adventure filled with discovery, inspiration, and the joy of connecting with a culture so profoundly rich and diverse. Cairo is ready to embrace you with open arms, and it is sure to leave you with memories you will cherish forever. Your extraordinary journey begins now.

Printed in Great Britain
by Amazon